APPLYING
TWELVE DIFFERENT LEARNING THEORIES TO IMPROVE CLASSROOM TEACHING

Ways to Close the Achievement Gap

APPLYING
TWELVE DIFFERENT LEARNING THEORIES
TO IMPROVE CLASSROOM TEACHING

Ways to Close the Achievement Gap

George R. Taylor
Stephanie Johns Hawkins
Delores S. Harvey

With a Foreword by
Leontye Lewis

The Edwin Mellen Press
Lewiston•Queenston•Lampeter

KH

Library of Congress Cataloging-in-Publication Data

Taylor, George R.
 Applying twelve different learning theories to improve classroom teaching : ways to
close the achievement gap / George R. Taylor, Stephanie Johns Hawkins, Delores S.
Harvey ; with a foreword by Leontye Lewis.
   p. cm.
 Includes bibliographical references and index.
 ISBN-13: 978-0-7734-4975-6
 ISBN-10: 0-7734-4975-2
 1. Learning, Psychology of. 2. Multiple intelligences. 3. Cognitive styles. 4. Social
learning. I. Hawkins, Stephanie Johns. II. Harvey, Delores S. III. Title.
 LB1060.T286 2008
 370.15--dc22

                              2008038656

hors série.

A CIP catalog record for this book is available from the British Library.

      The Edwin Mellen Press   The Edwin Mellen Press
            Box 450   Box 67
      Lewiston, New York   Queenston, Ontario
       USA 14092-0450   CANADA L0S 1L0

                    The Edwin Mellen Press, Ltd.
                    Lampeter, Ceredigion, Wales
                    UNITED KINGDOM SA48 8LT

               Printed in the United States of America

11/2/09

Dedication

This textbook is dedicated to all professionals and classroom teachers in the public and private sectors who may have limited background and experiences in integrating and infusing learning theories in their instructional programs.

Table of Contents

Appendices

List of Tables

Preface

This textbook was written to provide a functional and realistic approach to making practical application of human learning to the classroom. Frequently, classroom teachers may be aware of the many theories of learning, but are unable to transpose these theories to practical classroom applications in improving learning for all children regardless of their cultural diversities. This book is designed to accomplish such a purpose. It was written to provide teachers and other human service personnel serving and teaching children with hands on activities. Practical examples are given for classroom applications in each chapter. The school of thought, which underpins this text, is that all learning theories and principles proceed from the simple to the complex, the known to the unknown, and the concrete to the abstract. This school of thought is directly related to how children learn. Consequently, instruction should follow this format.

This book contains 18 chapters. Chapter 1 covers the goals and psychology of education, Chapter 2 overviews the learning experiment, Chapter 3 discusses the emotions and motivation in learning, Chapter 4 highlights the contributions of early theories, Chapter 5 provides the application of behavioral theories, Chapters 6 highlights the social learning strategies, Chapter 7 reports the social learning theories, Chapter 8 discusses the field of cognitive psychology, Chapter 9 covers the impact of early cognitive theorists, Chapter 10 lists the major components of concept learning, Chapter 11 discusses critical thinking and problem solving, Chapter 12 provides information on holistic learning and education, Chapter 13 discusses reciprocal teaching, Chapter 14 contains information on the theory of multiple intelligence, Chapter 15 summarizes the most recent research on Brain-Based Learning, Chapter 16 discusses integrating learning styles into the curriculum, Chapter 17 provides a proposed model for closing the achievement gap, and Chapter 18 provides some concluding remarks.

Foreword

I have had the opportunity to read this work written by George R. Taylor, Stephanie Johns Hawkins, and Delores S. Harvey. This interesting manuscript provides a body of knowledge that explains how to apply learning theories in closing the achievement gap. The structure of the information is excellent for educators to instruct individuals on all achievement levels. The definitions provide practical information for educators to use in applying theories of psychology, sociology, and education to close the achievement gaps prevalent among diverse groups of children.

Taylor, Hawkins, and Harvey write from their own experiences working with and researching the values of infusing learning theories into instruction. They clearly articulate the process of incorporating a theoretical base into practical applications of learning.

The chapters on applications of learning theories are important for many reasons, most notably for explaining how to convert the theories into practical application strategies in the classroom to meet the needs of all children, including children with disabilities. The authors have given excellent examples of how to accomplish this. This is an excellent manuscript, appropriate to use on the graduate level. It is an outstanding resource for educators, social workers, and other professionals involved in closing the achievement gap. The authors have done a superior job in explaining and of infusing and integrating these theories into practical and workable techniques.

I am pleased to have reviewed this excellent manuscript and comment the authors for addressing such a vital topic, which will serve to educate educators about the treasure we have in all our citizens, including our children.

Leontye Lewis, Ed.D, Dean

School of Education

Fayetteville State University

Acknowledgements

Many individuals are responsible for the final version of this textbook. First, we wish to acknowledge the contributions of students in Dr. Taylor's learning theory classes who constantly reminded us to associate principles of learning with practical classroom applications.

We also wish to thank our colleagues who reviewed chapters. We extend our gratitude to Dr. Charity Welch, Dr. Daniel Joseph, all of Coppin State University, for their timely and relevant comments, and to Dr. Judith Wilner and Malik Saher for proof reading the final draft. The staff at Mellen Book Publishing Company was instrumental in bringing this textbook to its conclusion. Their professionalism extended "beyond the call of duty."

We would certainly be remiss if we did not especially thank Ms. Ruth Petty for her secretarial competencies and assistance in typing and retyping the manuscript until the final draft was accepted.

Chapter 1

The Goals and Philosophy of Education

Introduction

The goals of education for all children is to assist them in becoming competent as well as well-adjusted individuals, now and as well as in the future, by creating an atmosphere that supports learning. To be effective this philosophy must be shared by children and they must have an essential part in developing it through communicating their interests.

Littky's[1] assessment of learning goals is in agreement with the philosophy of the authors. He listed five goals:

1. Empirical Reasoning—How do I improve it? Children can be taught how to employ scientific method in solving problems and formulating general concepts which can be applied to many situations.

2. Quantitative Reasoning—How do I measure or represent it? Children can be taught practical mathematical concepts such as size, length, weight, width, large, small, time, measurement, how to find averages, and rating. These concepts can be expressed in numerical terms and used in measuring.

3. Communication Reasoning—How do I take in and express information? Educators should assess the learning styles of children and represent information which address their strongest modalities. The cultural styles of children must also be considered.

---

[1] D. C. Littky, *The Big Picture: Education is Everyone's Business* (Alexandria, VA: Association for Supervision and Curriculum Development, 2004).

4. Social Reasoning—What do other people have to say about this? Appropriate social skills and graces must be modeled and demonstrated for children to emulate. These skills should be integrated within the curriculum. Both human and physical resources should be available to accommodate the instruction.

5. Personal Qualities—What do I bring to the process? The abilities, needs, cultural experiences and background, and interests of children should be collectively assessed and discussed in planning instructional programs.

Achievement of these goals will assist educators in creating an atmosphere that supports learning by making children part of the democratic process. In order for the aforementioned goals to be achieved, educators must have a comprehensive understanding of learning. Even through learning has been defined in many ways, there are similarities in the definitions, with most of them indicating changes in behavior that result from experience. Two common definitions of learning are: (a) a potential change in behavior, and (b) the acquisition of information, or psychological learning is an invisible, internal neurological process. Generally, changes in behavior are a result of taking drugs, physical fatigue, biological or physical growth, and from an injury. Psychologically speaking, learning may be defined as a relatively permanent change in potential for behavior that results from experience, but changes are not the result of fatigue, maturation, drugs, disease, or physical injury.[2]

With these and many other considerations, concluded that learning is a change in performance through conditions of activity, practice and experience,[3] we can conclude that learning is a change in performance through conditions of activity, practice, and experience. This is an operational definition that is derived in part from scientific investigations. In the classroom, the activities and

---

[2] G. R. Lefransios, *Theories of Human Learning* (Sanford, CA: Ct. Wadsworth/Thompson, 2000).

[3] J. E. Ormrod, *Human Learning, 3rd ed.* (New Jersey: Prentice Hall, Inc., 1999).

experiences that lead to change in performance involving telling and listening, judging, reading, reciting, observation of demonstrations, experimenting pupils interacting, and individual learning and activities, it is hoped that both sporadic practice and formal drill in reading, writing, competing, and speaking will carry over to performance in daily life. Living and working with others, and supplementing the feedback that comes from reflecting and discussing while engaged in classroom learning will lead to improved and continued learning during and beyond the school years.

Learning begins with the organism. It is the means through which we acquire not only skills and knowledge, but values, attitudes, and emotional reactions as well. Our learning may be conditioned by our sensory acuity. If our vision on reading is impaired, because of a bad cold, our learning may be influenced. Hearing may be influenced by the physiology of one's emotion. There can be no doubt that pupil's learning abilities are affected by the speed with which nerve messages move and are sorted and combined and by the degree of permanence of the impression they make. Whether this physical base is hereditary, congenital, or developmental in origin, it influences the natural and speed of learning. Learning depends on the inclination and ability to receive and respond to stimulation.

Physical Aspect of Learning

There are physical aspects of learning that cannot be ignored by the teacher, such as vision and hearing. Biochemical factors affect the comfort and satisfaction that an individual derives from learning. Such influences bear heavily on personality, orientation, and on the teaching-learning processes.[4] Learning includes not only the acquisition of subject matter, but also that of habits, attitudes, perceptions, preferences, interests, social adjustments, skills of many

---

[4] G. R. Taylor, *Curriculum Models and Strategies for Educating Individuals with Disabilities in Inclusive Classrooms* (Springfield, IL: Charles C. Thomas, 1999).

4

types, and ideals. Even such seemingly simple things as learning to spell and add involve varied forms of learning.

It is quite likely that researchers are coming closer to knowing what chemical, electrical, biological, and neurological changes occur during the process of learning.[5] We do not know so much about those changes as is desirable, but much is known about the conditions under which learning takes place most effectively. Some conditions and the ways in which they may be improved are, at least in part, subject to the control of teachers. While other conditions, such as cultural deprivation and physical and physiological handicaps, are beyond the control of teachers. Even so, those factors are part of the psychological field with which teachers must be concerned.

Learning also involves the modification of perception and behavior. Not all behavior change is positive learning. A child may eat more because his/her stomach enlarges and because his/her energy needs increase, but the changed behavior is not learning. He/she may, however, learn to eat more because of parental example or because of psychological needs that appear to be satisfied through food. The loss of a hand modifies behavior, but the loss itself is not learning. The person may, though, learn to compensate for the loss of his/her hand by learning new skills. Modification does not necessarily result in improved learning.

The permanent affects of learning may not be immediately apparent. Sometimes the results of learning is latent due to the capacity or condition of the individual performing the behavior, as well as the impact of the environment, and culture may impact on how intelligence is assessed.

---

[5] D. Goleman, *Emotional Intelligence* (New York: NY: Banton Books, 1995); J. LeDoux *The Emotional Brain: The Mysterious Underlining of Emotional Life* (New York, NY: Simon and Schuster, 1996).

Learned Intelligence

The impact of the environment on learning has been well established. It is commonly believed that instructional activities, use of community resources, as well as human and physical resources within the school and the community can significantly facilitate learned intelligence.[6] The leadership of the school, competencies of teachers, infusion of culture experiences, individualizing instruction, involving children, parent, and the community in planning educational experiences can combine to enhance and expand the learned intelligence of pupils. This approach to learning negates that intelligence is fixed by heredity, and provides educators with practical and functional strategies needed to raise the achievement of all children.

There are many definitions of learned intelligence. For the purpose of this text, "learning intelligence is defined as a continuum of experiences which begins at birth and ends at death." Research findings by Cattell[7] defined intelligence as crystallized and fluid. Crystallized intelligence involves knowledge of facts, forming generalizations, and principles about the world, and enhances students' background and knowledge. Many of the instructional experiences afforded to students in school designed to promote achievement may be attributed to crystallized intelligence.[8] Activities designed to promote crystallized intelligences include:

---

[6] J. M. Reilly, *Mentorship: The Essential Guide for School and Business* (Dayton, OH: Psychology Press, 1992); G. Clinton, Setting up a school-based mentoring program, *The Prevention Research,* 9 (1), 4-7, 2002); J. Pilgreen & S. Krashen, Sustained silent reading with English as a second language: High school students impact on reading frequency, and reading enjoyment, *School Library Media Quarterly*, 21-23, 1993; M. Pressley, *Reading Instruction That Works: The Case for Balanced Teaching* (New York, NY: Guilford, 1998).

[7] R. B. Cattell, *Intelligence: Its Structure, Growth, and Action (Rev. Ed.)* (Amsterdam: North Holland Press, 1987, original work published 1971); P. O. Ackerman, A theory of adult intellectual development: Process, personality, interests, and knowledge, *Intelligence,* 22 (1996): 227-257.

[8] R. L. Marzano, *What Works in School: Translating Research into Action* (Alexandria, VA: 2003); F. Dochy, M. Segers, & M. M. Buehl, The relationship between assessment practices and

1. Mentoring relationships with the community where adults assist youth who need support in any area of functioning.

2. Vocabulary development is a good indicator of crystallized intelligence.[9]

Strategies for improving vocabulary Instruction:

1. Expose children to wide reading strategies. There are many reading programs which will promote vocabulary development. For specific reading strategies designed to promote vocabulary development refer to the listed sources:

   a. Hunt, L. C. (1970). Six Steps to the Individual Reading Program (IRP). *Elementary English*, 48, 27-32.

   b. Holt, S. B., & O'Tuel. (1989). The Effect of Sustained Silent Reading and Writing on Achievement and Attitudes of Seventh and Eighth Grade Students Reading Two Years Below Grade Level. *Reading Improvement*, 26 (4), 290-297.

The National Institute of Child Health and Human Development[10] on teaching children to read provides an evidence-based assessment of the scientific research literature on reading and its implications for reading instruction. In the opinion of Marzano,[11] the more fluid intelligence an individual processes, the more easily they can acquire crystallized intelligence to assist them in solving problems in their environments. Marzano's work concerning the two types of

---

outcomes of studies. The case of research on prior knowledge, *Review of Educational Research*, *69 (2)* (1999), 145-186.

[9] J. S. Chall, Two vocabularies for reading: Recognition and meaning. In M. G. Keown and M. E. Curtis (eds.), *The Nature of Vocabulary* Acquisition (Hillsdale, NJ: Erlbaum, 1987); Coleman et al., *Equality of Educational Opportunity* (Washington, DC: U.S. Printing Office, 1996); W. E. Nagy & P. A. Herman, *Limitations of Vocabulary* Instruction (Tech. Rep. No. 326) (Urban, IL: University of Illinois, Center for the Study of Reading, 1984 [ERIC Documented Reproduction Service No. ED248-498].

[10] The National Institute of Child Health and Human Development. Report on the National Reading Panel: *Teaching Children to Read* (2000).

[11] R. L. Marzano, *What Works in School: Translating Research into Action* (Alexandria, VA: 2003).

intelligences has provided us with information which may assist teachers in providing strategies to promote the two types of intelligences. He voiced that:

"a student's background knowledge can enhance crystallized intelligence. It is certainly true that students who have high fluid intelligence and access to a variety of experiences will quite naturally acquire substantial crystallized intelligence. Students with low fluid intelligence in the same experience--rich environment--will have lower crystallized intelligence because of lack of opportunity to acquire it. Only the confluence of high fluid intelligence and a rich experimental base is conducive to highly crystallized intelligence."

Educators must plan functional and cultural experiences to develop crystallized intelligence in children. Children who participate in crystallized intelligent activities usually perform higher than their peers, and have a higher G.P.A. in high school, and have a greater chance of enrolling and completing college.

Sternberg[12] wrote

"the danger is that we overlook many talented people in any field of study because of the way we measure intelligence, and some of the best potential psychologists, biologists, historians, or whatever may get derailed because they are made to think they don't have the talent to pursue a career in any field. To be successfully intelligent is to think well in three different ways: analytically, creatively, and practically. Typically, one analytical intelligence is valued on tests and in the classroom. Yet, the style of intelligence the schools most readily recognize as smart may well be less useful to many students in their adult lives than creative and practical intelligence."

---

[12] R. J. Sternberg, What is successful intelligence? *Education Week*, 16 (11) (November 1996), 37.

Concerning the theoretical constructs of intelligence, Gardner[13] and Sternberg[14] appear to be the fore runners. Both authors have advanced the concepts of "Multiple Intelligence." They have advocated that human intelligence manifest itself in many avenues of human functioning. Gardner's eight states of intelligences are:

1. verbal –linguistic,
2. logical-mathematical,
3. visual-spatial,
4. bodily-kinesthetic,
5. musical-rhythmic,
6. interpersonal,
7. interpersonal, and
8. naturalist (refer to Chapter 11 for details).

Sternberg proposed three types of intelligence:

1. analytical,
2. creative, and
3. practical

There are differences and similarity in the two approaches; however, both authors support the premise that intelligence is a capacity to solve problems and that it is fluid rather than fixed. Additionally, they support that individuals have strengths in one or more intelligence in which they favor, and that instructional strategies should be aligned with individual intelligence preferences. Much of what we know and understand about learning may be attributed to contributions made by early psychologists.

---

[13] H. Gardner, *Multiple Intelligences: The Theory in Practice* (New York, NY: Basic Books, 1993).

[14] Sternberg, 1996.

Early Contributors to Learning Theories

Experimentations with learning theories can be traced to William James and Edward Tichener. They attempted to explain behavior based upon instinct and emotions. These researchers instructed individuals to examine their own feelings and motives to discover information relevant to their learning and behavior.

Wilhelm Wundt[15] is considered by many psychologists to be the father of psychology. He established the first psychological laboratory in Leipzig, Germany in 1879. Wundt and his associates experimented with mental attributes, such as consciousness, sensations, feelings, imagining, and perceiving. They attempted to use the scientific method to study these mental attributes.

These early contributors to the field of psychology laid the groundwork for our present understanding of learning theories by attempting to systematically observe and experiment with human behavior. Early experimentation was mainly based upon a method called introspection. William James is frequently called the father of psychology because of his work in introspection. Individuals were simply asked to look inside their mind, and describe what they were thinking. It would take the works of Pavlov and Thorndike to develop a more objective approach to the study of learning, one which was based upon observable behaviors rather than on having an individual describe mental events. The contributions of these researchers will be discussed in greater detail in Chapters 4, 5, and 6. Their contributions to the learning theory had a significant impact on how educators can abstract learning principles for theories to assist children in mastering learning.

Theory Defined

In attempting to explain phenomena, scientists constructed hypotheses to test theories. A hypothesis attempts to explain a limited set of facts, whereas a theory attempts to involve a broad range of facts. To be useful, a hypothesis must

---

[15] Lefransios, 1999.

be testable. It must lead to predictions that may be validated as true or false. A single experiment may disprove a hypothesis, but rarely disclaim a hypothesis. Several disapproved hypotheses are needed to disclaim a theory. A new theory with few hypotheses or facts to support it soon is abandoned.

Theories of Learning

Ormrod[16] voiced that theories of learning provide explanations about the process involved in the learning process. They permit investigators to summarize research findings from several research studies and extrapolate and classify them according to principles of learning. Theories provide insensitive to conduct new research. They suggest possible approaches which may be employed to conduct the study, as well as interpreting research findings in light of the theoretical framework. Additionally, theories can assist us in understanding how humans learn and factors which may agree that no one learning theory can completely cover all aspects of human leaning and behavior. Educators should draw from various theories and formulate their own theories relevant to the learning process.

Classification of Learning Theories

The first systematic study of learning according to Lefrancios[17] is behaviorism. Behavioristic theories of Pavlov and Skinner will be addressed in greater details later in the text. Cognitivism theories include those of Robert Rescorlla, Allen Wagner, Wilson, Donal Hebb, Edward C. Tolmen, Kurt Koffla, and Wolfgang Kohler. The theoretical framework of these theories has lead to evolutionary psychology, sociology, stimuli, responses, reinforcement, and mediation behavioral orientations. Unlike behaviorists, cognitive psychologist place values on perception, decision-making, processing and understanding information. Gestalt psychologists were one of the first cognitive psychologists to indicate the importance of the organizational process in perception, learning, and

---

[16] Ormrod, 1999.

[17] G. R. Lefrancios, *Theories of Human Learning* (Sanford, CA: Brooks Cole Publishing Company, 2000).

problem solving.[18]   The work of Piaget concerning developmental and information processing will be expanded in Chapter 9.

Behaviorism and Cognitivism approaches differ in that behaviorisms focused on external behavior can be shaped and modified (the blank state concept), and learning principles may be applied to all species. Cognitivism emphasizes the mental process and maintains that global learning principles cannot be applied to all species. It maintains that many types of learning are reserved for the human species only. Both approaches support the premise that the study of learning should be studied objectively and based upon scientific research. Both approaches will be related to how they may be employed in closing the achievement gap among children.

Scientific Theory

A scientific theory is a set of principles and laws which are related and explains a broad spectrum of learning behaviors. Hergenhahn and Olson[19] added additional clarity to scientific theories by stating that a theory has a formal aspect, which includes the words and symbols that theory contains as well as having an empirical aspect, which consists of the physical events that the theory is attempting to explain.

Regardless of the complexity of theories, they all begin and end with observation. To support assumptions based upon observations, hypotheses may be formulated to test the validity of the observations. If hypotheses are supported, they aid in strengthening the theory; thus, generalizations may be made concerning the theory. If generalizations are strong, they may help form principles and laws. Theories provide starting points for summarizing, concluding, and making sense of research findings, as well as assisting us in designing learning environments that facilitate human learning.

---

[18] Ormrod, 1999.

[19] B. R. Hergenhahn & M. H. Olson, *An Introduction to Theories of Learning (5th ed) (New Jersey: Prentice Hall, 1997).*

Principles of learning identify specific factors that consistently influence learning and describe the particular effects of these factors. Principles are most useful when they can be applied to a wide variety of situations in solving problems. When a principle is observed countless times, and results are repeated, principles may be laws.[20]

In support of this view, Lefrancois[21] stated that laws are statements whose validity and accuracy have been well established. They are conclusions that are based on what appears to be undeniable observations and irrefutable logic. Unlike principles, laws are not ordinarily open to exceptions and doubt. An understanding to the characteristics of theories will aid educators in understanding the many factors involved in developing theories.

Characteristic of Scientific Theory

Hergenhahn and Olson[22] summarized characteristics of scientific theory as follows:

1. A theory synthesizes number of observations.
2. A good theory must generate hypotheses that can be empirically verified. If such hypotheses are confirmed, the theory gains strength; if not, the theory is weakened and must be revised or abandoned.
3. A good theory is heuristic; that is, it generates new resources.
4. A theory is a tool and as such cannot be right or wrong, it is either useful or it is not.
5. Theories are chosen in accordance with the law of "parsimony" of two equally effective theories, the simpler of the two must be chosen.
6. Theories contain abstractions, such as numbers of words, which constitute the formal aspect of a theory.

---

[20] Ormrod, 1999.

[21] Lefransios, 1999.

[22] Hergenhahn & M. H. Olson, 1997.

7. The formal aspects of a theory must be correlated with observable events, which constitutes the empirical aspect of a theory.

8. All theories are attempts to explain empirical events and they must, therefore, start and end with empirical observations.

The Scientific Method

The scientific method is used to solve problems in the solution of problems. According to Leedy[23] there are six steps to this method:

1. Definition of the problem
2. Statement of hypothesis
3. Design the experiment survey
4. Deductive reasoning
5. Collection and analysis of data
6. Confirmation or rejection of the hypothesis

The scientific method is objective, reliable, and replicable. It contains only those results which have been replicated by others used as a basic format and under similar conditions. It is an objective way for developing and testing a learning experiment.

---

[23] P. D. Leedy, *Practical Research: Planning and Design (6th ed.)* (New York, NY: MacMillan, 1997).

Chapter 2

The Learning Experiment

The learning experiment begins with observations. Observations provide the initial approach to begin scientific inquiry in both quantitative and qualitative research methods. Observations may be supported by reviewing the professional literature. Review of the literature in qualitative research is usually conducted after the study, the reverse is usually true for quantitative research. Educators must become competent in applying and using research to determine best practices and strategies for promoting learning in the classroom.

Reviewing the literature is important when learning experiments using quantitative and qualitative research methods. The use of the review of literature has different purposes when using the two methods. In quantitative research, the review is conducted after the study has been completed. The researcher, using the qualitative method, may find minimal use of the review, since he/she will be constructing theory there may not be current research on the topic. The quantitative researcher would use the review liberally, since he/she will be testing theory based upon current models and research findings. In quantitative research, the review of literature will enable the researcher to use it inductively, so that the researcher's review will not have a significant impact upon the question being posed. In quantitative research the review of literature is used deductively, where the researcher is drawing from general principles and theories in the field in developing and conducting his/her research.

Identification, Selection, and Statement of the Problem

Identification, selection, and statement of the problem are frequently minimized by the research in both quantitative and qualitative research. The areas must be carefully considered and weighted against such factors as:

1. Values and needs of the study.
2. Prospects of making a contribution to the field.
3. Training and experience of the research.
4. Availability of human and physical resources to conduct the study.
5. Interest and motivation in the study.
6. Use of expert advice in identifying and selecting the problem.
7. The attended audiences for the study.

A systematic and detailed investigation of the above factors will assist the researcher in determining the feasibility of pursuing the problem in greater depth, or to change and modify procedures.

Development of Testable Hypotheses and Research Questions

Once the research topic has been selected and the problem formulated, the next step is to develop testable research questions or hypotheses to scientifically guide the study. In quantitative research, questions and hypotheses are developed to test theory; whereas in qualitative research, questions and hypotheses are designed to test theory. Researchers may employ a variety of techniques in developing research questions or hypotheses for the two paradigms. In quantitative methods, various types of hypotheses may be used. The null and alternative hypotheses are frequently used. In qualitative methods, research questions are most frequently used.

Validating and Establishing Reliability of Instruments

The use of validated instruments are required and necessary in conducting quantitative research, but it is not a prerequisite for conducting qualitative research. In conducting quantitative research, many researchers choose standardized instruments in which validity and reliability have already been established. When a researcher constructs his/her own instrument, validity and reliability will need to be established. Cresswell[24] provides an excellent approach to validating and establishing reliability for instruments.

Experimental Conditions

An essential part of quantitative research is the experimental condition, sometimes referred to as the intervention or treatment. This aspect closely follows the scientific method. Variables are systematically identified and controlled. Subjects are randomly selected and matched in the experimental and control groups and performances of the two groups are compared at the end of the experiment. In qualitative research, experimental conditions are not employed, they are not required. By deleting the experimental conditions, researchers may readily use the research design to conduct qualitative research.

Statistical Analysis

Various statistical tools to test data quantitatively may be explored. Both parametric and non-parametric statistics may be used to test hypotheses. Various methods and procedures for testing different types of experimental designs may be selected based upon sampling, instruments, and experimental conditions. Statistical analysis is limited in qualitative research. Some descriptive statistics may be used such as graphs, charts, percentages, and measures of control tendency. Descriptive analysis is the most frequently used technique.

Descriptive Analysis

Descriptive analysis may be used in both designs, such as graphs, mean scores, percentiles, and correlations. Generally, researchers categorize and develop themes when using qualitative methods. The themes provide narrative descriptions of the behaviors. The process can be completely voided of numerical data. Numerical data may add to the understanding and the interpretation of the research questions or hypothesis under study. Quantitative research has more structure and narrative interpretations are limited. Observations and interviews

---

[24] J. W. Cresswell, *Research Design: Qualitative and Quantitative Approaches* (Thousand Oaks, CA: Sage Publications, 1994).

are used in both designs. In quantitative research, description and inferential statistics are used to analyze data. In qualitative research, analysis is continuous and infrequently employ the use of the statistics.

Constructing Theory

Qualitative research attempts to construct theory using observational and interviewing techniques to define human behavior. Experiences are documented, identified, and described. Patterns and categories are developed in an attempt to provide theoretical explanations to human behavior. The theory is used inductively and is developed at the end of the study. Data are collected and analyzed before the theory is developed.

Testing Theory

Quantitative research attempts to test theory deductively. The theory provides the framework for conducting the study and is usually placed before the experimental conditions. In essence, the theory guides the type of research conducted. The major emphasis is to test or verify a theory. Instruments are developed or selected, data are analyzed to test the hypotheses.

Findings/Results

Data are analyzed in both quantitative and qualitative research. In quantitative research, statistics are employed to determine to what degree the hypotheses have been accepted or rejected. Some degree of objectivity is inherited in the process. Findings in qualitative research are usually reported in narrative form. Data must be coded, classified, and categories formed in order to appropriately analyze data. Findings are subjective and are frequently not considered obsolete.

Triangulation

Today, attempts are underway to combine the two paradigms in the collection and analysis of data. The process is referred to as triangulation. The trend is to objectify techniques by combining the two approaches in research activities. Computer programs have been developed to assist in the interpretation of the massive amount of data generated through the qualitative method. Computer programs can assist greatly in using the two paradigms in evaluating research. Using maps is another technique that may be employed by making diagrams of the relationships among data through the use of computerized hypertext techniques. Descriptive types of statistics may be employed to assist in analyzing data from the two methods. Data sources, such as interviews and demographic information, may yield qualitative data which may be analyzed through descriptive statistics. These data can enhance quantitative data reported in the research.

The learning experiment outlined can assist the researcher in conducting either qualitative or quantitative research. The research design provides a mechanism by which both qualitative and quantitative approaches can be used employing the scientific method. In both methods the scientific method begins with observations and proceeds through analysis of and reporting results. Ethical issues must be considered in conducting any type of research.

Ethical Issues in Conducting Research

Historically, issues related to subjects have constituted the greatest concern to society in the violating of human rights during the early part of this century. Specific guidelines are developed for researchers to follow under the listed areas:

1. Consent
2. Harm
3. Privacy
4. Deception

Consent

Subjects must be given a choice to determine whether or not they wish to participate in the study. Subjects must be both mentally and physically able to make the choice or someone must be designated to act on their behalf. Assessment should also be made of the legal qualifications of the subjects.

Subjects under the age of 18 years should not be permitted to participate in the study unless a parent or guardian gives written permission.[25]

Guidelines

1. Type of intervention or treatment to be conducted. Specific procedures for conducting the research should be clearly articulated. Length of time as well as human and physical resources needed to conduct the research should be addressed.

2. Impact upon the normal activities of subjects. The researcher should address to what extent the research will affect the normal activities of the subjects. There should be strategies to restore subjects to the normal routines of the inclusion of the research.

3. Informed consent. It is incumbent upon the researcher to inform the subjects what is expected of them and what they will be expected to do. A consent form usually accomplishes this.

4. Right of withdrawal. Subjects should be told and given the right to withdraw from the research at any time. A statement should be developed outlining the procedure.

Harm

Subjects participating in research should be assured that no harm will come to them as a result of their participation. Harm covers physical and psychological factors which may adversely affect the functioning or the well being of the subjects. The extent and possible harm that subjects may experience should be clearly articulated in the questionnaire or survey completed by the subjects. Treatment should not leave the subjects more psychologically depressed or physically incapacitated than they were before the treatment began.[26]

---

[25] V. Kimmell, *Ethical Issues in Behavioral Research* (Cambridge, MD Blackwell Publisher, 1996).

[26] D. N. Robinson, *Social Discourse and Moral Judgment* (San Diego, CA: Academic Press, 1992).

Guidelines

1. Safeguarding subjects from harm. The researcher should ensure the subjects that no physical or psychological harm will come to them as a result of participating in the research. The researcher should inform subjects concerning any possible risks associated with the research.

2. High-risk subjects. Researchers should consider the characteristics of the subjects involved in the experiment such as age, physical or mental disabilities. These subjects may be unable to make realistic decisions on their own, thus, placing them "in harms way" for certain types of experiments.

3. Assurance to subjects. It is incumbent upon the researcher that subjects are returned to their original physical and psychological conditions when they are no longer needed in the experiment.

4. Results of other experiments. The researchers should provide subjects with how other studies safeguarded subjects or how the lack of safeguards brought harm to subjects, and relate how his/her study will avoid some of the pitfalls.

Privacy

Our privacy in this country is considered to be a valued right as reflected in local, state, and federal mandates. Subjects participating in research should be guaranteed the right that sensitive data collected through the research process will be confidential. Researchers should assure subjects that sensitive data will be held in the strictest confidence in order to protect their anonymity.[27]

Guidelines

1. Selection of the site. The rationale for choosing the site should be outlined and clearly articulated. The researcher should consider the setting in which the study is to be conducted. Settings in public places are not

---

[27] M. Kurtines, *The Role of Values in Psychology and Human Development* (New York: NY: John Wiley and Sons, 1992.

generally considered conducive for assuring privacy. Other factors which should be considered are:

- The reputation and competencies of the staff.
- Safeguarding of information.
- Protecting information for individuals not involved in the research.

2. Making results of the research available. Subjects should have an opportunity to review a draft copy of the report in order to determine invasion of privacy. This is especially true when some of the data may be damaging to the institution or subject. Feedback should be incorporated into the final report providing that the hypotheses and findings are not altered.

3. Feedback. Researchers should assure subjects that they will provide an opportunity for them to obtain accurate information relevant to the research, and that he/she will respond to all of the participants' concerns.

4. Confidentiality. Confidentiality should be maintained at all times. The proposal should indicate that names will not be used or revealed with the data.

Deception

Misleading subjects, under or over representing facts are forms of deception. There should be no hidden agenda relevant to the treatment process. Any deception which is an integral part of the research must be explained to the subjects as soon as feasible.[28]

Guidelines

1. Limitations. Factors such as finances, time, resources, and data sources should not be a standard for using deception.

2. Consent. Subjects should be given an accurate description of what tasks they will be required to perform.

---

[28] R. E. Jensen, *Standards and Ethics in Clinical Psychology* (Lanham, MD: University Press of America, 1992).

3. Justification. Any deception employed should be clearly justified by the researcher and clearly explained to the subjects at an appropriate time.

The researcher should indicate what the subjects will gain from the research in the areas of improved treatment, innovative methods, in-service training needs, and the need for additional physical or human resources.[29]

It should be incumbent upon the researcher to safeguard all subjects involved in experiments. Certain ethical concerns should be considered. These considerations may involve submitting a research proposal to an ethics committee for approval. In some cases, an oral presentation may be required.

Summary

The many branches of psychology all have one basic principle, the study of human behavior. Objective measures are employed in studying human behavior. Learning theories have greatly aided researchers in study learning by organizing and systematizing what is known about human learning. These theories provide information needed for predicting and controlling human behavior and learning. Learning experiments provide researchers with an outlet for testing theories and determining to what degree hypotheses are supported. Factors such as defining the problem, statement of hypothesis, instrument construction, testing or developing theory, data analysis, and the findings must all be clearly articulated in the design. Learning experiments should follow the scientific method, starting with observations and proceeding to the analysis and reporting of results. The issues of using humans and animals in research should be conducted with published guidelines as articulated earlier in the chapter.

The two major divisions of learning theories are behaviorism and cognitivism. Behaviorism is an approach that deals with observable behaviors, whereas cognitivism is concerned with mental traits such as perception, information processing, concept formation, and understanding. Each of the

---

[29] C. Marshall & G. B. Rossman, *Designing Qualitative* (Newbury Park, CA: Sage Publishing Company, 1989); R. C. Bogdan & S. K. Biklen, *Qualitative Research for Education: An Introduction to Theory and Methods* (Boston, MA: Allyn & Bacon, 1992).

divisions provide information into how individuals learn and how educators can modify the learning environment so that all individuals can reach their optimum levels of functioning.[30]

The text is designed to provide a blueprint for educators to use when instructing individuals. Although various approaches to learning have been summarized, we have emphasized that no one theory can cover completely the gamut of human learning and behavior. Educators must draw from the various theories, those attributes which they consider important for facilitating learning and closing the achievement gap, to which the remaining chapters will address.

---

[30] R. Epstein, Skinner, creativity, and the problem of spontaneous behavior, *Psychological Science*, 2 (1991), 363-370; R. E. Reynolds, G. M. Sinatra & T. L. Jetton, Views of knowledge acquisition and representation: A continuum from experience centered, *Educational Psychologist*, 31 (1996) 93-104; T. Gilovich, *How We Know What Isn't So: The Fallibility of human reason in everyday life* (New York, NY: Free Press, 1991).

Chapter 3

Emotions and Motivation in Learning

Introduction

Neuroscience research, during the present decade, has shed valuable information about the development of emotional and social competence. Goleman[31] stands out as one of the pioneers in this area. He defines "Emotional Intelligence" as a form of intelligence relating to the emotional side of life, such as the ability to recognize and manage one's own and others' emotions, to motivate oneself and restrain-impulses, and to handle interpersonal relationships effectively.[32]

Developmental psychologists, initially focused on cognitive development, set the stage for current research on social and emotional development in children. However, in recent years child development research has expanded its scope of study to the development of children's social and emotional lives. The result has been a new understanding of what makes a child socially adept or better able to regulate emotional distress. This new strata of scientific understanding can be of immense help in informing the practical efforts of the emotional literacy movement.[33] Their research in this area has resulted in a clearer understanding of a child's social adaptations, ability to monitor emotions, and cope with emotional distress. This information served as a basis for teaching reading to students who find difficulty in interacting with the literature on any level due to prior emotional

---

[31] T. Goleman, *Emotional Intelligence* (New York, NY: Banton Books, 1995).

[32] Goleman, 1995.

[33] D. Sluyter & P. Salovey (eds.), *Emotional Development and Emotional Intelligence: Implications for Educators* (New York: Basic Books, 1997).

experiences that may have a negative impact on normal development and learning.

The brain, which controls the emotions and the impetus for social interactions, is the last organ of the body to mature anatomically, and continues to grow and shape itself throughout childhood into adolescence (see Chapter 12 for additional details). Similarly, as the development progresses, circuits that control emotional competence seem to be the last part of the brain to mature. Because of the plasticity of the brain, it can reshape itself as it responds to repeated experiences that strengthen the circuits. Children are more adept at making new brain connections than are adults, and consequently, they integrate new experiences at an incredibly fast rate.[34] Therefore, a rich learning environment yields more comprehensive brain pathways proven to be advantageous for organizing and connecting meaning to learning experiences.[35] What this means is that childhood is the most optimum time to provide children with repeated experiences that help them to develop healthy emotional habits for self-awareness and self-regulation, for empathy and social skill.

Children's emotions must be recognized and integrated in the instructional program, if not learning and achievement are significantly impeded. Research by Sylwester[36] reveal that emotions drive attention, and in turn, drive learning and memory. Since more neural fibers project from the brain's emotional center into the logical/rational center than the reverse, emotion tends to determine behavior more powerfully than rational processes. Thinking is an integrated process of the

---

[34] J. Newberger, New brain development research: A wonderful window of opportunity to build public support for early childhood education, *Young Children*, 52 (1997) 4-9; C. Toepher, Curriculum design and neuropsychological development, *Journal of Research and Development in Education*, 15 (1982) 1-10.

[35] L. Galloway, Billingualism: Neuropsychological considerations, *Journal of Research and Development in Education*, 15 (1982, Spring) 12-28; J. Newberger, 1997; D. Sousa, *How the Brain Learns* (Reston, VA: The National Association of Secondary School Principals, 1995).

[36] R. Sylvester, How emotions affect learning, *Educational Leadership*, 52 (2) (1994, October) 60-68.

body/brain system. According to Sylwester,[37] the emotional system is located in the brain, endocrine, and immune systems and affects all organs of the body. Therefore, chronic emotional stress has adverse effects on the entire body. Stressful school experiences and environments inhibit learning, while positive classroom atmospheres encourage neural connections in the brain to help children learn. Children naturally seek out and thrive in places where their needs are met. Integrating emotional expressions of children in the classroom can improve memory and stimulates learning.

These findings may be employed to assist children who are victims of a culture and an environment often violent, hostile, and threatening, and present unique challenges for new teachers who leave teacher education programs equipped with literacy theories that often do not take into consideration the impact of negative experiences on the brain. Emotional intelligence has proven to be effective for those who are faced with negative experiences, such as poor self-worth and self-images that may stagnate their learning.

Sylwester[38] contends that curricula must include many sensory, cultural, and problem layers that stimulate the brain's neural networks. He recommended that the classroom be closely related to real experiences of the children. Other studies support the critical role adults play in facilitating an early stimulating environment for children, but if caregivers are unable to provide early stimulation, children stagnate and brain activity is limited at a time when they are most receptive to stimulation.

Studies have shown that a growing number of students demonstrate an inability to control emotions; therefore, school-based programs have surfaced across the country in an effort to address the emotional and social development of

---

[37] Sylwester, 1994.

[38] R. Sylwester, *A Biological Brain in a Cultural Classroom: Enhancing Cognitive and Social Development Through Collaborative Classroom Management* (Thousand Oaks, CA: Corwin Press Incorporated, 2003).

children. These programs have several names from "social development," "life skills," "self-science," and "social competency," but generally, they all address the same issues in providing students with coping mechanisms which are socially acceptable and self-fulfilling.[39] The Collaborative for Social and Emotional Learning, begun at the Yale Child Studies Center in New Haven, Connecticut, has provided school districts with quality programs that offer practical assistance in this area. The Nueva School in Hillsborough, California, was the first to start such a program, and New Haven was the first city to implement such a program in public school districts. We recommend that educators seek professional advice and review these programs and current research findings before initiating their own programs.

The Role of Emotions in Learning

The role of emotions in learning has been well established through research conducted by Gazzainga[40] Collectively, these authors postulated that human beings have little control over their emotions, because emotions can flood consciousness. Emotions are primary motivators that often override an individual's system of values and beliefs relative to their influence on human behavior. Most individuals find causes for their emotions, but when factual reasons are not available, they make up reasons and support them. It appears safe to conclude that all learning is driven by emotions.

Leading research on the aspect of intelligence called emotional intelligence (social emotional development) also highlights the connection between emotional development and learning. Research conducted by The

---

[39] Sluyter & Salovey, 1997.

[40] M. S. Gazzainga, *Nature's Mind: The Biological Roots of Thinking, Emotions, Sexuality, Language, and Intelligence (New York: Bantam Books,* 1992); J. E. LeDoux, Emotion, memory, and brain, *Scientific American,* 270 (6) (1994) 50-57; R. M. Restak, *The Modular Brain* (New York: Touchstone, 1994).

Research Triangle Institute,[41] found that the base of meaning and memory formation is emotion. We remember and apply what resonates in our relationships and our feelings. Thoughts that make us *feel* are the thoughts we retain. How we feel about school, the environment, peers, and our teacher impacts our learning experience and thus achievement ability in a particular setting.

The notion that emotion informs thought is the basis for the understanding that information and cognition alone—without emotion or relationships—loses its meaning. If one bit of information is just as important as another—we have no basis to prioritize, to assign meaning, to put the knowledge in a context. One early example of this was a "natural" brain experiment from 1848. A railroad worker named Phineas Gage was in an accident that drove a steel bar through his skull. He recovered and could speak and appeared to have normal intellect. However, he never again was able to function adequately in society. What he appeared to lose was his social reasoning, his sense of responsibility for himself and for others—his empathy, his ability to abide by social conventions and maintain human connections. In short, his emotional intelligence. He could learn and retain facts—he would probably be able to pass most of our school readiness and end of grade tests—but without the ability to put social meaning to the facts, he was condemned to a marginal life without human content.[42]

Thus, academic learning depends on effective connections between perception, emotion, and thought. And if we truly understand this, it becomes obvious why emotional intelligence is a necessary component of general intelligence and thus a critical aspect of learning.[43]

---

[41] Research Triangle Institute, *Developing Emotional Intelligence* (Research Triangle Park, NC: Early Childhood Resource Center, 2002).

[42] A. Damasio, *Descarte's Error: Emotion, Reason, and the Human Brain* (Avon Books, 1994), 3-19.

[43] Encouraging Connections, 2004.

Sylwester[44] voiced that children's emotions must be recognized and their importance in learning considered. He further articulated that emotions drive attention, memory and behavior, and is more powerful than rational processes. He considers thinking and emotions as an integrated part of the body/brain system, and any factors affecting this system can have adverse affects on the emotional state of the body. Reduction on stressful school experiences can improve memory and reduce emotional stress. Use of an application of emotional principles by educators can have a profound affect on learning and achievement in the classroom.

Motivation

The role of motivation in learning has been well documented. The works of Steinkamp and Maehr, Bandura, Covington, and Harter[45] have supported the importance of motivation in learning. These authors have identified the theoretical components of learning:

1. Drive,
2. Attribution,
3. Self-worth,
4. Emotion, and
5. Self-system.

In essence, these theoretical concepts explain why individuals are motivated to complete certain tasks. Individuals may employ one or a combination of these constructs in completing a task. These components, if not properly incorporated, may impede learning and task completion.

---

[44] R. Sylwester, What the biology of the brain tells us about learning, *Educational Leadership*, 51 (4) (1994), 22-26.

[45] M. W. Steinkamp & M. L. Maehr, Affect, ability, and science achievement: A quantitative synthesis or correlational research, *Review of Education*, 53 (3) (1983) 369-396; A. Bandura, *Self-efficacy: The Exercise of Control* (New York: W. H. Freeman and Company, 1997); M. V. Covington, *Making the Grade: A Self-worth Perspective on motivation and School Reform* (New York: Cambridge University Press, 1992); S. Harter, *The Construction of the Self: A Developmental Perspective* (New York: The Guilford Press, 1999).

Drive Theory

Atkinson and Atkinson and Raynor[46] laid the foundation for our understanding of drive theory. They identified two components of drive theory, striving for success and the fear of failure. Students employ both of these strategies in the classroom. Students striving for success are motivated to engage and complete new tasks. Successful completion of these tasks provide emotional rewards for them. Students displaying fear of failure are not motivated to learn new tasks because of fear of failure. These students may develop strategies which impede the normal operation of the classroom, such as setting unrealistic goals, excuses for failing, and procrastination.

Attrition Theory

Attrition theory for students as defined by Weiner; Wiener, Friezel, Kulka, Reed, Rest, and Rosenbaum[47] demonstrates that students perceive the causes of their prior successes or failures is a better determinant of motivation and persistence than is a learned success or failure avoidance orientation. This theory is associated with the following attributes: ability, effort, luck, and task difficulty. Covington[48] contends that effort is the most important attribute. His rationale is justified by the following statement:

---

[46] J. W. Atkinson, Motivation determinants of risk-raking behavior, *Psychology Review*, 64 (1957) 359-372; J. W. Atkinson, *An Introduction to Motivation* (Princeton, NJ: Van Nostrand, 1964); J. W. Atkinson, *Michigan Studies of the Failure*, in F. Halisch & Huhl (Eds.), *Motivation, Intention, and Volition* (Berlin: Springer, 1987); J. W. Atkinson & J. O. Raynor, *Motivation and Achievement* (New York: Wiley, 1974).

[47] B. Weiner, *Theories of Motivation: From Mechanisms to Cognition* (Chicago: Markham, 1972); B. Weiner, L. Friezel, A. Kulka, L. Reed, S. Rest & R. Rosenbaum, Perceiving the causes of success and failure. In E. E. Jones, D. E. Kanouse, H. H. Kelly, R. E. Nisbett, S. Valins, & B. Weiner (Eds.), *Attribution Perceiving the Behavior* (Morristown, NJ: General Learning Press, 1971).

[48] M. V. Covington, *Making the Grade: A Self-worth Perspective On Motivation and School Reform* (New York: Cambridge University Press, 1992).

32

"One of the most important features of attribution theory is its focus on the role of effort in achievement. This emphasis is justified for several reasons. For one thing, if students believe their failures occur for a lack of trying, then they are more likely to remain optimistic about succeeding in the future. For another thing, trying hard is known to increase pride in success and to offset feelings of guilt at having failed. And, perhaps, most important of all, the emphasis on the role of effort in achievement is justified because it is widely believed that student effort is modifiable through the actions of teachers."

Other views indicate that motivation is not a fixed drive within this theory; motivation can be changed by understanding our attributions.[49]

According to Covington,[50] the search for self-acceptance is one of the highest human priorities. It strives best within an environment where one's status is accepted. If teachers maintain acceptable high academic standards in the classroom, only those students demonstrating high performances will succeed and obtain a high degree of self-worth. Through instituting a system of rewards, teachers can motivate insecure students to strive for success and become high performers.

The concept advanced by Berliner[51] has relevance for promoting unmotivated students. It was advocated that educators should:

---

[49] M. E. P. Seligman, *Helplessness: On Depression, Development, and Death* (San Francisco, CA: Freeman, 1975); M. E. P. Seligman, S. F. Maier & J. Greer, The alleviation of learned helplessness in the dog, *Journal of Abnormal Psychology,* 73 *(*1968) 256-262; M. E. P. Seligman, S. F. Maier & Solomon, Unpredictable and uncontrollable aversive events. In F. R. Brus (Ed.), *Aversive Conditioning and Learning* (New York: Academic Press, 1971).

[50] M. V. Covington, The motive of self worth. In R. Ames and C. Ames (Eds.), *Research on Motivation in Education* (New York: Academic Press, 1984); M. V. Covington, The role of self-processes in applied social psychology, *Journal of the Theory of Social Behavior,* 15 (1985); M. V. Covington, *Achievement Motivation, Self-attributions, and Exceptionality* (Norwood: NJ: Ablex, 1987).

[51] D. C. Berliner, Reaching unmotivated students, *Education Digest,* 69 (5) (2004, January) 46-47.

1. Create positive learning environments by accepting students viewpoints, offering encouragement, de-emphasizing competition, establishing school-wide programs and collaboration for solving problems, involve students in developing rules and consequences. Educators should demonstrate and model these strategies and behaviors initially.

2. Teach engaging content by infusing the interest, ability, learning and culture, opinions and experiences of students. Instructional strategies offered to students should be designed to develop self-expression and positive peer relationships. Educators should sequence curricula into small manageable steps and require students to demonstrate their mastery of the learning task.

3. Choose instructional strategies that motivate student involvement by setting high standards and realistic expectations, systematically evaluate students work with timely feedback, and use a variety of concrete materials in teaching to develop metacognition strategies, use strategies to promote self-worth. It is desirable that educators use flexible grouping and creative expression of students to promote academic and social skills.

Self-System

Harter's[52] view of self-esteem is described as a system which helps us to decide whether to engage in a new task. Cskszentimihaly[53] provided us with a more universal definition. He postulates that:

> "The self is no ordinary piece of information...in fact, it contains (almost) everything...that passes through consciousness: all the memories, actions, desires, pleasures, and pains are included in it; and more than anything else, the self represents the hierarchy of goals that we have built up, bit by

---

[52] S. Harter, *The Construction of the Self: A Developmental Perspective* (New York: The Guilford Press, 1999).

[53] M. Cskszentimihaly, *Flow: The Psychology of Optimal Experience* (New York: Harper and Row, 1990).

bit over the years… At any given time we are usually aware of only a tiny part of it….”

An essential part of the self-system is self-regulation of learning, which may enable students to develop a positive approach and attitude toward self-motivation and dispositions that must be mastered: (1) planning, (2) knowledge awareness, (3) metacognition, (4) productive reflection, (5) self-efficacy, and (6) social efficacy.[54]

Planning

This aspect of self-regulation is associated with the student's ability to set functional and realistic goals. Regardless of the curriculum area in question, the student must have an interest in the area, and be motivated to achieve the goal. Educators must provide prerequisite skills to assist the student and ultimately lead him/her to develop intrinsic motivation needed to achieve the stated goal.

Knowledge Awareness

In order to achieve this self-regulation strategy, students must have a knowledge base in the selected subject area. Having a keen awareness of the content area will assist the students in understanding the dynamic of their strengths and weaknesses in the selected area. Educators must assess the knowledge bases of students to assist them in perfecting their own personal knowledge.

Metacognition

This strategy will equip students to reflect upon their own thinking. Students employing this strategy tend to inspect the extent of their planning and strategy. Based upon examination of the strategy, a student will have information to adjust, revise, or modify how the goal will be attained.

---

[54] D. Wittenburg & R. McBride, *Dispositions for Self-Regulation of Learning for Four Pre-service Physical Education Teachers.* (Manuscript submitted for publication, 2004).

Proactive Reflection

Proactive reflection denotes when students examine potential outcomes to reflect upon what might occur in the future based upon assumptions. The term is frequently referred to as forethought. The process is critical for setting functional and realistic goals to be achieved in the future. Educators should provide strategies to assist students in achieving their established goals; students will then be able to realistically project how long it will take to achieve their projected goals.

Self-Efficacy

This strategy refers to how a student feels about the inabilities to obtain goals in a content area. Self-efficacy can be low or high. A low self-efficacy tends to retard the achievement of goals; however, a high self-efficacy promotes the achievement of goals. According to Bandura,[55] if educators really want to assist students they must provide them with competencies and build opportunities for them to develop the competencies.

Social-Efficacy

Students' perceptions of what their peers and others think about them is referred to as social-efficacy. Perceptions do not have to be true; however, it can affect students' self-efficacy. Students tend to be influenced by peer standards. Both appropriate and inappropriate behaviors may be associated with peer standards and pressures. When appropriate behaviors are demonstrated and modeled, students usually show positive behaviors. When peer relations show pro-social skills, there is usually an increase in students internalizing appropriate behaviors.[56]

---

[55] A. Bandura, *Self-Efficacy: in Changing Societies* (Cambridge, MA: University Press, 1995).

[56] G. R. Taylor, *Curriculum Strategies: Social Skills Intervention for Young African-American Males* (Westport, CN: Praeger, 1997); S. J. Salend & C. R. Whittaker, Group evaluation: A collaborative peer-mediated behavior management system, *Exceptional Children*, 59 (1992) 203-209.

36

Summary

Maslow's[57] in-depth study of motivation has clearly shown that if motivation strategies are not employed in educating individuals their learning growth will be impeded. To ensure that education is a positive force in the student's life, educators need to make sure that certain motivational factors exist, which includes that the student's primary motivation, their calling, or vocation be nurtured. Additionally, Maslow articulated that motivation is involved in the demonstration of all learned responses. A learned behavior or response will not occur unless energized.

Motivation has a positive affect and influence on emotions and behaviors. Children tend to learn if teachers expect them to learn. An effective teacher will find creative ways to motivate each individual student, such as determining what rewards and/or incentives will motivate each student to achieve his/her best. Application of the motivational theories outlined in this chapter can assist teachers in identifying thoughts, emotions, dispositions, skills, and behaviors of children, and provide appropriate motivational strategies needed to encourage children to achieve at their optimal levels.

---

[57] A. H. Maslow, *Motivation and Personality* (New York: Harper, 1954).

Chapter 4

Contributions of Early Theories

Introduction

The first systematic study of human behavior may be traced to behaviorism. Prior to behaviorism, there was no systematic study of human behavior. Ivan Pavlov and Edward Thorndike were the first theorists to objectively study human learning. Major contributions of these theorists will be discussed in greater detail later in the text. Behaviorism advocates that principles of learning apply equally to humans and animals. Research findings from animals have been applied to humans premised upon the belief that animals and humans principally learn in the same way.

To the behaviorists, learning can be studied objectively by measuring and observing behavior by the researcher observing stimuli in the environment and responses that organisms make to those stimuli, frequently referred to as S-R Psychology.[58] The role of cognitive and internal processes in learning is not considered necessary or important in observing and measuring human behavior and learning by behaviorists. Additionally, they maintained: (1) if there has been no change in behavior, then no learning has occurred, (2) the mind is a blank tablet at birth for humans, and environmental factors shape behaviors, other than some instincts, of all organisms (humans and animals). Application of principles in this theory can assist educators in modifying, reducing, or eliminating inappropriate behaviors, which may interfere with learning.

Contributions of Early Theorists

Several theorists have made major contributions to behaviorism. The work of those who have influenced education and classroom practice in this

---

[58] J. E. Ormrod, *Human learning* (3rd ed.) (New Jersey: Prentice Hall, Inc., 1999).

country include Ivan Pavlov, Edward L. Thorndike, John Watson, Edwin Guthrie, and B. F. Skinner. We will address the contributions of Pavlov and Skinner and discuss in detail their significant contributions to behaviorism.

There are two excellent texts concerning contributions of Guthrie, Watson, Hebb, Thorndike, Watson, and Guthrie to the field of human learning. Therefore, their work will only be summarized. Refer to Hergenhan & Olson and Ormrod[59] for detailed analyses.

Edward L. Thorndike

Thorndike believed that the major components of learning are stimuli and responses connections. He called this connection Connectionism. Thorndike conducted several experiments with humans and animals. He concluded that animals that completed tasks took several trials, which he called trial and error learning. Based upon his experimentation with animals he formulated several laws of learning: (1) The Law of Effects, (2) The Law of Exercise, (3) The Law of Readiness, and (4) Subsidiary Laws. Refer to the glossary for examples and explanations of the laws. Thorndike transferred his trial and error learning to humans by inferring that they learn the same way as animals.

Thorndike's theories, principles, research and findings represented his views of learning theories. His experimentation and research supported the notion that learning consisted of the formation of physiological connections between stimuli and responses. Thorndike also made significant contributions to the field of education and teaching by applying psychological principles of learning to develop, teach, and evaluate the effectiveness of teaching.

John B. Watson

John Watson is frequently called the father of behaviorism. He introduced the term in the early twentieth century. It was Watson who first called for the scientific study of the psychological process by focusing on observable rather

---

[59] B. R., Hergenhahn & M. H. Olson, *An Introduction to Theories of Learning* (5th ed.) (New Jersey: Prentice Hall, 1997); Ormrod, 1999.

than non-observable behaviors. Watson's work was greatly influenced by early behaviorists, Pavlov and Thorndike. He employed their classical conditioned process as well as a model to conduct his experiments in human learning.

He proposed two laws: (1) The Law of Frequency, where the importance of repetition was stressed in learning, and (2) The Law of Recency, where the importance of timing was stressed. He believed that past experiences were essential for mostly all behaviors. He refuted the role of heredity factors in behavior and learning. He defended his view with the following quote:

> "Give me a dozen healthy infants, well-formed, and my own specified world to bring them up in and I'll guarantee to take any one at random and train him to become any type of specialist. I might select—doctor, lawyer, artist, merchant, chief, and yes, even beggar-man and thief, regardless of his talents, penchants, tendencies, abilities, vocations and race of his ancestors."[60]

Edwin R. Guthrie

Guthrie's[61] work was based upon John Watson's theory in that it emphasized the S-R connections. He did not support the role of rewards in modifying behaviors. Guthrie supported the view that only observable behaviors could be employed to understand learning. Unlike some behaviorists, Guthrie did not produce significant publications, he only produced one major publication, *The Psychology of Learning*, published in 1935 and revised in 1952. Guthrie compounded one theory of learning, where he explained all behaviors based upon the following principle: A stimulus that is followed by a particular response will, upon its recurrence, tend to be followed by the same response again. This S-R

---

[60] R. I. Watson, *The Great Psychologists* (3rd ed.) (Philadelphia, PA: Lippincott); G. Windholz, (1996a), Hypnosis and inhibition as viewed by Hdidenhain and Pavlov, *Integrative Physiological and Behavioral Science*, 31, (1971), 155-162.

[61] R. I. Watson, 1971.

connection gains its full strength on one trial. Guthrie conducted little research to support his premise.

Ivan P. Pavlov

Pavlov was born on September 14, 1849 in Russia. Pavlov had a mediocre school career. He was educated first at the church school in Ryazan and then at the theological seminary. He had planned on a career in theology, but was so influenced by Russian translations of Western scientific writings, and particularly with their Darwinian overtones, that he abandoned his religious training.[62] In 1870, he enrolled in physics, mathematics, and took courses in natural science. Natural science caused him to become absorbed with physiology and medicine.

Five years later, in 1875, Pavlov completed the courses and was awarded the degree of candidate of Natural Sciences. He continued his education in physiology at the Academy of Medical Surgery and was awarded a gold medal four years later. In 1883, he developed the basic principles of the function of the heart and the nervous system. Pavlov's experiments showed that there was a basic pattern in the reflex regulation of the activity of the circulatory organs. His worked earn him a Nobel Prize in 1904.

This research led the way for new advances in medicine. He clearly showed in one of his experiments that the nervous system played a significant part in regulating the digestive process. His research into the digestive process led him to create a science of conditioned reflexes. From his research findings, Pavlov was able to study all psychic activity objectively.[63]

---

[62] Windholz, 1997.

[63] I. P. Pavlov, *Conditioned reflexes* (G. V. Anrep, Tran.) (London: Oxford University Press, 1927).

Classical Conditioning

Pavlov's experiments with conditioning reflexes in his dog are well reported in the professional literature.[64] He devised a series of experiments in classical conditioning, which is essentially sign language. In his experiments, he demonstrated that the pairing of a neutral stimulus with an unconditioned stimulus until the formal comes to substitute for the latter in eliciting a response. The first response to be conditioned by Pavlov was the salivary reflect.

According to Ormrod,[65] Pavlov's experiment in conditioning his dog is reflected by a stimulus response sequence. The sequence is modified premise upon a three-step method.

1. A neutral stimulus (NS) is a stimulus to which the organism does not respond. In the experiment the bell was originally a neutral stimulus that did not elicit a salivation response.

2. The second stimulus is called an unconditioned stimulus (UCS) and the response is called an unconditioned response (UCR), because the organism responds to the stimulus unconditionally, without having had to learn to do so. In Pavlov's experiment, meat power was an unconditioned stimulus to which the dog responded with the unconditioned response of salivation.

3. When steps 1 and two are paired, step (1) the neutral stimulus now elicits a response. The NS has become a conditioned stimulus (CS) to which the dog has learned a conditioned response (CR). The US and UR are an unlearned stimulus-response unit called a reflex.

The main features of Pavlov's classical conditioning procedure are discussed in this chapter. Before conditioning, the UCS naturally elicits the UCR.

---

[64] S. B. Klein, *Learning: Principles and Applications* (3rd ed.) (New York, NY: McGraw-Hill, Inc., 1996); B. R. Hergenhahn, & M. H. Olson, *An Introduction to Theories of Learning* (5th ed.) (New Jersey: Prentice Hall, 1997).

[65] Ormrod, 1999.

A neutral stimulus (such as tone) has no eliciting effect. During conditioning, the neutral stimulus is paired with the UCS. Through its association with the UCS, the neutral stimulus becomes a CS and elicits similar to the UCR.

Classical conditioning is also referred to as learning through stimulus substitution, since the conditioned stimulus, after being paired with the unconditioned stimulus often enough, can then be substituted for it. The CS will evoke a similar, but weaker, response. It is also referred to as signal learning, because the CS serves as a signal for the occurrence of the UCS.

Most responses that can reliably be elicited by a stimulus can be classically conditioned. For example, the knee-jerk reflex, the eye-blink reflex, and the pupilliary reflex can all be conditioned to various stimuli.[66]

The more time between the signal and the subsequent event, the better the animal can prepare for the event, and this is of special importance when the event is noxious or potentially harmful. A longer preparation time requires longer interval between the CS and the UCS, such as occurs in either delayed or trade conditioning, both of which require a nervous system that can maintain excitation after the stimulus has ceased to act. Such animals have more time to prepare for oncoming events, which means that they can employ strategy and tactics instead of only reflexes.

The Classical Conditioning Model

Classical conditioning has been conducted on a number of organisms and humans.[67] The classical conditioning model becomes active when two stimuli are presented to an organism at approximately the same time. When a stimulus elicits

---

[66] Lefrancois, 1999.

[67] L. P Lipsitt, & H. Kaye, Conditioning sucking in the human newborn, *Psychonomic Science*, 1 (1964), 29-30; H. W., Reese, & L. D. Lipsitt, *Experimental Child Psychology* (New York, NY: Academic Press, 1970); A. Macfarlane, What a baby knows, *Human Nature*, 1 (1978), 74-81; R. Thompson, & J. McConnell, Classical conditioning in the planarian, dugesia doroto cephala, *Journal of Comparative and Physiological Psychology*, 48 (1955), 65-68.

response, the stimulus brings about a response automatically within the organism; in essence, the organism has no control over the response.[68]

In classical conditioning the CS precedes the UCS, and, as with most sequential events, the time relations between these two stimuli are crucial. Conditioning is faster when the CS is followed almost immediately by the unconditioned stimulus. The best interval in humans is about half a second, which is approximately the optimal interval between the warning stimulus and the signal to respond in a reaction time experiment. Half a second is also roughly the time estimated for the reticular formation to alert the cerebral cortex to its optimal level of arousal for acting on incoming stimuli. All these time relations suggest that the CS acts as a signal that prepares the organism for the oncoming UCS.

At intervals slower than half a second or greater than two seconds, conditioning is slower. In terms of the time interval between the CS and UCS, there are three possibilities: simultaneous, delayed, and trace conditioning.[69]

Simultaneous Conditioning

The CS and UCS start and end at the same time, but very little conditioning results. An example, according to Klein,[70] would be an individual walking into a fast food restaurant. The restaurant (CS) and food (UCS) would occur at the same time. This simultaneous conditioning in this case would lead to weak hunger conditioned to the restaurant.

Delayed Conditioning

The (CS) onset proceeds (UCS) onset. When the CR first appears, it occurs immediately after the onset of the conditioned stimulus, but eventually it is delayed until just prior to the onset of the UCS. A darken sky that proceeds a

---

[68] Hergenhahn & Olson, 1977; K. L. Hollis, Contemporary research on Pavlovian conditioning: A new functional analysis, *American Psychologists*, 52 (1997), 956-965.

[69] S. B. Klein, *Learning: Principles and Applications* (3rd ed.) (New York, NY: McGraw-Hill, Inc., 1996).

[70] Klein, 1996.

severe storm is an example of delayed conditioning. A person having experienced this condition may become afraid when a dark sky appears.

Trace Conditioning

The CS starts and terminates before the onset of the UCS. Presumably, the response is conditioned to the neutral trace of the conditioned stimulus, hence, the name trace conditioning. With this conditioning the CS is presented and terminated prior to the USC onset. A parent who calls a child to dinner is using trace conditioning.[71]

Backward Conditioning

This time relation requires brief mention. In backward conditioning, the UCS precedes the CS. Tait and Saladin, 1986, explanation provides some clarity to backward conditioning. They indicated that backward conditioning may not produce the intended CS but may result in the development of another type CR. The backward conditioning paradigm is also a conditioned inhabitation procedure where the CS is paired with the absence of the UCS. In some instances, a person would experience a conditioned inhibition rather than conditioned excitation when exposed to the CS.

Extinction

So long as the CS and UCS are paired, the CR is likely to occur, but if the CS is presented repeatedly without the UCS, the CR gradually dissipates. The process is called extinction, and it continues until there is no longer any CR.

When the organism no longer responds to the CS, it might appear that the effects of the conditioning process are eliminated, but they are not. After a brief time CR reappears, though it is weaker. This phenomenon is called spontaneous recovery. It may require repeated extinctions to eliminate all the effects of the original conditioning.

---

[71] Klein, 1996.

Higher Order Conditioning

A UCS is usually part of a stimulus response reflexive unit that is programmed in the nervous system. Pavlov's experiment with his dog provided an excellent example of higher order conditioning. After the dog had been conditioned to salivate at the sound of a bell, the bell was later rang in conjunction with a NS such as a flash of light. This NS would also elicit a salivation response, even though it had never been directly associated with meat.[72] The flash of light, through its association with the bell, will eventually elicit the conditioned flexion response, which is called higher order conditioning. It consists of using a previously CS (the bell) as an UCS with which a new, NS (the flash of light) can be paired to obtain another CS.

First order conditioning is nothing more than the process of conditioning explained. Second order conditioning consists of using the CS from first order conditioning as the UCS in a subsequent conditioning procedure. Pavlov has demonstrated third order conditioning, but is extremely difficult to obtain.

Higher order conditioning is difficult to accomplish because of the ever-present problem of extinction. When the CS is presented without the UCS, the CR is extinguished. Thus, when the light and the bell in the example are paired, the CR to the tone weakens because the original UCS (the electric shock) is absent. This tendency can be counteracted by interspersing trails of first-order conditioning (pairing of the bell with electric shock), thereby, strengthening the original CR. These difficulties in obtaining higher order conditioning underscore the limitations of classical conditioning: it cannot be separated very far from the unconditioned stimuli that comprise one half of the innately programmed reflexive units.

Discrimination

Survival often involves a choice of alternative responses, and the ability to choose requires the ability to discriminate among objects and events in the

---

[72] Ormrod, 1999.

46

environment. Such discrimination is easy to condition, even in so primitive an animal as the flatworm. Discrimination can be induced by two ways, prolonged training and differential reinforcement. First, if a CS is paired with a UCS many times, the tendency to respond to stimuli related to the CS. But for those stimuli not identical to the CS, the response level decreases. The second way of bringing about discrimination is through differential reinforcement. This process involves presenting a high frequency tone with a low frequency tone that will occur during extinction. Only the high frequency tone is followed by reinforcement after such training. When the animal is presented with tones other than high frequency tones during extinction, it tends not to respond to them.[73]

Classical Conditioning in Human Learning

The principle of classical conditioning has been successfully used to control or condition human behaviors in the areas of involuntary responses, fears, and phobias.[74] Involuntary responses can be induced through hunger. When animals or people are exposed to food, they exhibit a set of UCRS that prepare them to digest, metabolize, and store ingested foods. These unconditioned feeding responses, are involuntary and include the secretion of saliva, gastric juices, pancreatic enzymes, and insulin. Powley's[75] research claimed that these unconditioned feeding responses in humans can be controlled.

Miller[76] and Staats and Staats[77] research have reported the development of fear through classical and conditioning in animals and humans. Their findings

[73] Hergenhahn & Olson, 1997.

[74] J. S. Bruner, J. Goodnow, & G. Austin, *A Study of Thinking* (New York, NY: Wiley and Sons, 1956).

[75] R. L Powley,. The ventro media hypothalamic syndrome, satiety, and a cephalic phase hypothesis, *Psychological Review*, 84 (1977), 89-126.

[76] N. E. Miller, Studies of fear as an acquirable drive: Fear as motivation and fear reduction as reinforcement in learning of new response, *Journal of Experimental Psychology*, 38 (1948), 89-101.

supported the premise that fear is conditioning when a novel stimulus (CS) is associated with an aversive event. An example, given by Klein,[78] provides some clarity to this premise. He states that an examination is an aversive event, and explains that when an individual takes a test (UCS), the examination elicits an unconditioned pain reaction (UCR). The psychological distress experienced when an instructor hands you a test is one aspect of your pain reaction, and the increased physiological arousal is another part of your response to receiving an examination. Although the intensity of the aversive event may lesson while you are taking a test, you will not experience relief until you complete it.

More recently Ormrod[79] indicated that individuals who are unusually afraid of failing may have previously associated failure with unpleasant circumstances, such as associating failure with pain punishment. Educators should be careful to make certain that this type of association with failure does not become such strong CS for children that they resist engaging in new activities and attempting challenging problems.

Ivan Pavlov's research in conditioning had a significant impact on the development of psychology in the world. His experiments with salivation responses in dogs were instrumental in developing classical conditioning. The impact of his work received worldwide recognition, and in 1904, he was awarded a Nobel Prize in Medicine and Physiology for his work on digestion.[80]

Pavlov's experiments have provided a theoretical framework for the continuation of scientific studies in contemporary psychology and related medical research activities. Additionally, his research in classical conditioning has

---

[77] C. K., Staats & A. W. Staats, Meaning established by classical conditioning, *Journal of Experimental Psychology*, 54 (1957). 74-82.

[78] S. B. Klein, *Learning: Principles and Applications* (3rd ed.) (New York, NY: McGraw-Hill, Inc., 1996).

[79] Ormrod, 1999.

[80] G. P. Smith, Pavlov and appetite, *Integrative Physiological and Behavioral Science*, 30 (1995), 169-174.

48

assisted us in understanding human fears and phobia in humans, and has provided
a model for educators to employ in reducing, controlling, or eliminating fears and
phobia, as well as providing strategies for modifying, reducing, eliminating, or
controlling behaviors of humans and animals in their natural or constructed
environments.

Burrhus Frederic Skinner

Burrhus Frederick Skinner is an American psychologist who was one of
the many giants of behavioral psychology in the 20th century. He was born in
Susquehannah, Pennsylvania in 1904. Skinner, since his early days, was an
avowed behaviorists who found psychology intriguing. In 1931, he received his
Ph.D. in Psychology, and then spent several years conducting research projects.
The Behavior of Organisms was his first major publication. It was published in
1938 and provided the framework for his principles of operant conditioning. He
was famous for his popular book *Walden Two.*[81] Through his writings and
research, over a span of two decades, Skinner was recognized as the leader in the
behaviorism movement. He held and promoted this leadership until his death.[82]

Respondents and Operant Behavior

In Lefranscios'[83] view responses elicited by a stimulus are called
respondents. Responses emitted by an organism are called operants. In
respondent behavior the organism acts on the environment. Other differences
between the two behaviors may be seen in the following ways, respondent
behaviors are shown by the organism's involuntary behaviors to a stimulus,
whereas operant behaviors are more voluntary.

---

[81] B. F. Skinner, *Walden Two* (New York, NY: Macmillan, 1948).

[82] B. F. Skinner, The science of learning and the art of teaching, *Harvard Educational Review*,
124 (1954), 86-87; B. F. Skinner, Teaching machines, *Science*, 128 (1958), 969-977; B. F.
Skinner, *Beyond Freedom and Dignity* (New York, NY: Knopf, 1971); J. G., Holland & B. A.
Skinner, *The Analysis of Behavior: A Program for Self-instruction* (New York, NY: McGraw Hill,
1961).

[83] Lefranscios, 1999.

Operant Conditioning

Operant conditioning is a form of learning "in which the consequences of behavior lead to changes in the probability of its occurrence,"[84] Skinner prescribed to this theory and furthered it with his own work that evolved into what has been called, "The Behavior Analysis Model," which is commonly referred to as behavior modification. This model is a systematic shaping process that uses positive and negative reinforcers to obtain desired behaviors or extinguish inappropriate ones. This technique can be used in the context of child rearing or diminishing simple deviant social behaviors (e.g., getting towed if parked in a reserved parking space), but is most widely known for its use in the classroom. The technique has been well demonstrated by several authors Ormrod and Hergenhahn and Olson.[85] Its benefits are felt even more profoundly in the special education classroom, where behavior problems abound, as it is widely used to change inappropriate behaviors or teach appropriate ones. Skinner's entire theory is based upon the use of reinforcers.[86]

Skinner experimented with the use of positive and negative reinforcers and the timing in which they were given in an effort to shape a desired behavior. He created a learning apparatus called the Skinnerean Box, which was designed for "teaching" rats to push a lever in order to get food pellets. Immediately after the rat made any movement toward the lever, it received a food pellet (positive reinforcer). With each successive move it made toward the lever, it was compensated with a food pellet and this reinforced the rat's movement toward the level (successive approximations). It was ultimately rewarded with food when it

---

[84] Skinner, 1948.

[85] Ormrod, 1999; Hergenhahn & Olson, 1977.

[86] D. L. Miller, & M. L. Kelley, The use of goal setting and contingency contracting for improving children's homework performance, *Journal of Applied Behavior Analysis*, 27 (1994), 73-84; Hergenhan & Olson, 1997; S. B. Klein, *Learning: Principles and Applications* (3rd ed.) (New York, NY: McGraw-Hill, Inc., 1996); M. V. Covington, *Making The Grade: A Self-worth Perspective on Motivation and School Reform* (Cambridge, UT: Cambridge University Press, 1992).

50

finally reached the lever and pushed down hard enough to receive the pellets from the dispenser.[87] The idea of shaping the rat's behavior was extended beyond the laboratory and used to shape human behavior as well.[88] Key components that are integral in achieving successful behavior modification are timing, consistency, and effectiveness of the reinforcers. Skinner discovered the importance of the timing of the reinforcer. If the food pellet was not given to the rat immediately after he moved toward the lever, the movement was not being reinforced. In order for behavior modification to be successful, the delay between the response and the reinforcer should be minimal. At the same time, Skinner concluded that consistency is equally important. Initially, the reinforcer must be given after every response; and then after some learning has taken place it is not always necessary, or in some cases, desirable, to reinforce each response.

Lastly, Skinner discovered that the reinforcer being used must, in fact, be rewarding for the learner.[89] If student's behaviors are being reinforced with candy and the student hates candy, then little learning will occur. Therefore, it is often necessary to experiment with different options for different students. Another important factor is that not all reinforcers are contrived; natural consequences of one's actions can be an equally or more effective reinforcer. Skinner developed the concept of two kinds of reinforcers: primary and secondary. Primary reinforcers are innately reinforcing and have not been learned (i.e., food, warmth, sexual gratification), while secondary reinforcers are learned through classical conditioning.[90] When these two reinforcers are paired together, learning naturally occurs. For example, in teaching a dog to sit, a treat (primary reinforcer) is given

---

[87] I. H. Iverson, Skinner's early research: From reflexology to operant conditioning, *America Psychologist*, 47, 1318-1328, 1992.

[88] D. J. Delprato, & B. D. Midley, Some fundamentals of B. F. Skinner's behaviorism, *American Psychologist*, 47 (1992), 1507-1520.

[89] Ormrod, 1999.

[90] Hergenhahn & Olson, 1999.

each time the dog sits as the owner says "good dog" (secondary reinforcer). The dog eventually associates the treat with "good dog," as the positive reinforcer in the absence of the treat. This pairing of reinforcers is done regularly without premeditation of child rearing, on the job, and in many other social situations.

Reinforcement

Skinner considered that animal trainers, parents, and educators could not realistically walk around with primary reinforcers in their pockets and devote all of their time to rewarding behaviors in a timely, consistent manner keeping in mind all of the different reinforcers that were effective for each individual person. With this in mind, Skinner developed six different schedules of reinforcement and tested each of their effects on behavior.

The first schedule is continuous reinforcement schedule, in which the investigator used continuous reinforcement for every correct response made. The second schedule is fixed interval reinforcement schedule where the animal is reinforced for a response made only after a set interval of time. The third schedule is fixed ratio reinforcement schedule, which is employed whenever the response made by the animal is reinforced. The fourth schedule is variable interval reinforcement, with that schedule, the animal is reinforced for responses made at the end of time intervals of variable durations. The fifth schedule is variable ratio reinforcement where the reinforcer is received after a varying number of responses have occurred, this schedule produces the highest response rate. The six schedule is concurrent schedules and matching law where reinforcement is delivered under different schedules.

Positive and Negative Reinforcements

According to Skinner,[91] a positive reinforcer, either primary or secondary, is something that, when added to the situation by a certain response, increases the probability of that responses recurrence. Skinner,[92] also utilized and experimented

---

[91] Skinner, 1953.

[92] Skinner, 1953.

52

with negative reinforcers in an effort to shape behavior. Negative reinforcers are often confused with punishment, when, in fact, they are quite the contrary. Negative reinforcers remove unpleasant situations and in doing so reinforce the behavior that aided the learner in escaping the unpleasant situation. Negative reinforcers support a behavior that stops a negative event from happening or prevents it from happening at all. Using another sidewalk on a rainy day rather than the usual one prevents you from getting splashed by the puddles as cars passes. The use of another sidewalk (target behavior) is reinforced by avoiding the wet splashes (negative reinforcer) punishment that otherwise would have occurred.

Punishment, unlike negative reinforcers, is a negative consequence that leads to the reduction in the frequency of the behavior that produced it. Punishment suppresses a response as long as it is applied, the habit is not weaken and will return. According to Skinner:[93]

"Punishment is designed to remove awkward, dangerous, or otherwise unwanted behavior from a repertoire on the assumption that a person who has been punished is less likely to behave in the same way again. Unfortunately, the matter is not that simple. Reward and punishment do not differ merely in the direction of the changes they induce. A child who has been severely punished for sex play is not necessary less included to continue, and a man who has been imprisoned for violent assault is not necessarily less inclined toward violence. Punished behavior is likely to reappear after the punitive contingencies are withdrawn."

In summary, Skinner's major disagreement with punishment is that it is not effective in changing behavior in the long run.

According to Skinner,[94] punishment is used so widely because it is reinforcing to the punisher. He stated that we instinctively attack anyone whose

---

[93] Skinner, 1971.

[94] Skinner, 1953.

behavior displeases us. The immediate effect of the practice is reinforcing enough to explain its currency.

Skinner has provided us with some alternatives to punishment.

Change the circumstance causing the undesirable behavior. For example, to rearrange the seating of a child may reduce or eliminate the behavior.

The undesirable behavior can be satisfied by permitting the organism to perform the act until it is tired of it.

Some behaviors are considered normal for the development stage of the child, simply waiting for the child to outgrow the behavior is a recommended procedure.

Skinner recommended by letting time pass and ignoring behavior may be an effective method for controlling the behavior.

Probably the most effective alternative process according to Skinner[95] is probably extinction. He further stated that behavior persists because it is being reinforced. To reduce or eliminate undesirable behavior one needs to find the source of reinforcement and remove it.

Extinction

Once the reinforcement has been withdrawn, the amount of time required before the organism stop responding deviates from organism to organism due to continuous schedules of reinforcement, fixed schedules of reinforcement.[96] When a response is not reinforced it gradually return to its baseline. During the initial stage of extinction there may be a brief increase in the behavior being extinguished.[97]

---

[95] Skinner, 1953.

[96] Ormrod, 1999.

[97] D. C Lerman, & B. A. Iwata, Prevalence of the extinction burst and its attenuation during treatment, *Journal of Applied Behavior Analysis*, 28 (1995), 93-94.

54

An excellent example, according to Lefrancios,[98] is a behavior that has been extinguished through withdrawal of reinforcement often appears without any further conditioning when the animal is again placed under the same experimental conditions. The extinction period following spontaneous recovery is almost invariably much shorter than the first. Assume that the pigeon that Skinner conditioned to peck at a disk is taken out of the cage and not allowed to return to it for a considerable period of time. If it does not peck at the disk when it is reintroduced into the cage, one can infer that forgetting has occurred. One of Skinner's experiments showed at least one pigeon that had still not forgotten the disk-pecking response after six years. He also reported one instance of a pigeon that emitted 10,000 pecks prior to extinction.

Shaping

Slavin[99] wrote that shaping is employed in behavioral learning theories to refer to the teaching of new behaviors by reinforcing learners for approaching the desired final behavior. Shaping is considered to be an important tool in classroom instruction. Teachers may model and teach skills to children step by step until the children are ready to perform certain tasks in the skills and finally to complete the total skill. Shaping is also employed in training animals to complete tasks or acts when they do not ordinarily perform. The environment must be controlled if shaping is to be effective. The Skinnerean box is an excellent example of controlling the environment. The box included a mental bar that, when pushed down, causes a food tray to swing into reach long enough for the rat to grab a food pellet. By conducting the tasks, the rat was reinforced with food pellets.

Chaining

"Chaining" may be defined as the linking of a sequence of responses. It is an important component used in operant conditioning. All training works

---

[98] Lefrancios, 1999.

[99] R. E. Slavin, *Educational Psychology: Theory and Practice* (6th ed.) (Boston, MA: Allyn and Bacon, 2000).

backward from a primary reinforcer. The investigator reinforces one response, then two responses in a row, followed by reinforcing a sequence of three or more responses. Ormrod's[100] example provided clarity to the process:

"students in a first-grade classroom might learn to put their work materials away, sit quietly at their desks, and then line up single file at the classroom door before going to lunch." These behaviors or actions often require one step at a time, which is frequently identified as chaining.

Programmed Learning

Skinner's principles of learning have been applied to programmed learning. In Skinner's and Fletcher's[101] views, programmed learning is most effective when the information to be learned is presented in small steps, when rapid feedback is given to the learners concerning the accuracy of their responses, and the learners are permitted to learn at their own pace. According to Skinner, a teaching machine meets the prerequisite for programmed learning. In an article written by Skinner in 1958, he outlined the values of teaching machines. Since his views on the matter have been succinctly reported elsewhere, we will simply summarize his views. A teaching machine:

1. Simply brings the student into contact with the person who composed the materials it presents
2. Is a labor-saving device because it can bring one programmer into contact with many students
3. Provide constant interchange between program and student
4. Induces sustained activity
5. Insists that a given point be thoroughly understood, either frame by frame or set-by-set, before the student moves on
6. Presents just the material for which the student is ready

---

[100] Ormrod, 1999.

[101] Skinner, 1958; Fletcher, 1992.

7. Assist the student in arriving at the correct answer

8. Reinforces the student for every correct response, using immediate feedback

Research findings involving the effectiveness of program learning are inconclusive. Research conducted by Schramm and Lumsdaine[102] pinpointed the controversy in the field. Approximately half of the studies summarized by Schramm found programmed learning to be effective when compared with traditional programs. Data from these studies tend to support the notion that additional research is needed investigating the various components of programmed instruction that make it an effective teaching device.

The concepts of programmed learning have been infused into computer-assisted instruction. Computer software programs are used to instruct students in a variety of skills.[103] Polloway and Patton[104] alluded to the value of CIA in teaching mathematics. Bakken and Goldsten[105] stated that computers have the ability of presenting information in a multisensory mode, which make them suitable for individuals with various types of disabilities.[106]

These programmed devices have had minimum impact on educational practices today. However, it is believe that the impact in the future will be significant on educational changes and reforms.

---

[102] W. Schramm, *The Research on Programmed Instruction: An Annotated Bibliography.* (Washington, DC: U. S. Office of Education, 1964); A. A. Lumsdaine, Educational technology, programmed learning, and instructional sciences. In E. R. Hilgard (Ed.), Theories *of Learning and Instruction* (Chicago, IL: University of Chicago Press, 1964).

[103] J. S. Choate, *Successful Inclusion Teaching* (Boston, MA: Allyn & Bacon, 1977).

[104] E. A., Polloway & J. R. Patton, *Strategies for Teaching Learners with Special Needs* (New York, NY: Merrill, 1993).

[105] J. A. Bakken, Evaluating the World Wide Web, *Teaching Exceptional Children*, 36 (6), (1998), 48-52; C. Goldstein, Learning at cyber camp, *Teaching Exceptional Children*, 30 (5), (1998), 16-26.

[106] K. Ryba, L. Selby, & P. Nolan, Computers empower students with special needs, *Educational Technology*, 53 (1995), 82; E. Cornish, The cyber future: 92 ways our lives will change by the year 2025, *The Futurist*, 6 (1996).

Summary

Skinner's work in behaviorism makes him the indisputable spokesperson in the field.[107] He raised experimentation in animal behavior to a scientific level through the use of the Skinnerean Box. Other contributions, included experimenting with the teaching machine and programmed learning. These experiments still have a significant impact on educational reforms today. It would be remiss if Skinner's contributions in operant conditioning were not summarized. His principles of operant conditioning were based on a system of controlling behavior through positive and negative reinforcement.

Few fields in American psychology have received more attention in the past decades than that of operant conditioning, and none has been attacked more vigorously by critics of all persuasions for its practices and theories, particularly in the area of educational and social control. Whatever the arguments for or against the methods or the theory of their operation, the fact remains that rigorous psychophysical methods have successfully been developed for animals with the aid of operant techniques.

Lafrancios[108] sums up operant conditioning by stating that, "it involves a change in the probability of a response as a function of events that immediately follow it. Events that increase the probability of a response are termed reinforcers. Aspects of the situation accompanying reinforcement become discriminative stimuli that serves as secondary reinforcers." These reinforcers may be positive or negative, primary or secondary, and a variety of reinforcement schedules may be applied to record and evaluate behaviors.

Skinner's experiments with humans and animals have been supported by a preponderance of research studies. Many of them, which were conducted by him,

---

[107] Skinner, 1945, 1953, 1954, 1958, 1966b, 1971. 1989.

[108] G. R. Lefrancios, *Theories of Human Learning* (Stamford, CA: CT Wadsworth/Thomson, 2000.

are reflected throughout this chapter. Most of the studies support the premise of immediate consequences, which implies that behavioral changes are based upon immediate reinforcement. In addition, pleasurable consequences, increases the frequency of a behavior, whereas negative consequences reduce the frequency of behavior.

Skinner objected to speculation concerning unobserved behaviors. He believed that most theories of learning were wasteful and unproductive because they were not based upon observable behaviors.

Chapter 5

Application of Behavioral Theories

Today, behaviorism owes much of its survival to theorists such as Pavlov, Watson, Skinner, and Guthrie. Principles of behaviorism are currently being used by researchers to evaluate human and animal learning. Historically, behaviorists place little or no emphasis on intrinsic traits. Today, behaviorists also recognize that the value of intrinsic traits such as motivation and interests in affecting learning or punishment has changed from the view of early theorists. Early theorists maintained that punishment has little or no affect on behavior. Present-day theorists support the notion that punishment may affect learning.[109] Historically, behaviorists divorced themselves from the role of cognitive factors in learning. Present day behaviorists recognize the role of cognitive traits and environment in understanding learning.[110]

Early behaviorists were not concerned with the role of mental traits in the learning process. They inferred that evaluation of learning could not be achieved through observations, but through introspection. This view was held until the late nineteenth century when the study of learning was scientifically studied. The works of Pavlov, Thorndike, and Skinner added significantly to the movement. Pavlov's experiments assisted in making the study of learning a scientific process. Thorndike developed several laws of learning using scientific procedures. The law of effect has implications today for classroom implications.

---

[109] H. Rachlin, *Introduction to Modern Behaviorism* (3rd ed.) (New York, NY: W. H. Freeman, 1991).

[110] R. M. Church, Human models of animal behavior, *Psychological Science*, 4 (1993), 170-173; S. H. C. Hulse, The present status of animal cognition: An introduction, *Psychological Science*, 4 (1993), 154-155; Rachlin, 1991; E. A. Wasserman, Comparative cognition: Toward a general understanding of cognition in behavior, *Psychological Science*, 4 (1993), 156-161.

60

Skinner was concerned with the relationships between behavior and its consequences. He articulated that if an individual's behavior is immediately followed by pleasurable consequences, the individual will engage in that behavior more frequently. The use of pleasant and unpleasant consequences to change behavior is often referred to as operant conditioning.[111] Principles of operant conditioning and Skinner's experiments and their scientific relevance will be overviewed in Chapter 5.

The Impact of Behaviorism

The impact of behaviorism on classroom practices emphasizes the role of drill and practice, rewards, and breaking negative behaviors in the classroom. In order to fully realize the impact of behaviorism in the classroom, the learning must be actively engaged in the process. Strangers must be introduced thereby enabling the reader to assess the learner's behavior and learning by objectively noting changes in behavior. According to behaviorists, implications of behavioral strategies in the classroom by teachers should involve drill, practice, behavioral intervention strategies, and appropriate rewards and reinforcement for changing negative behaviors. Essential to the process are rewards and reinforcement. Rewards can be either or external and internal. External rewards may include tangible items, such as food, praise, toys, gold stars, etc. Internal rewards are associated with the personality. Educators should design educational experiences which deflate the id and develop the ego and superego. When this strategy is employed, children's egos can be developed to guide their efforts and reward their successes in achieving their goals and mastering their behaviors. Individually designed instrumental units based upon culture experiences and learning styles can assist children in integrating external and internal rewards.

---

[111] E. A. Wasserman, Comparative cognition: Toward a general understanding of cognition in behavior, *Psychological Science*, 4 (1993), 156-161.

Behavioral Strategies

Behaviorism continues to influence educational practices. According to Kohn,[112] education cannot avoid behaviorism entirely. Reinforcement will always be an important tool for shaping behavior. Principles of conditioning are reflected in many aspects of learning. We will summarize these strategies we believe to have relevance for education.

Mastery Learning

According to Guskey,[113] mastery learning is one of the most well researched instructional models in this country. The model had its inception in the works of Camenius, Pestalozz and Herbant. Research conducted by Guskey and Gates,[114] indicates that mastery learning significantly improve achievement of children engaged in the process.

Mastery learning is based upon the behaviorist's approach and supports the belief that gives appropriate environmental conditions, such as reinforcing appropriate behaviors. People are capable of acquiring many complex behaviors. Mastery learning requires that conditioning concept of shaping. Refer to Chapter 4 for techniques to develop shaping techniques.[115]

---

[112] A. Kohn, *Punished by Rewards: The Trouble with Gold Stars, Incentive Plans, A's, Praise, and Other Bribes* (Boston, MA: Houghton Mifflin, 1993).

[113] T. R. Guskey, Mastery learning. In J. H. Block, S. T. Everson & T. R. Guskey (Eds.), *School Improvement Programs* (New York, NY: Scholastic, 1995).

[114] T. R. Guskey, & S. L. Gates, Synthesis of research on the effects of mastery learning in elementary and secondary classrooms, *Educational Leadership*, 43 (8) (1986), 73-80.

[115] Ormrod, 1999.

Mastery Learning Defined

Mastery learning is an educational theory developed by Benjamin S. Bloom, with the basic principle that all children can learn when provided with conditions that are appropriate for their learning.[116] Mastery learning is defined in various ways. In its simplest form, mastery learning means that a learner must be able to demonstrate mastery or attainment of specific criteria in the following areas: cognitive, affective, and psychomotor domains, and to encompass all phases of education from the pre-primary to the graduate.[117] In essence, mastery learning is a theory about teaching and learning that is closely tied to a set of instructional strategies.[118] The Hunter[119] model provides specific ways that it can be used in teaching.

The Hunter Model

In a recent publication by Danielson and McGreal,[120] they overviewed the Hunter Model. They articulated that it was a theory based upon a behavioristic approach to learning. Learning concepts in the model embrace motivation, retention, and transfer. These concepts formed the bases for the authors to develop a set of prescriptive learning and instructional practices designed to improve student learning and instructional practices. The authors further voiced that the Hunter Model dominated views of teaching into the 1980's and commenced a trend toward increased instructional focused staff development that persists to the present.

---

[116] P. Chance, Master of mastery, *Psychology Today*, 21 (4) (1987), 42-46.

[117] M. J. Palardy, Mastery learning: A mixed view. *Education*, 107 (4) (1987), 424-427.

[118] T. R. Guskey, Rethinking mastery learning reconsidered, *Review of Educational Research*, 57 (2) (1987), 225-229.

[119] M. C. Hunter, *Mastery Teaching* (Thousand Oaks, CA: Corwin Press, 1982).

[120] C. Danielson, & T. L. McGreal, *Teacher Evaluation to Enhance Professional Practice* (Alexandria, VA: Association for Supervision and Curriculum Development, 2000).

The effect of the Hunter Model assisted in developing teacher-centered and structured classrooms. Many school districts in the country adopted the model and employed Hunter's seven steps in designing instructional strategies and lesson plans. The steps include:

1. Anticipatory set.
2. Statement of objectives.
3. Instructional input.
4. Modeling.
5. Checking for understanding.
6. Guided practice.
7. Independent practice.

These steps became the major evaluative techniques used to evaluate the effectiveness of the model. As a result, the model was displayed as encouraging a single view of teaching, which has persisted into the present century. Despite the misuse of research, the Hunter Model has made a significant contribution to the field by assisting educators in developing a knowledge base in the field.[121]

The Hunter model[122] is based upon the mastery-learning model. Hunter referred to that model as mastery teaching. Hunter defined master teaching as:

"A way of thinking about and organizing the decisions that all teachers must make before, during, and after teaching. These decisions are based on research but should be implemented with artistry."

Components of Mastery Learning

Mastery learning is premised upon the fact that most students can learn curricula skills provided that they are broken down into small sequential steps. In addition, Slavin[123] maintained that teachers must state objectives clearly,

---

[121] Hunter, 1982.

[122] Hunter, 1982.

[123] R. E. Slavin, *Educational Psychology: Theory and Practice* (6th ed.) (Boston, MA: Allyn and Bacon, 2000).

determine the type of instruction to employ, assess abilities and disabilities of children, and provide individualized and enrichment activities for the varying needs and abilities presented by children. Each of the points advanced by Slavin will require planning and assessment of children.

In support of Slavin's beliefs relevant to mastery learning, Ormrod[124] reflected that in order for mastery learning to be effective the following components should be evident:

1. Instruction should be broken down into small management and discrete units.

2. Units should be sequenced such that basic concepts and procedures are learned first in order to build a foundation for more complex concepts. Instruction should move from the simple to the complex (task analysis) from the known, and from the concrete to the abstract.

3. Mastery should be demonstrated at the conclusion of each unit by showing that skills have been mastered through tests or other objective measures determined by the teacher.

4. A concrete, observable criteria for mastery of each unit should be clearly articulated to students.

5. Additional remedial and/or enrichment activities should be provided for students who need them in order to master the units.

What is mastery learning and what is not mastery learning has caused a great deal of controversy. The label mastery learning has been applied to a broad range of education materials and curricula which bears no resemblance to the ideas described by its founder and refined by its advocates. In the mastery-learning framework, students are given a pretest. The items of the pretest are correlated to a set of learning objectives. The pretest gives the teacher a clear picture of what the student knows or lacks for the purpose of devising

---

[124] Ormrod, 1999.

instructional strategies to enrich their knowledge or improve their weaknesses. Students are constantly given feedback and correctives as they move through the learning objectives.

Feedback and correctives are means of monitoring students' progress and providing activities to remediate their deficits. At the end of the unit, the students are given a post-test to determine the extent to which they have mastered a unit's objectives. In essence, all mastery learning programs must have feedback and corrective activities. If teaching strategies are not congruent with feedback and corrective activities, then you do not have mastery learning. For example, suppose an English teacher was to provide feedback to students relating to grammar and punctuation, but are evaluated on content and organization of their composition. In the mastery-learning framework, the feedback students receive should always be congruent with specific learning criteria and the procedures used to evaluate their learning.[125] Mastery learning is equal to a set of behavioral objectives plus feedback and corrective activities, tied together by effective instruction to produce the competent learner.

Proponents of Mastery Learning

There have been a variety of approaches used by educational systems around the country and the world to improve the quality of education received by our young people. However, mastery learning has attracted a great deal of attention and controversy within the last score. Many studies have shown that the quality of instruction and highly effective schools consistently point to the components of mastery learning as an integral part of successful teaching and learning. According to Guskey,[126] many school systems believe that the implementation of mastery learning can indeed lead to striking improvements in a wide range of student learning outcomes. Research findings have shown that

---

[125] Guskey, 1987.

[126] Guskey, 1987.

mastery learning can improve students' achievement and promote positive self-esteem.[127]

Several studies have found mastery learning to be of significant benefit for low achieving children.[128] The research indicated that when mastery-learning strategies were not in conjunction with corrective techniques, achievement gains were not noted.

Classroom Implications

According to Kulik, Kulik, and Bangert-Downs,[129] learning for mastery, students clearly do better than other students on tests developed to fit local curricula and do slightly better than others on standardized tests that sample objectives from many school systems and many grade levels. Even though mastery learning students only do slightly better than other students on standardized tests, they continue to do better academically. Many researchers have found evidence that standardized tests do not always cover what they are assumed to cover, such as the basic skills curriculum contained in textbooks.[130] Standardized tests are better measures of the long-term effects of schooling rather than the short-term effects of instruction, because of their broad, stable knowledge structures, which are more indicative of ability than recently acquired curricular knowledge.

Contrary to many critics, mastery learning places no restrictions on the scope, depth, or level of the objectives that are to be taught or that the students

---

[127] C. L. Kulik, J. A., Kulik, & R. L. Bangert-Drowns, Effectiveness of mastery learning programs: A meta-analysis, *Review of Educational Research*, 60 (2) (1990), 265-299; G. B, Semb, J. A., Ellis, & J. Araujo, Long-term memory for knowledge learned in school, *Journal of Educational Psychology, 55 (1989), 137-155.*

[128] B. S. Bloom, The sigma problem: The research for methods of instruction as effective as one-to-one tutoring, *Educational Research*, 13 (1984), 4-16; Kulik & Kulik, 1990.

[129] Kulik et al., 1990.

[130] L. W. Anderson, & R. B. Burns, Values evidence and mastery learning, *Review of Education Research, 57* (2) (1987), 215-223.

should learn.[131] In essence, mastery learning is neutral in regard to curricular issues. Feedback and correctives are essential elements of mastery learning. Students who are having problems with a particular objective are allotted additional time to address their weakness(es). However, feedback and correctives are obstacles for high achieving students to move on. Mastery learning should be highly individualized, with a great deal of focus placed on the extent of achievement, rate, and style of learning.[132] The learner should not wait for others to master the material. Guskey[133] stated the following rebuttal against the critics who believe that mastery learning does nothing else but teaching a test.

> "The element of congruence has led to the criticism of mastery learning being nothing more than teaching a test. This is not the case. If a test serves as a basis of the teaching, and if what is taught is determined primarily by the test, one who is teaching the test. Under these conditions, the content and format of the test guide and direct what is taught and how. With mastery learning, however, the learning objectives, which are generally determined by individual teachers, are the basis of the teaching the primary determiner of what is taught. In using mastery learning, teachers simply ensure their instructional procedures and test match what they have determined to be important for their students to learn. Instead of teaching to the test, these teachers are more accurately testing what is taught. After all, if it is important enough to test, it ought be important enough to teach. And if it is not important enough to teach, why should it be tested?"

---

[131] Guskey, 1987.

[132] Palardy, 1987.

[133] Guskey, 1987.

Critics of Mastery Learning

Several authors have voiced their opposition to mastery learning.[134] These authors claimed that students who learn quickly receive less instruction than their classmates and sometimes must wait for their slower classmates; consequently, they learn less than they normally would. Some students have greater difficulty passing mastery tests, despite repeating testing. Mastery learning does not permit, as such, interaction among students as other strategies.

The advantages and disadvantages of mastery learning is summarized below:

1. The effect of mastery learning is far greater on experimenter-made tests than on standardized tests.
2. Mastery learning restricts the teacher's ability to cover other areas or objectives that are not part of the unit objectives.
3. High achieving students are held back in group mastery learning programs until the majority has reached mastery.
4. Mastery learning only teaches a test.

Some researchers feel that standardized tests are more appropriate than criterion reference tests in measuring students' achievement in coverage (the amount of content learned) as well as mastery. Other critics of mastery learning feel that standardized tests tap a broad, stable knowledge structure more indicative of ability than recently acquired curricular knowledge.[135]

Behavior Analysis

The entire premise of the Behavior Analysis Model as it applies to the classroom, which is based on the above described work of Skinner, is based on

---

[134] M. Arlin, Time, equality, and mastery learning, *Review of Educational Research,* 54, (1984), 65-68; D. C. Berliner, The place of process-products research in developing the agenda for research on teaching thinking, *Educational Psychologist,* 24 (1989), 325-355; D. M. Sussman, PSI: Variations on a theme. In S. W. Bijou & R. Ruiz (Eds.) *Behavior Modification: Contribution to Education* (Hillsdale, NJ: Erlbaum, 1981).

[135] Guskey, 1987.

the analyzing of one's behavior. It includes gathering baseline data and clearly defining the behavior in measurable and observable terms that is undesirable, the target behavior. In order for the shaping to occur, behavioral objectives must be chosen, defined, and committed to in writing. Graphing random samples, observing student in several areas, and keeping daily anecdotals will aid in the overall effectiveness as well. Clearly defining the steps necessary in shaping the target behavior in writing before the behavior is modified, helps in noting and showing progress being made toward the ultimate behavioral goal. Similar to Skinner's rats, students' behaviors must be shaped in gradual successive approximations with timely, effective reinforcements consistently being awarded. This technique can be time consuming and intrusive in the classroom setting, but it ultimately helps students gain self-control of their own behaviors. Effective reinforcers must be identified, followed by a specific intervention plan based upon the target behavior to be changed. Both baseline data and data yielded from treatment are compared and measured.

The Application of Behavior Through a Token Economy System

A token economy system is based upon behavior modification principles. As in a behavioral modification system, positive and negative reinforcers are part of the system. A token system may be employed to assist students in identifying and improving their target behaviors.

Several researchers have summarized what they consider to be important components of a token economy system:[136]

1. A set of rules, developed with input from students, delineating specific behaviors which will be reinforced.

---

[136] J. G. Osborne, Free time as reinforcer in the management of classroom behavior, *Journal of Applied Behavior Analysis*, 2, (1969), 113-118; H. S. McKenzie, M. Clark, M. M. Wolf, R. Kothera, & C. Benson, Behavior Modification of children with learning disabilities using grades as tokens and allowances as back-up reinforcers, *Exceptional Children*, 34, (1968), 745-752.

2. Immediate reinforcement of tokens when appropriate behaviors are demonstrated.

3. Have in hand alternative reinforcers for back up or for special events.

4. A place where tokens can be used or exchanged for reinforcers.

School-Wide Token Economy System

Each student in the program should be individually evaluated by all staff and goals assigned to each student. The majority of the students participate in the development of behavioral goals with their therapist and/or homeroom teacher guiding them through this process. The students are split in two groups: returning students and new students. New students to the program should be evaluated at the end of each 45 minute period by a staff member. If the goal was accomplished for the majority of the period, the student receives a reward. If the student achieves the goal for at least half of the period, the student receives a partial reward. Points are tallied at the end of every period, at the end of the day, and at the end of the week. The student receives a paycheck every Friday for the amount of points earned in the week. Returning students follow a similar system, rather than staff evaluating their behaviors, students evaluate themselves at the end of every period. Staff has the opportunity to agree or disagree with the evaluation. These students use the traditional A,. B, C, and D system to grade themselves rather than the 2, 1, and 0. This system empowers students to become reflective and self-monitoring. It also rewards those students who can accurately self-evaluate rather than just those who can achieve their goals.

The students keep a working checkbook of the money they make on their point sheets. The money can be used to buy items from the school store (candy, microwaveable lunches and breakfasts, hair products, chips, etc.), and privileges (getting lunch out in the community, music listening privileges, applying for "credit"). Students must pay monthly rent of $600.00 in order to make use of both the school store and other privileges.

Contingency Contracting

Hergenhahn[137] articulated that contingency contracting comes from the fact that an agreement is made between teacher and student that certain activities will be reinforced that otherwise may not have been. In essence, the contract rearranges the reinforcement contingencies in the environment, causing them to be responsive to behavior patterns that one hopes to modify in some way. The teacher and student specify the conditions in the contract. When the conditions are approved, both teacher and student sign and date the contract.

Contracts may be designed to serve a variety of purposes, such as modifying classroom behavior, completing homework assignments, improving social behaviors, improving attendance rate, and academic performance are to name but a few types. Specific rewards are identified with each contract, amount, and frequency of the rewards are also specified in the contract.

Computer Technology and Technological Services

Today, computers are widely used in educating individuals.[138] Many computer software programs teach children a variety of skills. Other programs are used to develop social and emotional skills. The instructional units developed in this text can be facilitated through the use of computer software. Benefits from the use of microcomputers in improving the performance of children in the contract areas have been thoroughly documented.[139]

---

[137] Hergenhahn, 1997.

[138] J. M. Pena, How K-12 teachers are using computer networks, *Educational Leadership*, 53 (1995), 15-18; M. K. Frazier, Caution: Students on board the Internet, *Educational Leadership*, 53 (2) (1995), 26-27.

[139] R. T. Hughes, Computers in the classroom, *The Clearinghouse*, 4 (1996); M. K. Frazier, 1995; S. P. Walters, Accessible web design, *Teaching Exceptional Children*, 30 (6) (1998), 42-47; J. Fodi, Kids communicate through adaptive technology, *Exceptional Parent*, 36 (1991); B. Bader, Measuring progress of disabled students, *American Teacher*, 15 (1998); M. P. Lester, Connecting to the world, *Exceptional Parent*, 26 (11) (1996), 36-37; E. A. Polloway, & J. R Patton, *Strategies for Teaching Learners with Special Needs* (New York, NY: Merrill, 1993).

One of the major reasons why computers and other technological devices are not in great supply in many classrooms is due to expense. Many school districts simply do not have funds to equip their classroom. To assist school districts, the Clinton Administration proposed increased spending for computer technology.[140] Subsequently, the passage of the telecommunication act in 1996 included goals and provisions to network classrooms to the Internet by the year 2000. On January 1, 1998, approximately 2.3 billion dollars of annual, additional funding was made available to schools to offset connectivity costs. This law enabled school districts to use technology to enhance their instructional programs by having access to the World Wide Web. The North Carolina Department of Public Instruction appears to be in the forefront by profiting from the new federal regulation. The department has advanced a plan to have computers in every classroom by the next decade.

Advantages of Using Computers and Other Technical Devices

Computers are based upon principles of operant conditioning. Instruction is programmed in small sequential steps by computers and reinforcement is supplied immediately after the student supplies the correct response.

Generally, in computer technology, the drill-and-practice type programs lend themselves nicely in developing fluency on a skill. Currently, the best research suggests that when a student is in the fluency stage of learning, his/her use of drill-and-practice software will result in very positive student gains. Perhaps the best example of why these features are necessary can be seen in the area of mathematics.[141] Students who have difficulty in any area can spend time looking at the very creative artwork on the introductory screen while they gather their thoughts. This is considered to be a constructive use of learning time.

Prior to starting to use the computer, the teacher may wish to introduce computer-based vocabulary words to the students. Words such as information

---

[140] Hughes, 1996.

[141] Polloway et al., 1993.

highway, on board, user-friendly, or e-mail, help the student become familiar with some computer terminology. A vocabulary list that is user-friendly to the student can be a source on which the teacher can motivate students' interest.

The impact of the computer and other technological devices have been well entrenched into the American culture. Computers have impacted upon all aspects of society. The impact of computers on education is too numerous to be adequately covered in this chapter in any great detail. There are adequate texts which comprehensively address the issue. Our intention is simply to summarize what we consider to be major advantages of using the computer and technological devices in the classroom.

- Computer lab teachers are better able to teach classes of students with divergent abilities. Individual needs of children with disabilities can be successfully met through the use of integrated media systems.[142]

- While at one sitting, the student can literally visit a Web Site in virtually any country, or research a topic anywhere in the city, state, country, or world.[143]

- Students choose the computer to complete assignments when they are functional and real.[144]

- Since classrooms are information-rich environments, the computer offers a slow student an opportunity to sit down and repeat the right answer as many times as possible.[145]

- Video conferencing can be offered in one class via camera and computer screen, with a class in another wing of the school.[146]

---

[142] E. Cornish, The cyber future: 92 ways our lives will change by the year 2025, *The Futurist*, 6 (1996).

[143] M. P. Lester, 1996.

[144] Bolger, 1996.

[145] Polloway, 1993.

[146] J. S. Choate, *Successful Inclusion Teaching* (Boston, MA: Allyn & Bacon, 1977).

- Cyberism, the creed of information, will become a practical solution to some of the problems faced by students with disabilities.[147]

- The integration of technologies such as computers and telephones combined, and other assistive devices can open a source of information to children with disabilities, which have historically been denied to them.[148]

- Digital technology has the potential for making polished presentations of research findings and publications.

- Computer software has the potential for remediating skills in any content area.[149]

- Modifications and adaptations in Web Site designs and computer software packages are needed for many children to use effectively.[150]

- Computers have the ability of presenting information in a multi-sensory mode.[151]

Lester[152] contended that computers and high technologies offer children the ability to access databases. Ryba[153] remarked that adaptations of computers enable many children full access to them. Adaptations of other technological devices such as laser-scanners, alternative keyboards, and voice recognition, allow children to achieve their optimal level of growth.

---

[147] J. Fodi, Kids communicate through adaptive technology, *Exceptional Parent*, 36 (1991).

[148] M. P. Lester, Connecting to the world, *Exceptional Parent*, 26 (11) (1996), 36-37.

[149] J. S. Choate, *Successful Inclusion Teaching* (Boston, MA: Allyn & Bacon, 1977).

[150] J. R. Necessary & T. S. Parrish, The relationship, *Education*, (1996), 116-117; J. L. Bigge, *Teaching Individuals with Physical and Multiple Disabilities* (New York, NY: Macmillan, 1991); K. Ryba, L. Selby, & , P. Nolan, Computers empower students with special needs, *Educational Technology*, 53 (1995), 82.

[151] C. Goldstein, Learning at cyber camp, *Teaching Exceptional Children,* 30 (5), (1998), 16-26.

[152] Lester, 1996.

[153] K. Ryba, L. Selby, & P. Nolan, Computers empower students with special needs, *Educational Technology*, 53 (1995), 82.

Integrating Technology in the Classroom

The importance of integrating technology in the classroom was clearly articulated by the Alliance for Childhood.[154] The Alliance offered the following guidelines for the appropriate use of technology:

1. Learning occurs in context.
2. Learning is active.
3. Learning is social.
4. Learning is reflective.

Learning Occurs in Context

Duffy & Cunningham, Riebe, Honebein, and the Cognition and Technology Group at Vanderbilt[155] contended that technology can expand learning by providing cultural relevant information that engage learners in solving complex problems in their environments. Research conducted by the Cognition and Technology Group at Vanderbilt[156] supported the above premise. An interactive video was shown to a student that prevented mathematical problems to be solved in concluding how much fuel was needed to fly an aircraft. The student had to use mathematics to solve the problem. The equipment clearly demonstrated how previously learned skills and content can be transferred to solve new problems.

---

[154] Alliance for Childhood. Fool's gold: A critical look at computers and childhood. Available online: http://www.allianceforchildhood.net/projects/computers/Computers reports_ foods_gold_contents.htm, 2000.

[155] T. M. Duffy & D. J. Cunningham, Constructivism: Implications for the design and delivery of instruction. In D. H. Jonasse (Ed.) *Handbook of research for Educational Communications and Technology* (New York, NY: Macmillan, 1996); L. Rieber, Seriously considering play: Designing interactive learning environments based on the blending of micro-worlds, simulations, and games, *Educational Technology Research and Development*, 44, (1996); P. C. Honebein, Seven goals for the design of constructivist learning environments. In B. G. Wilson (Ed.) *Constructivist Learning Environments: Case Studies in Instructional Design* (Englewood Cliffs, NJ: Educational Technology Publications, 1996); Cognition and Technology Group at Vanderbilt. *The Jasper Project: Lessons in Curriculum, Instruction, Assessment, and Professional Development* (Mahwah, NJ: Lawrence Erlbaum Associates, 1992).

[156] Cognition and Technology Group at Vanderbilt.

Learning is Active

Students must be actively involved in the learning process. Educators must experiment and create innovated approaches to accomplish this goal by permitting students to make connections between what they know and solving new problems through constructing meaning from their experiences. Scandamilia[157] supports the use of technology in facilitating the process. Hannatin, Land, Oliver, and Pena.[158] have expressed similar views. The position taken by these authors imply that some learning using technology, such as brainstorming and concept mapping software, may assist students in improving memory, in collecting and analyzing data, and experimenting with solving complex social problems.

Learning is Social

School personnel have long considered the importance of promoting social skills in children through work and solving learning tasks.[159] Social skills should be designed to develop cooperative activities among students. The Computer-Supported Intentional Learning Environment (CSILE), according to Scardamalia and Bereiter,[160] is a technological device that can be used to foster collaborative learning activities among students, between schools, and larger communities. Community involvement is essential in providing quality education for children.

Research findings by Taylor, Booth and Dunne, Epstein, Graft and Henderson, and Hamlett[161] have all alluded to the values of collaboration. It is

---

[157] Scandamalia, 2002.

[158] Hannatin, 1999.

[159] E. Wenger, *Communities of Practice: Learning, Meaning, and Identity* (New York, NY: University Press, 1998).

[160] M. Scarmalia, & C. Bereiter, Computer support for knowledge-building environments, *The Journal of the Learning Sciences*, (3) (1994), 265-283.

[161] G. R. Taylor, Parenting Skills and Collaborative Service for Students with Disabilities, (Lanham, MD: Scarecrow Press, 2004); A. Booth, & L. Dunner, Family School Links: How do they Affect Educational Outcomes? (Hillsdale, NJ: Erlbaum, 1990); J. L. Epstein, School,

incumbent upon the schools to develop, direct, supervise, and support collaboration efforts in the community.

Learning is Reflective

Opportunities should be provided for students to reflect on their learning. One promising technique is for the teacher to provide feedback about students' thinking. Students should be required to make revisions and reflect their thinking in the critical thinking areas. Technologies should be selected to improve communication, and made student friendly for feedback, reflection, and revisions to occur. Technology can be infused with strengthening the critical thinking in the areas of analysis, synthesis, and evaluation. Students may demonstrate through technology how their thinking will reflect high levels of thinking in solving problems.

Cornish[162] predicts by the year 2025 teachers will be better able to handle classes of students with widely different abilities. Children will be the beneficiaries of infotech-based education by having sophisticated technological devices and equipment. The assistance of computers offered to special education children is a little short of miraculous. Many children with disabilities who may posses writing or math blocks and are unable to produce even one neat page of handwritten text often discover labor-saving word processing programs. Computers can give independence, employment, knowledge, and accessibility to the outside world for children. Additionally, they promote individualization of instruction and have high interest values for children.

---

family, community partnerships: Caring for childhood we share, Phi Delta Kappan, 77 (9), (1995), 701-712; O. L. Graft, & B. Henderson, Twenty-five ways to increase parental participation, *High School Magazine*, 4 (1997), 36-41; H. E. Hamlette, Effective parents: Professional communication, *Exceptional Parent*, 27 (1997), 51.

[162] E. Cornish, The cyber future: 92 ways our lives will change by the year 2025, *The Futurist*, 6 (1996).

The Internet

The Internet can serve as a lure or a magnet to attract children to the computer and make them work. The attraction of the Internet for children has been widely discussed on television and radio. While all of the material obtained via the Internet can be validated, the informational and research use of the Internet cannot be denied.

Technology is a tool that can assist the teacher by providing children with a multisensory environment. The Internet can provide information so children can make associations between information and transfer information to solve problems. The Internet arranges information hierarchically. Broad topics are presented first, and information is narrowed down by requesting more specific facts. The process enables children to employ critical thinking skills to solve problems. Additionally, the Internet can give children the opportunity to work at their own pace. By the school providing early Internet training to children, it is equipping them to be prepared for the challenges they will face in competing for employment in the job market of the future.[163] Hannafin, Land, and Oliver[164] claimed that technology tools provide "the means through which individuals engage can manipulate both resources and their own ideas." The collaborative visualization project provides visualization software designed to assist students in collecting and analyzing climatologically data.

According to Andrews and Jordan,[165] multimedia technology allows one to develop stories in two or more languages, or present information in different formats. This technology has many benefits for instructing children because video dictionaries of sign language can be built right into the stories. The

---

[163] C. Goldstein, Learning at cyber camp, *Teaching Exceptional Children,* 30 (5), (1998), 16-26.

[164] M. Hannafin, S. Land, & K. Oliver, Open learning environments: Foundations, methods, and models. In C. M. Reigeluth (ed.) *Instructional Design Theories and Models: A New Paradigm of Instructional Theory* (Vol. II,) (Mahwah, NJ: Lawrence Erlbaum Associates, 1999), p. 128.

[165] J. E Andrews, & D. L. Jordon, Multimedia stories for deaf children, *Teaching Exceptional Children, 30* (6), (1998), 28-33.

technology allows a child to explore information at his or her own pace. Computer technology combines printed text, narration, words, sound, music, graphics, photos, and movies and animation on one computer page.

Many children have difficulties accessing information over the Internet due to poor Web Site designs.[166] Many of the Web Sites create barriers for some children. Children who have vision problems have difficulty accessing the Web because the Web requires a degree of vision acuity. Students who have reading problems will not be able to access the Web appropriately because information is in a text format. Children with attention deficit disorders will have problems accessing the Web due to their short attention span and inability to stay focused for an extended time. Other children with disabilities, without the aforementioned disabilities, can easily access the Web. Specific modifications and adaptations for improvement in order that the Web can be accessible for all children have been recommended to Web designers.

Summary

Waal[167] wrote that several decades ago thoughts about animal behavior and human behavior had opposite views. Animal behavior was characterized as instinctive and human behavior as learning. Currently, behaviorists view all behavior as the product of trials and error learning. They premised their beliefs on the assumption that differences among species were irrelevant and that learning applied to all animals, including humans.

This view began to change with scientific studies involving learning. Behaviorists began to realize that learning is not the name for all conditions, situations, and species. For example, animals are specialized learners, being best at those conditions that are most important for survival, which include strategies for adaptation to the environment.

---

[166] S. P. Walters, Accessible web design, *Teaching Exceptional Children*, 30 (6) (1998), 42-47.

[167] F. B. Waal, The end of the nature versus nature, *Scientific American*, 6 (281) (1999), 49-99.

Klein[168] stated that behaviorism is a school of thought that emphasizes the role of experience in governing behavior. Klein further alluded that according to this principle, the import processes governing behavior are learned. Both the drives that initiate behavior and the specific behaviors motivated by these drives are learned through our interactions with the environment. The major goal of behaviorists is to determine the laws governing learning. The impact of early theorists, Pavlov, Thorndike, Watson, Guthrie, and Skinner all contributed to shaping today's concepts in behaviorism. Although these theorists had separate views, each made major contributions to the field of psychology. Conditioning and behaviorism have made a significant impact upon learning: mastery learning, behavior analysis, and computer technology are to name but a few.

The results reported in this chapter have shown that when the basic elements of mastery learning (feedback and correctives) are congruent, students' test scores on criterion reference test are extremely high. Even though students who are exposed to a mastery learning program only perform slightly better than other students on standardized tests, mastery learning students continue to perform better. It has also been shown that when cooperative learning strategies are paired with mastery learning strategies, students' test scores are even higher.[169] Both mastery learning and cooperative learning strategies compliment each other, promote positive self-esteem, and student involvement.

Other studies have shown that the use of computer base instruction and high technology has helped learning disabled students learn more complex content such as earth science, chemistry, fractions, health promotion, reasoning skills, and vocabulary.[170] Mastery learning is not the cure all for our educational

---

[168] S. B. Klein, *Learning: Principles and Applications* (3rd ed.), (New York, NY: McGraw Hill, 1996).

[169] T. R. Guskey, Cooperative mastery strategies, *Elementary School Journal*, 91 (1) (1990), 33-42.

[170] D. Carnine, 1989.

woes, but if used correctly, mastery learning can improve students' achievement and self-esteem.

Computer technology is here to stay. The values of computers in increasing achievement and ability to solve problems have been well documented in this chapter. When used appropriately, computer technology is a valuable tool that can augment instructional programs and enable children to become self-sufficient and more independent.

As indicated in this chapter, the application of behaviorism has provided innovative and creative ways of changing inappropriate behaviors of learners as well as providing educators with strategies for improving learning and achievement.

Chapter 6

Social Learning Strategies

Introduction

During the last two decades we have witnessed the rediscovery, creation, or the validation of a great diversity of social learning theories. These theories have provided us with a common language concerning learning theories on academic performance of disabled and other individuals.

The study of social learning theories enables the school to better understand both how individuals think about school-related processes and how the children are likely to be feeling about themselves in relation to the process. The school's understanding of both the cognitive and the affective characteristics of individuals may be termed as empathic. One way of showing empathy to children is through designing effective classroom environments that considers the cognitive and affective levels of the children.[171]

The conceptual basis of this research is based upon the social imitation theory of Bandura and Walters.[172] The common threads uniting these theories and concepts are imitation, modeling and copying, and behavior intervention. Children imitate, model, and copy behavioral techniques from their environments. These models and techniques are frequently inappropriate for the school environment and create conflict and tension between children and the school. Learning, culture, and behavioral styles of these children should be incorporated and integrated into a total learning packet. Social learning theories also provide a

---

[171] O. B. Butler, Early help for kids at risk: Our nations best investment, *NEA Today*, 7 (1989), 51-53; A. G. Hilliard, Teachers and cultural styles in a pluralistic society, *NEA Today*, 7 (1989), 65-69.

[172] A. Bandura, & R. H. Walters, *Social Learning and Personality Development* (New York: Holt, Rinehart, and Winston, 1963).

concrete framework for the schools to begin to implement additional social skills strategies into the curriculum.

Throughout the latter half of this century social learning theory emerged as an integral part of behaviorism. As researchers defined learning paradigms, while the opponents of classical and operant conditioning offered a lawful relationship of behavior and the environment, social learning theory postulated that an individual could acquire responses by observing and subsequently imitating the behavior of others in the environment.[173]

"Social learning theory" is defined as a psychological theory that emphasizes the learning of socially expected, appropriate, and desirable behavior.[174] Social learning theorists view behavior as an interaction between an individual and the environment. From its inception, social learning theory was an attempt to integrate the stimulus-response and the cognitive theories. Advocates of this school of though felt that theorists must include both behavioral and internal constructs in any theory of human behavior and learning.[175]

Vzgotsky's Theory

Vzgotsky's theory, according to Moll,[176] lends support to the concept that natural properties as well as social relations and constraints make possible the social construction of a child's higher psychological processes. The three major components of Vzgotsky's theory are: overviewed: (1) the internalization of culture means; (2) the interpersonal, or social process of mediation; (3) a child's

---

[173] J. Rotter, Generalized expectancies for internal versus external control of reinforcement, *Psychological Monographs: General and Applied*, 30 (1966), 80; A. Bandura, & R. H. Walters, *Social Learning and Personality Development* (New York: Holt, Rinehart, and Winston, 1963); M. Coleman, *Behavior Disorders: Theory and Practice* (Englewood Cliffs, NJ: Prentice Hall, 1986).

[174] K. Kahn, & J. Cangemi, Social learning theory: The role of imitations and modeling in learning socially desirable behavior, *Education*, 100 (1979), 41-46; J. Rotter, 1966.

[175] J. Rotter, 1966; A. Bandura, 1963.

[176] I. Moll, The material and the social in Vzygotsky's theory of cognitive development, Clearinghouse on Teacher Education. ED 352186, 1991.

knowledge is formed within the zone of proximal developmental cognitive space defined by social relational boundaries.

One of the major postulates of Vzgotsky's theory, according to Moll,[177] is that there is a functional relationship between the affects of the culture on cognitive development and biological growth. The physical, biological, and neurological determinants are more readily understood and generally agreed upon. However, the impact of the cultural determinants are not as easily understood. The cultural determinants include social processes that transforms naturally through the mastery and use of cultural signs. In essence, on the one hand, the natural development of children's behavior form the biological conditions necessary to develop higher psychological processes; on the other hand, culture provides the conditions by which the higher psychological processes may be realized.

Commonality Among Theories

The common threads uniting these theories and concepts are imitation, modeling, and copying behavior.[178] Individuals imitate, model and copy behaviors directly from their environments. These models and techniques are, however, considered inappropriate and create conflict and tension between children, society and the school. Learning, culture, and behavioral styles of individuals should be, as much as possible, incorporated and integrated into a total learning packet. Social learning theories provide a concrete framework for society and the school to begin to implement additional social skills strategies into the curriculum.

Social skills is a phrase used to describe a wide range of behaviors varying in complexity and is thought to be necessary for effective social function and

---

[177] Moll, 1991.

[178] Bandura, A., & R. H. Walters, *Social Learning and Personality Development* (New York: Holt, Rinehart, and Winston, 1963).

academic success. Behaviors that constitute social skill development may vary depending upon situation, role, sex, age, and disabling conditions of individuals.

Social Cognitive Theory

By 1986, Bandura, defined his position by using new terminology. Social learning theory was replaced by the term social cognitive theory.[179] Social cognitive theory is an attempt to explain human behavior from a natural science perspective by integrating what is known about the effects of the environment and what is known about the role of cognition. It suggests that people are not merely products of their environment nor are they driven to behave as they do by internal forces. Social cognitive theory presents a cognitive interactional model of human functioning that describes behavior results from reciprocal influences among the environments, social, physical, personal, thoughts, feelings, perceptions and the individual's behavior itself.[180]

In summation, social cognitive theory reconceptualizes that thought and other personal factors, behavior, and the environment all operate as interacting determinants. Because of the reciprocal causation, therapeutic efforts can be directed at all three determinants. Psychosocial functioning is improved by altering faculty thought patterns, by increasing behavioral competencies and skills in dealing with situational demands and by altering adverse social conditions.[181] Bandura uses the term "traidic reciprocality" to describe the social cognitive model. Because we have systems with which to code, retain, and process information, several human attributes are incorporated into the social cognitive theory.

---

[179] A. Bandura, Human agency in social cognitive theory, *American Psychologist,* 44 (1989), 1175-1184; K. Corcoran, Efficacy, skills, reinforcement, and choice behavior, *American Psychology,* (February 1991).

[180] J. Kauffman, *Characteristics of Emotional and Behavioral Disorders of Children and Youth* (New York, NY: Merrill, 1993).

[181] A. Bandura, 1986.

Social learning theory is concerned with acquisition of new behaviors that occur as unlearned or previously learned responses that are modified or combined into more complete behaviors. This process, according to social learning theory, is speeded up by direct reinforcement or expected reinforcement through imitation.[182]

Miller and Dollard

N. E. Miller and E. Dollard[183] were influenced by the earlier work of Hull. Theories developed by Miller and Dollard investigated the circumstances under which a response and a cue stimulus become connected. Accordingly, both a cue and a response must be present in order for social learning to exist. Four factors of psychological principles are outlined by Miller and Dollard: drive, cure, response, and reward.

Drive

"Drive" is defined as the first factor in learning that impels action or response. It is the motivating factor which allows the individual to view a situation and react toward a stimulus. Individuals have primary or innate drives and secondary or acquired drives. The behavior that the drive leads to will be learned if there are results in a reduction of drive.[184] Reinforcement always results from reduction of drive.[185]

Cues

Cues determine when the individual will respond, where and which response he/she will make. In social learning, the individual waits for cues from society and then responds to those cues. Society can control the individual by

---

[182] N. E. Miller & J. Dollard, *Social learning and imitation* (New Haven, CN: Yale University Press, 1941).

[183] N. E. Miller & J. Dollard, 1941.

[184] N. E. Miller & J. Dollard, 1941.

[185] K. Kahn, & J. Cangemi, Social learning theory: The role of imitations and Modeling in learning socially desirable behavior, *Education*, 100 (1979), 41-46.

sending out various cues and rewarding the response, either positively or negatively. The presence or absence of cues, number of cues, and/or types of cues can determine the resulting amount and type of learning that occurs.

Response

The response is the most integral part of assessing whether or not the individual has learned, and to what degree learning exists. It is the result of the individual's reaction elicited by cues.

Reward

Reward determines if the response will be repeated. If a response is not rewarded, the tendency to repeat that response is weakened. Similarly, responses that are rewarded are likely to be repeated. Moreover, a connection can be made between the stimulus and the reward, thereby strengthening the response. Rewards may be positive or negative and can themselves become a motivating factor or drive.

Miller and Dollard[186] outlined the following phrases to describe imitation.

Same Behavior

Same behavior is created by two people who perform the same act in response to independent stimulation by the same cue. Each has learned independently to make the response. The behavior may be learned with or without independent aides.

Matched-Dependent Behavior

Matched-dependent behavior primarily consists of leadership by which followers are not presently aware of the consequences of their action, but rely totally on the leadership of others, and follow without question. The individual is controlled by the cues which the leader exhibits and the response from the individual becomes a predictable source for the leader to maintain. Most behavior is demonstrated in this matched-dependent mode. No immediate reward criteria

---

[186] D. L. Miller, & M. L Kelley, The use of goal setting and contingency contracting for improving children's homework performance, *Journal of Applied Behavior Analysis*, 27 (1994), 73-84.

need be present at this time. The actions of the individual can become motivating within themselves. The participation and interaction the individual is allowed to take part in becomes the rewarding factor.

Copying Behavior

Copying behavior is demonstrated when an individual duplicates his or her attitudes and responses so that it matches that which has been deemed socially acceptable by the peer group of the individual. The individual is rewarded for modeling after a select group of peers and the acceptance of their norms. Miller and Dollard[187] have suggested that the child's tendency to copy is an acquired secondary drive that can account for the psychoanalytic concept of identification.

Julian B. Rotter

Rotter[188] combined a social learning framework and behavioral approaches with applications for clinical, personality, and social psychology. While Rotter was inspired through his work with his former teacher Kurt Lewin, he rejected Lewin's and Hull's position because he felt that they did not conceptualize past experiences. Thus, they did not explain and predict all behavior. According to Rotter,[189]

> "Cognitive approaches were of little value in predicting the behavior of rats; and approaches that did not take into account the fact that human beings think, generalize along semantic lines, and are motivated by social goals and reinforced by social reinforcements, were extremely limited in their explanations or predictions."

Rotter turned into the learning theorist, wherein his thinking was strongly influenced by Alfred Adler. Beginning in 1946, immediately following World

---

[187] Miller & Dollard, 1941.

[188] J. Rotter, *Social learning and clinical psychology* (New York, NY: Prentice Hall, 1966); J. Rotter, Generalized expectancies for internal versus external control of reinforcement, *Psychological Monographs: General and Applied,* 1954; J. Rotter, Internal versus external control of reinforcement: A case history variable. *American Psychologist,* 45, (1990), 489-493.

[189] J. Rotter, 1966.

War II, Rotter culminated work from his masters' thesis and his doctoral dissertation and published the work in *Social Learning and Clinical Psychology* in 1954.

From a construct point of view, Rotter[190] outlined seven principles of social learning theory as follows:

1. The unit of investigation for the study of personality is the interaction of the individual and his/her meaningful environment. This principle describes the social learning position of an interactionist approach.

2. Personality constructs are not dependent for explanation on constructs in any other field. Rotter contended with this principle that scientific constructs should be consistent across all fields of science.

3. Behavior as described by personality constructs takes place in space and time. According to Rotter, any constructs that describe events themselves are rejected because constructs must describe physical as well as psychological variables.

4. Not all behavior of an organism may be usefully described with personality constructs. Behavior that may be usefully described by personality constructs appear in organisms at a particular level or stage of complexity and development. This postulate recognizes that events are amenable to specific terms. Likewise, they are not amenable to others.

5. Personality has unity. In this context, Rotter defines unity in terms of relative stability and interdependence. The presence or relative stability does not, however, exclude specificity of response and change.

6. Behavior as described by personality constructs has a directionality aspect. Behavior is said to be goal directed. This principle is the motivational focus of social learning theory. Social learning theorists identify specific events that have a known effect either for groups or for individuals as reinforcers.

---

[190] Rotter, 1966.

Environmental conditions that determine the direction of behavior also refer to goals or reinforcement. When reference is made to the individual's determining the direction, Rotter calls these needs. Both goals and needs are inferred from referents to the interaction of the person with his/her meaningful environment. Learned behavior is goal oriented and new goals derive their importance for the individual from their associations with earlier goals.

7. The occurrence of a behavior of a person is determined not only by the nature or importance of goals and reinforcements but also by the person's anticipation or expectancy that these goals will occur. This principle is an attempt to determine how an individual in a given situation behaves in terms of potential reinforcers.[191]

Rotter's expectancy-reinforcement theory stresses that the major basic modes of behavior are learned in social situations and are intricately fused with needs required for their satisfaction.[192]

Internal versus external, i.e., control, that is control of reinforcement often referred to as locus of control, is firmly embedded in Rotter's social learning theory.[193] Internal versus external control refers to the degree to which persons expect that a reinforcement or an outcome of their behavior is contingent upon their behavior or personal characteristic versus the degree to which persons expect that the reinforcement or outcome is a function of chance, luck or fate, or is under the powerful influence of others.

Basic to Rotter's position is the fact that reinforcement acts to strengthen an expectancy that a particular behavior will be followed by that reinforcement in the future. Once an expectancy for a reinforcement sequence is built, the failure

---

[191] Rotter, 1966.

[192] Kahn & Cangemi, 1979.

[193] Rotter, 1954, 1966, 1990; F. Strickland, Internal-external control expectancies from contingency to creativity, *American Psychologist*, 44, (1989).

of the reinforcement to occur will reduce or extinguish the expectancy. As an infant grows and has more experiences, he/she differentiates casual events from the events that are reinforcing. Expectancies also generalize along a gradient from a specific situation to a series of situations that are perceived as related or similar.[194]

Albert Bandura

Albert Bandura is considered the forerunner of social learning theory and is most often associated with empirical research in the area.[195]

Because concerns with subjective measurement create skepticism among scientists regarding social learning theory, Bandura insisted on experimental controls. Thus, he was able to transcend from empirical observations to experimental validity.[196] Bandura wanted a broader meaning of behaviorism which would include learning from the behavior of others. He too, was dissatisfied with the stimulus response theorists who contended that people acquire competencies and new patterns of behavior through response consequences.[197] He could not image how a culture could transmit its language and mores through tedious trial and error.[198]

---

[194] Rotter, 1966.

[195] A. Bandura, *Social learning and Personality* (New York, NY: Holt, Rinehart, and Winston, 1965); A. Bandura, Human agency in social cognitive theory, *American Psychologist*, 44 (1989), 1175-1184; M. Coleman, *Behavior Disorders: Theory and Practice* (Englewood Cliffs, NJ: Prentice Hall, 1986); R. Evans, *Albert Bandura: The Man and His Ideas: A Dialogue* (New York, NY: Praeger, 1989); R. Tudge & P. Winterhoff, Vzgotsky, Piaget, and Bandura: Perspectives on the relations between the social world and cognitive development, *Human Development*, 36, (1991) 61-81; A. Bandura, & R. H. Walters, *Social Learning and Personality Development* (New York: Holt, Rinehart, and Winston, 1963); O. Weignan, O. Kuttschreuter & B. Baarda, A longitudinal study of the effects of television viewing on aggressive and prosocial behaviors, *British Journal of Social Psychology*, 31, (1992).

[196] J. Rotter, Generalized expectancies for internal versus external control of reinforcement, *Psychological Monographs: General and Applied*, 30 (1966); A. Bandura & Walters, 1963; Tudge & Winterhoff, 1991.

[197] Bandura, 1986.

[198] R. Evans, *Albert Bandura: The Man and His Ideas: A Dialogue* (New York, NY: Praeger, 1989).

Bandura's major concern was in the social transmission of behavior. Two prevailing principles support the theory. The first is the element of observational learning and second is the inclusion of a model or an individual who might serve as an example for another.[199] Learning through imitation is called observational learning.[200] Modeling is a process of teaching through example that produces learning through imitation. The basic assumptions underlying Bandura's position is that behavior is learning and organizing through central integrative mechanisms prior to motor execution.[201]

Observational Learning

Individuals acquire cognitive representations of behavior by observing models as previously indicated. These cognitive representations are in the form of memory codes stored in long-term memory. They may be either visual imagery codes or verbal propositional codes. Bandura uses the terms "observational learning" and "modeling" interchangeably to refer to learning that takes place in a social context. He prefers the term "modeling" (or "observational learning") over the term "imitation" because he believes that imitation is only one way in which we learn from models.[202]

Many behaviors are learned without benefit of reinforcement. Individuals learn many things by observing others.[203] That is, other people serve as behavioral models. This is the main principle of social learning theory proposed by Bandura and his colleagues.[204] What is the difference between observational learning and

---

[199] Kahn & Carnegie, 1979; Bandura, 1966.

[200] Bandura & Walters, 1963.

[201] Bandura, 1971.

[202] P. H. Mussen, *Handbook on child psychology* (*4th* ed.) (New York, NY: Wiley, 1983).

[203] D. L. Best, Inducing children to generate mnemonic organization strategies: An examination of long-term retention and material, *Developmental Psychology*, 29 (1993), 325.

[204] Bandura & Walters, 1963.

imitation? Best takes the following episode as an example. Suppose you watch someone at a party eat a mint from a tray of candies. The person turns blue, falls to the floor, and thrashes about, moaning loudly. You then eat a mint from the same tray. Even though you imitated the model's behavior, could you conclude that you learned very little from observing the model. McCormick and Pressley[205] conducted a similar study having a skilled gymnast watching another gymnast's routine. The skilled gymnast had no trouble performing the acts, whereas the less skilled gymnast did.

In observational learning, people learn through vicarious experiences. That is, when they see others experience reinforcements and punishments, they form expectations about the reinforcements or punishments that they might receive for their own behaviors. In an experiment, Bandura[206] had young children view a film in which a child exhibited some very novel physical and verbal aggressive behaviors to a set of toys. At the completion of the film, the child model was either punished for the aggression (spanked and verbally rebuked), reinforced for it (given soft drinks, candy, and praise), or provided no consequences. After watching the film, the children were left alone in the room where the film was made with an opportunity to play with the toys seen in the film. Children who had watched the film in which the child model was spanked for aggression were much likely to exhibit the aggressive behaviors when interacting with the toys than if they had watched the film depicting reward or no consequences for the aggression. Then, all children in the experiment were offered stickers and fruit juice if they would show the experimenter the aggressive behaviors that the film model exhibited. The children had little difficulty reproducing the behavior.

---

[205] C. B. McCormick, & M. Pressley, *Educational Psychology: Learning, Instructions, and Assessments* (New York, NY: Longman, 1997).

[206] Bandura, 1965.

McCormick and Pressley[207] viewed this as a situation where the children had clearly learned the aggressive behaviors in question because they could reproduce those behaviors when given an incentive to do so. They were less likely to perform the aggressive behaviors when given an incentive to do so. However, they were less likely to perform the aggressive behaviors after viewing the film in which the child model had been punished because they had learned to expect punishment for aggressive behavior from the film. Performance of a behavior depends on knowing a response as well as the expectation of reinforcements. Data from Bandura's study suggested the fun of playing with the toys aggressively was not worth the risk of getting spanked or verbally rebuked if no reward was given. Social learning theory stresses not only principles of behavioral learning theory, but also many aspects of cognitive theory as well.

Modeling and Imitation

Bandura believed that the basic way that children learn is through imitation of models in their social environment and the primary mechanism driving development is observation.[208] Imitation is to copy, to follow a model, or to repeat, rehearse, or reproduce.[209]

Bandura identified two kinds of processes of identity by which children acquire attitudes, values, and patterns of social behavior. Direct imitation is described as explicit directives about what adults, most often parents and teachers, want the child to learn; they attempt to shape the child's behavior through rewards and punishments and/or through direct instruction. Active imitation, through which personality patterns are primarily acquired, consists of parental attitudes and behaviors, most of which the parents have not attempted to teach.[210]

---

[207] McCormick & Pressley, 1997.

[208] Bandura, 1966.

[209] Bandura & Walters, 1979.

[210] Bandura, 1967; Kahn & Canegemi, 1979.

Bandura pointed out that human subjects in social settings can acquire new behaviors simply by seeing them presented by a model. He maintains that even if the observer does not make the response, and even if at the time neither he/she nor the model is reinforced for the behavior, the observer may learn the response so that he/she can perform it later. The observer acquires internal representational responses, which mediate subsequent behavioral reproduction or performance.[211]

A second subprocess is retention of the observer behavior. Bandura contends that observational learning can be retained over long periods of time without overt response. Retention depends in part upon sufficient coding or mediating the event and upon covert rehearsals.

A third subprocess is motoric reproduction. The observer may be able to imagine and to code behaviors of which he/she is motorically incapable. Motor responses are most readily acquired when the observer already possesses the competent skills and needs to synthesize them into new patterns.

Several constructs have been applied to the modeling process. The first construct, imitation, is the process wherein the person copies exactly what he/she sees the model doing. The model's example is repeated, rehearsed, or reproduced. The observer's next step is identification, the process that requires incorporation of personality patterns. The observer has to determine how and/or if the behavior response pattern embodies his/her personality. In most cases, the observer performs the learned behavior embellished with his/her idiosyncrasies rather than imitating the model's actions precisely.[212] Bandura felt that imitation was too narrow, identification, too diffuse. The third construct is social

---

[211] Bandura, 1969.

[212] Edwards, 1993.

facilitation. In this process, new competencies are not acquired and inhibitions serve as social guides.[213]

Actual performance depends upon incentive or motivation. The absence of positive incentives or negative sanctions may inhibit the response or the individual may have a reason to make the response. For example, parental prohibitions against foul language by their child and/or the child that is not given an opportunity to talk, dress, or feed himself or herself, may have acquired the necessary responses through observations, but this child will not deem it necessary to actually perform the response.

Bandura acknowledges the important influences of personal factors, endowed potentialities, acquired competencies, and stresses reciprocity between internal mechanism and the social environment.[214]

According to Bandura,[215] there are three effects of modeling influences. First, modeling can facilitate the acquisition of new behaviors that did exist in the observers repetoire. Second, previously acquired responses can strengthen or weaken inhibitory/responses in the observer (disinhibitory effect). Finally, observation can serve to elicit a response that has been previously exhibited by the model. This response facilitation effect was demonstrated in studies conducted by Bandura in which children observed aggressive behaviors by models that were rewarded or punished for their aggressive acts.[216] Voluminous amounts of literature support the use of modeling as an effective teaching strategy.[217]

---

[213] Bandura, 1963.

[214] S. Moore, *Piaget and Bandura: The Need for a Unified Theory of Learning.* Paper Presented at the bi-annual Meeting of the Society for Research in Child Development, Baltimore, MD: April 23-26, 1987.

[215] Bandura, 1977.

[216] Bandura, 1965.

[217] A. Bandura, D. Ross, & S. A Ross, Transmission of aggression through imitation of aggressive models, *Journal of Abnormal and Social Psychology*, 63 (1961), 575-582; Tudge & Winterhoff,

98

During the 1960s, Bandura & Walters[218] conducted a classic series of experimental studies on imitation. By introducing actions of the model as the independent variable, Bandura was able to observe the effects on the behavior of children who had observed the model. Furthermore, by systematically varying the behavioral characteristics of the models (for example, from nuturant to powerful, to cold to neutral) they were able to assert the kinds of persons who were the most effective models.[219] They noted specifically that other adults, peers, and symbolic models are significant in the learning process of children. When exposed to conflicting role standards as represented by adults, peers, and other observed models, children will adopt different standards than if adults alone provided the model. Peer modeling, however, is no more effective than child-adult interaction. The attitude of the child toward the model, and the personal characteristics of the model, whether or not the model is rewarded for his/her behavior, is more important.[220]

Vicarious learning as it relates to television viewing has been investigated extensively.[221] Bandura's work in the 60's and 70's demonstrated the powerful effects of both live and filmed models on young children's behavior. Viewing of television violence was found to correlate significantly with children's aggressive behavior.[222]

1991; Bandura, 1989; A. Bandura, Gusec & Menlow, Observational learning as a function of symbolization and incentive set, *Child Development*, 37, (1966), 499-506.

[218] Bandura & Walters, 1963.

[219] W. Damon, *The Social World of the Child* (San Francisco, CA: Jossey Bass, 1997).

[220] Bandura, 1986, 1989.

[221] Bandura & Walters, 1963; Bandura, Gusec & Menlow, 1966; Bandura & Ross, 1961, 1963.

[222] L. Eron, The development of aggressive behavior from the perspective of a developing behaviorism, *American Psychologist*, 42 (1987), 435-442.

Self-Efficacy

Bandura's most recent emphasis has been on individual factors in social-interactive contexts. Introduced in 1977, Bandura continued several decades of research regarding the basic source of motivation.[223] He outlined a theoretical framework in which the concept of self-efficacy received a central role for analyzing the changes achieved in clinical treatment of fearful and avoidant behavior. Because the results of the research showed good maintenance and transfer, adding a program of self-directed mastery expanded the concept of self-efficacy.[224] Bandura agreed that if individuals are allowed to succeed on their own, they would not attribute their success to the use of mastery aides or to the therapist. This clinical tool restored an individual's coping capabilities. He felt that the treatments that were most effective were built on an "empowerment model." Continued research suggested to the investigators that they could predict with considerable accuracy the speed of therapeutic change and the degree of generality from the extent to which the individuals perceived efficacy was enhanced. Bandura felt strongly that if you really wanted to help people you must provide them with competencies, build a strong belief, and create opportunities for them to develop the competencies.[225]

The self-efficacy theory addresses the origins of beliefs, of personal efficacy, their structure and function, the processes through which they operate and their diverse effects.[226] Four main sources of self-efficacy are cited.[227] The most effective way of creating a strong sense of self-efficacy is through mastery

---

[223] Bandura, 1976, 1977.

[224] J. Carroll, Self-efficacy related to transfer of learning and theory-based instrumental design, *Journal of Adult Education*, 22 (1993), 37-43.

[225] Evans, 1989; Bandura, 1995.

[226] Bandura, 1995.

[227] Bandura, 1977.

experiences. As individuals master skills, they tend to raise their expectations about their capabilities. Vicarious experiences provided by social models is the second method of creating efficacy beliefs. Seeing people who are similar in success raises the observer's level of aspiration. Bandura[228] noted, however, that this influence is most effective when the observer perceives him/her to be similar to the model. Social persuasion, or verbally encouraging persons that they have what it takes to succeed is regarded by Bandura as a weaker influence. Finally, emotional arousal is the source that serves as an indicator to an individual that he/she is not coping well with a situation, the self-regulating capacity.

As Bandura[229] examined psychological principles as a means of creating and strengthening expectations of personal efficacy, he made a distinction between efficacy expectations and response outcome expectancies. "Outcome expectancy" is defined as the individual's estimate that a given behavior will lead to specific outcomes. An efficacy expectation is the conviction that one can successfully execute the behavior that is necessary to produce the outcomes.

Perceived self-efficacy is referred as an individual's act of raising or lowering their self-efficacy beliefs. A major goal of self-efficacy research is an investigation of the conditions under which self-efficacy beliefs alter the resulting changes. The effects of self-efficacy in regulating human functioning are evident in human cognitive motivational effect and selectional process.[230] There are three levels of self-efficacy theory that are applied to cognition of interest to educators.

The first application is concerned with how children perceived how self-efficacy affects their rate of learning. This level of self-efficacy concerns the students' belief in their capacities to master academic affairs. In 1991, Moulton,

---

[228] Bandura, 1977.

[229] Bandura, 1977.

[230] Bandura, 1989; 1995.

Brown, and Lent[231] conducted a meta-analysis to determine the relations of self-efficacy beliefs to academic outcomes. The results revealed positive and significant relationships between self-efficacy beliefs, academic performance and persistence outcomes across a wide variety of subjects, experimental designs, and assessment methods. Moulton, Brown, and Lent supported earlier studies by Bouffard (1989) and Schunk (1987).[232] A second level of application examined how the teachers' perception in his/her instructional efficacy affects children academically. The classroom atmosphere, partially determined by the teacher's belief in his/her own instructional efficacy, affects children academically. The classroom atmosphere was partially determined by the teacher's belief in his/her own instructional efficacy. The recommendation for teachers is to teach children the cognitive tools with which to achieve and enhance their skills of efficacy so that they can use the skills effectively. Bandura[233] felt that skills are a general rather than a fixed trait. In addition, people with the same skills can perform poorly, adequately, or extraordinarily depending on how well the individual uses the subskills that they have developed. The third level of application is concerned with the perceived efficacy of the school. Collective efficacy of the school as a whole fosters academic achievement of the children in the school and creates an environment conducive to learning.[234]

Self-efficacy has been employed to enhance the academic skills of children who are learning disabled[235] to generate health related action,[236] to train in

---

[231] A. K., Moulton, S. Brown, & R. Lent, Relation of self-efficacy believes in Academic outcomes: A meta-analytic investigation, *Journal of Counseling Psychology*, 38 (1991), 30-38.

[232] Moulton, Brown & Lent, 1991.

[233] Bandura, 1989.

[234] Evans, 1989; P. T. Ashton, & R. B Webb, *Making a difference: Teacher's sense of efficacy and student achievement* (White Plains, NY: Longman, 1986).

[235] Schunk, 1985.

self-management[237] in achievement predictions in marketing,[238] to train self-confidence in sports,[239] to career choices and development and addictive behavior;[240] and in many other applications that are too numerous to mention here.

Summary

As with the information processing theory, the social learning theory is a framework or general theoretical approach that has encompassed the work of many theorists. The approach originated in the 1930s and 1940s by Miller, Dollard, and their associates, who proposed that imitation is the primary learning mechanism for most social behaviors. Subsequently, the social learning theory, spearheaded by Bandura and his colleagues,[241] initially attempted to explain the acquisition of aggression and other social behaviors through the mechanisms of observation and vicarious reinforcement.

Bandura laid out the conceptual framework of his approach in his book, *Social Learning Theory.*[242] Bandura's theory is based on a model of reciprocal determinism. This means that Bandura rejects both the humanist/existentialist position viewing people as free agents and the behaviorist position viewing behavior as controlled by the environment. Rather, external determinants behavior (such as rewards and punishments) and internal determinants (such as thoughts,

---

[236] Bandura, 1995; I. Rosenstock, V. Strecher, & M. Becker, Contribution of HBM to self-efficacy theory, *Health Education Quarterly*, 15, (1988), 175-183.

[237] C. Frayne & F. Lantham, Application of social learning theory to employee self-management of attendance, *Journal of Applied Psychology*, 72, (1987), 383-392.

[238] A. Kalecstein & S. Norwicki, Social learning theory and prediction of achievement in telemarketers, *Journal of Social Psychology*, 134 (1993), 547-548.

[239] T. George, Self-confidence and baseball performance: A causal examination of self-efficacy theory, Journal *of Sport and Exercise Psychology*, 16 (1994), 381-389.

[240] Bandura, 1995.

[241] Bandura & Walters, 1963.

[242] Bandura, 1977.

expectations, and beliefs) are considered part of a system of interlocking determinants that influence not only behavior but also the various other parts of the system. Each part of the system, behavior, cognition, and environmental influences, affect each of the other parts. People are neither free agents nor passive reactors to external pressures. Instead, through self-regulatory processes, they have the ability to exercise some measure of control over their own actions. As self-regulation results from symbolic processing of information, Bandura in his theorizing has assigned an increasingly prominent role to cognition. In 1986, he started calling his approach a social cognitive theory, rather than social a learning theory.

Bandura's theory is similar to the behavioral learning theory in that it is primarily concerned with behavioral change. The question lies in the definition of learning. Does behavior learning produce a relatively permanent change in behavior? A major difference between them lies in their concepts of how people acquire complex, new behaviors. Bandura found it hard to believe that learning a relatively permanent change in behavior is acquired through reinforcements as Burrhus F. Skinner claims. Reinforcement is the concept behaviorists use to describe the acquisition of complex behaviors. It is a process in which the organism is initially reinforced for responses that faintly resemble some target behavior. Over time, reinforcement is gradually reserved for behaviors that become increasingly similar to the target behavior until, at last, the target behavior is achieved. Bandura[243] offered the example of language where the child masters thousands of words and complex syntax and grammar by the time she/he enters school. The rapidly and seeming ease with which children acquire language does not fit well with the tedious process of reinforcing. Bandura pointed out that cognitive and social development would be greatly retarded if we learned only

---

[243] Bandura, 1986.

through the effects of our own actions. Fortunately, most human behavior is learned by observing the behavior of others.

Many of the differences between Bandura's and other theoretical approaches to human learning are made apparent by contrasting their views of where the causes of human behavior are located. Personal determinism claim that behavior is a function of instincts, traits, drives, beliefs, or motivational forces within the individual. Most cognitive theorists take the interactional view that behavior is determined by the interaction of internal forces and environmental influences. That is, the cognitive theorists believe that people's thoughts and beliefs interact with information from the environment to produce behavior. However, this model does not take into account how a person's behavior may lead to environmental changes that, in turn, may influence how he/she thinks about a situation.

Bandura viewed the relationship of behavior, person, and environment as a three-way reciprocal process in which he calls triadic reciprocality. Bandura suggested that the person, the environment, and the person's behavior itself all interact to produce the person's subsequent behavior. In other words, none of the three components can be understood in isolation of the others as a determiner of human behavior. Bandura[244] further stated that behavior can also create environments: "We are all acquainted with problem-prone individuals who, through their obnoxious conduct, predictably breed negative social climates wherever they go. Others are equally skilled at bringing out the best in those with whom they interact."

Bandura[245] pointed out that the relative influence exerted by personal, behavioral, and environmental factors will vary across individual and circumstances. In some cases, environmental conditions are all-powerful. For

---

[244] Bandura, 1977.

[245] Bandura, 1986.

example, if people are dropped into deep water, they will engage in swimming behavior regardless of any differences in their cognitive processes and behavior repertories.

The application of Bandura's social learning principles to social situations has wide implementations for the school and other social agencies charged with instructing disabled individuals. The principles outlined have been successfully demonstrated with many groups, including disabled individuals. Applications of these principles do not require extensive training or preparation.

According to Bandura,[246] most human behavior can be self-regulated by individuals if they are given practical models to imitate. He further articulated that an individual's moral behavior has to be internalized for immoral behaviors to be changed. In essence, individuals must observe and be given practical models to observe, which will aid them in internalizing their behaviors.

---

[246] Bandura, 1987.

Chapter 7

Application of Social Learning Theories

Introduction

The major emphasis of social learning theories is primarily on environmental learner interaction. The learning of behaviors that are socially accepted, as well as learning ones that are not, is called social learning. Stuart supports this view.[247] He maintained that social learning theories attempt to describe the process by which we come to know what behaviors should or should not be projected when we are in different types of social situations. The theories themselves are learning theories that have been applied to social situations. These theories have been generally behavioristic rather than cognitive[248] and they do not separate the parts from the whole; instead, they have as a major underlying concept the holistic and interactive nature of development. Various areas of development of the self do not exist separately from one another, and that movement toward maturity in one area can affect movement and learning in another area. Social learning theories also address individual differences and how such factors as personality temperament and sociological influences may interact with the developmental process.[249]

Social learning theories assist us in identifying how different individuals may manage, delay, progress through, or retreat from developmental tasks. These

---

[247] R. B. Stuart, Social learning theory: A vanishing or expanding presence? *Psychology: A Journal of Human Behavior*, 26, (1989), 35-50.

[248] A. Bandura, *A Social Learning Theory* (Englewood Cliffs, NJ: Prentice Hall, 1970).

[249] I. Moll, The material and the social in Vygotsky's theory of cognitive development, *Clearinghouse on Teacher Education* (ERIC Document Reproduction Service No. ED. 346988) (Washington, DC: 1991).

108

theories also suggest that there are persistent individual differences such as cognitive style, temperament, or ethnic background which interact with development. Additionally, these theories are a source of knowledge about individual types and styles that may be critical to our understanding of differing sources or reward and punishment for students.

Research is congruent in the fact that observational learning offers an important vehicle in teaching youth and adults.[250] According to Charles,[251] special education was the first segment of public education to recognize the power of Bandura's work. Modeling, when used in conjunction with behavior modification, produced results that surpassed those of any previous technique. The early evidence summarized by Bandura and Walters[252] indicated that all children with a history of failure, and institutionalized children, are all more prone than other children to social influence. Thus, special educators have applied modeling procedures to teach new behaviors, to increase behaviors, and to reduce or eliminate undesirable behaviors. Zaragoza, Vaugh, and McIntosh[253] reviewed twenty-seven studies that examined social skills intervention for children with behavioral problems. The most frequently used intervention was one or more of coaching, modeling, rehearsal, feedback, or reinforcement. Twenty-six of the twenty-seven studies reported some type of improvement in the social behaviors. The results of this research yielded positive changes in the self, teacher, and parental perceptions.

---

[250] A. Kazdin, *Behavior Modification in Applied Settings* (Homewood, IL: Dorsey, 1980).

[251] C. M. Charles, *Building Classroom Discipline* (New York, NY: Longman, 1985).

[252] Bandura & Walters, 1993.

[253] N. Zaragoza, S. Vaughn, & R. McIntosh, Social skill intervention and children with behavior problems: A review, *Behavioral Disorders*, 1 (6), (1991), 260-275.

Application of Modeling Techniques

Charles[254] believed that the powers of modeling are even more notable in the regular classroom. Modeling, he contends is their most effective method of teaching many of the objectives in the three domains of learning: psychomotor, cognitive, and affective.

Bandura[255] expanded the concept of modeling to include symbolic modeling. Bandura concluded that images of reality are shaped by what we see and hear rather than by our own direct experiences. We have images of reality that we have never experienced personally. A theory of psychology should, thus, be in step with social reality.

During the years that followed, Bandura[256] identified internal processes that underlie modeling. These processes are referred to as self-efficacy (self-efficacy is discussed later in the chapter). Bandura[257] identified information abilities as mediating links between stimulus and response. Observers function as active agents who transform, classify, and organize meaningful stimuli.

Aggression

"Aggression" is defined as behavior that results in personal injury and in destruction of property.[258] In reference to the theories of aggression, Bandura's first position, one in which he remained, was that the instinct theories did not explain how children from high-risk environments develop prosocial styles. Conversely, they did not explain how children from advantaged backgrounds and disabled individuals develop serious antisocial patterns of behavior. The drive-reduction theorists view was that aggression had cathartic effects. Conditions that

---

[254] Charles, 1985.

[255] Bandura, 1971.

[256] Bandura, 1989.

[257] Bandura, 1955.

[258] Bandura, 1976.

were likely to be frustrating to the child heightened the drive level, thereby leading to aggression. Once the aggressive drive was reduced, the belief was that the likelihood of participation in aggressive behavior was abated.[259] According to Bandura, a complete theory of aggression must explain how aggression develops, what provokes aggression, and what maintains aggressive acts. He points that individuals can acquire aggressive styles of conduct either by observing aggressive models or through direct combat experience--individuals are not born with repertories of aggressive behavior. Contrary to existing theories, Bandura's research showed that frustration could produce any variety of reactions and one does not need frustration to become aggressive. Moreover, he demonstrated that exposure to aggressive models tended to increase aggression.[260] The findings have significant implication for reducing aggressive behaviors in individuals. Social forces determine the form that aggression takes, where and when it will be expressed, and who is selected as targets.[261]

The different forms of aggressive elicitors are delineated to include modeling influences, aversive treatment, anticipated positive consequences, instructional control, and delusional control.[262] In search of a common element among the stressors within the environment that elicits aggression, he concluded a common trait is that they all produce a negative effect.

The third major feature concerns the conditions that sustain aggressive behavior. Bandura[263] proposed that behavior is controlled by its consequences. Therefore, aggression can be induced. However, social learning theory distinguishes the three forms of reinforcement that must be considered. These

---

[259] Eron, 1987; Evans, 1989; Bandura, 1971.

[260] Evans, 1989.

[261] Bandura, 1996.

[262] Bandura, 1976.

[263] Bandura, 1973.

include direct internal reinforcement, vicarious or observed reinforcement, and self reinforcement

Anger and Hostility

The aforementioned studies have consistently shown that negative behaviors such as anger and hostility, are learned behaviors which children imitate from their environments. These behaviors manifest themselves in hostile and destructive patterns of behavior, which frequently cannot be controlled by the schools, thus, creating conflict and tension between children, parents, and the schools.[264]

Expressing anger and hostility constructively requires a great deal of inner control. Internal awareness of anger must first be recognized. If one is not aware of his/her anger, it cannot be controlled. When anger is repressed or ignored, it will surface later and add to one's frustration. Usually by this time, anger will be expressed in aggressive behaviors such as attempts to harm someone, destroy something, insults, and hostile statements and actions. Aggressive behaviors manifest themselves in ways which infringe upon the rights of others.

Controlling anger and managing feelings are essential in developing appropriate interpersonal skills. Individuals should be taught how to control anger through application of the following:

1. Recognizing and describing anger
2. Finding appropriate ways of expressing anger
3. Analyzing and understanding factors responsible for anger
4. Managing anger by looking at events differently or talking oneself out of anger
5. Learning how to repress feelings
6. Expressing anger constructively
7. Experimenting with various and alternative ways of expressing anger

---

[264] R. L. Matsueda, & K. Heimer, Race, family structure, and delinquency: A test differential association and social control theories, *American Sociological Review*, 52 (1987, December), 826-840.

Teachers may employ a variety of strategies to assist pupils in controlling or reducing anger. Role playing, creative dramatics, physical activities, time out, relaxation therapy, writing and talking out feelings, assertive behavioral techniques, managing provocations, and resolving interpersonal conflicts through cooperative approaches are, to name a few, strategies and techniques that teachers may employ.

Social Skills Teaching Strategies

Teaching Apology Strategies

Apologies can restore relationships, heal humiliations, and generate forgiveness, if taught appropriately. They are powerful social skills that generally are not considered to be important by the school. It may be concluded that the school considers this skill to be a function of the home. As reflected throughout this book, the school must assume the leadership in teaching all social skills. This approach is especially true for a significant number of individuals with disabilities and for those children who do not have this type of modeling at home.

Like all social skills, appropriate ways to apologize must be taught; otherwise, they can strain relationships, create grudges, and instill bitter vengeances. Apologies are a show of strength because not only does it restore the self-concepts of those offended, but makes us more sensitive to the feelings and needs of others. Specific strategies have been outlined and developed to assist educators in teaching appropriate ways that individuals with disabilities can apologize without diminishing their "egos."

The examples of anger and hostility and the teaching of apology and other social skills strategies have been observed and associated with many of the poor social skills shown by many individuals. These skills appear to interface, interact, and are associated with many poor social skills.

Teaching Self-Regulation Skills

Instructional programs must be developed and designed to enable individuals to gain knowledge about appropriate interpersonal skills and to employ this newly acquired knowledge in solving their social problems. In order for this goal to be accomplished, they must be taught effective ways of internalizing their behaviors and assessing how their behaviors affect others. Helping individuals develop self-regulation skills appears to be an excellent technique for bringing behaviors to the conscious level where they can be controlled. Some of the more commonly used self-regulation skills are summarized.

Be Aware of One's Thinking Patterns

Provide "think-aloud" activities and model behaviors to reflect solving problems by working through tasks and asking questions such as: (1) What is needed to solve the problem? (2) Things are not working out, should I try another way? (3) What assistance do I need to solve the problem? As the teacher performs these think-aloud activities, he/she may ask for input from the students' viewpoint that is relevant to the type of self-regulation skills being demonstrated. Those skills may have to be modeled and demonstrated several times. Provide opportunities for individuals with disabilities to demonstrate them individually and in cooperative groups, as well as evaluate the effectiveness of their actions.

Making A Plan

Have individuals to identify specific examples where self-regulation is useful. Motivation may come from a story, file, tape, or creative dramatic activities. Instruct them to develop a plan to reduce, correct, or eliminate the undesired behaviors. As they demonstrate the behaviors, the teacher should reinforce and praise them.

Develop and Evaluate Long-Term Goals

Employ self-regulation strategies to assist individuals with disabilities in accomplishing long-term goals. Have them to identify social and behavioral goals. Record the goals and assist them in making a plan as outlined previously. Provide a scheduled time to meet with them to determine how well the goals are being achieved. In some instances, the goals will need to be modified or adapted in order to focus on specific behaviors. Self-regulation strategies make actions more controllable by making one aware of his or her own behavior. Once awareness is achieved, the plan outlined earlier may be taught to bring behaviors under control. These strategies frequently will need to be adapted and modified to meet the uniqueness of the class. A variety of techniques and strategies may be used to aid the teacher in developing the skills of self-regulation:

1. Role playing activities
2. Classifying behaviors and identifying types of self-regulation strategies to employ
3. Working in cooperative groups
4. Positively reinforce the mental habits
5. Reading and developing stories
6. Being sensitive to feedback and criticism
7. Teaching self-monitoring skills
8. Seeking outside advice when needed
9. Evaluating progress made

Self-regulation strategies are one of several strategies, which may be used to teach appropriate social skills to individuals. Appropriate social skills are essential for developing personal relationships and accepting the roles of authority figures. Social behaviors are learned, therefore, they can be changed and modified with appropriate intervention. They require that an individual evaluate the situation, choose the appropriate social skills, and perform the social tasks appropriately.[265] Unfortunately, many individuals have not been exposed to appropriate social models or do not possess enough prerequisite skills, such as maturity and self-control, to successfully perform the social skills. Development of social skills requires that individuals have appropriate models to copy and imitate, to recognize nonverbal clues and to adjust their behaviors accordingly.

---

[265] L. G. Katz, *The Teacher's Role in Social Development of Young Children*, ED Clearinghouse on Elementary and Early Childhood Education. ERIC 331642, 1991.

Matsueda and Heimer's[266] research supports the findings of Katz;[267] it indicates that negative behaviors are learned behaviors, which children imitate from their environments. The schools view these behaviors as hostile and destructive and respond to children in a negative fashion, thus, creating conflict and tension between schools and children.

Several researchers have directly or indirectly implied that social skills must be taught and integrated into the curriculum and assume a position of primacy along with the basic three R's (reading, writing, and arithmetic).[268]

Findings from other studies support the aforementioned research by concluding that many individuals with disabilities may have developed or adapted alternative ways and styles of coping with problems within their communities. These behavioral styles are frequently in conflict with the school and society in general and may be viewed as negative or destructive. Behavioral styles and models copied and imitated by many individuals may serve them well in their environments but are frequently viewed as dysfunctional by the school.[269]

Integrative Aspects of Social Skills Development

As indicated throughout this text, one of the major reasons that individuals' behaviors are frequently rejected by the school and social institutions may be attributed to the failure of them to display appropriate social skills needed

---

[266] Matsueda & Heimer's, 1987.

[267] Katz, 1991.

[268] Hilliard, 1989; D. Biken, Making differences ordinary, in W. Stainback and M. Forest (Eds.), *Educating all Children in the Mainstream of Regular Education* (Baltimore: Paul H. Brookes, 1989); Taylor, 1992; T. W. Collins, & J. A. Hatch, Supporting the social-emotional growth of young children, *Dimensions of Early Childhood*, 27 (1992), 17-21; M. Forest, *Maps and Cities*, Presentation at Peak Parent Center Workshop (Colorado Springs, 1990); T. W. Collins, & J. A. Hatch, Supporting the social-emotional growth of young children, *Dimensions of Early Childhood*, 27 (1992), 17-21; S. L. Kagan, Early care and education: Beyond the school house doors, *Phi Delta Kappan*, (1989), 107-112; W. Johnson, & R. Johnson, Social skills for successful group work, *Educational Leadership*, 47 (1990), 29-33.

[269] Taylor, 1992; 1998.

for different social interactions. The types of role models to which they have been exposed to do not frequently provide them with the appropriate behaviors to copy or transfer to other social functions in our society.

Various types of social skills instruction must be developed and systematically taught to individuals. The earlier the intervention, the sooner negative behaviors can be addressed, eradicated, or reduced. Both the home and the school should play dominant roles in developing pro-social skills for individuals.[270]

The school may be the most appropriate agency, along with parental input, to conduct the social skills training or intervention. Teaching students pro-social skills necessary to cope with the social demands of society creates a climate in which positive relationships can exist and empower students to direct their own successes. A safe, supportive environment tends to facilitate learning. Pro-social skills taught and practiced daily in a nurturing environment assist in reducing negative behavior and in promoting positive ones.

Social skills of individuals are developed through interactions with family, school, and community. Social skills are shaped by reinforcement received as a result of interaction with the environment. Often, children do not learn effectively from past experiences. Frequently, they are enabled to transfer one social reaction to another socially acceptable situation; thus, their behaviors are frequently interpreted as immature, inept, or intrusive. This negative feedback prohibits future social interactions. This is especially true for individuals with disabilities.

Research findings suggest that a significant relationship exists between social skills intervention and academic achievement. Many social skill procedures, such as attending and positive interaction techniques, have been

---

[270] D. P. Oswald, & N. Sinah-Nirbay, *Current Research on Social Behavior Modification*, 16 (1992), 443-447; H. Walker, M. Irvin, K. Larry, J. Noell, & H. S. George, A construct score approach to the assessment of social competence, *Behavior Modification*, 16, (1992), 449-452.

shown to increase academic performance. Oswald and Nirbay[271] wrote that social skills interventions appear to work in a naturalistic environment. Similar findings by Walker et al.[272] indicate that the probability of individuals failing and not adjusting to school and peer acceptance is significant. He further articulated that some individuals do not have sufficient social skills to be successful in school. Finally, he voiced that there is an urgent need for social skills training which should be integrated into the curriculum.

Individuals are faced with double challenges; lack of appropriate social training may not permit many of them to engage productively in many social events. Special techniques and interventions related to remediating poor or inappropriate skills must be addressed early in their school experiences in order to bring skills up to school standards. According to Taylor,[273] early intervention is needed to expose individuals with disabilities to appropriate social models.

Many individual cultural experiences have not provided them with appropriate social skills to be successful in the larger community or cope with appropriate social behavior. Changing inappropriate social behavior involves infusing principles of social learning theories, such as modeling, imitation, and behavioral techniques, with social skills instruction. Once social skills deficits have been identified, the aforementioned social learning principles may be used to reinforce or reward appropriate social behavior.[274]

Research findings have clearly demonstrated that diverse groups of children are at risk for developing appropriate interpersonal skills.[275] Social skills

---

[271] Oswald & Nirbay, 1992.

[272] Walker et al., 1992.

[273] Taylor, 1992.

[274] Taylor, 1998.

[275] T. Achenback & E. Zigler, Cue-learning and problem learning strategies in normal and retarded children, *Child Development*, 39, (1968), 837-848; Coleman, 1986; C. Cummings & A. Rodda, Advocacy, prejudice, and role modeling in the deaf community, *Journal of Social Psychology*, 129 (1989), 5-12; Kauffman, 1993.

deficiencies are commonly observed in this population. Several factors may attribute to these deficiencies such as childrearing practices, deprived cultural environments, and lack of understanding the social expectations or rules. These deficiencies may lead to demonstration inappropriate or inadequate social behaviors.

Social skills are learned throughout a lifetime from imitating or modeling both negative and positive behaviors. Consequently, many individuals lack basic interpersonal skills. These individuals are frequently at a disadvantaged in society. Some individuals tend to feel inadequate and use unproductive, inadequate, and socially unacceptable ways of relating and communicating with others.

Many individuals may have developed or adapted alternative ways and styles of coping with problems. These behavioral styles are frequently in conflict with the school and society in general and may be viewed as negative or destructive. Behavioral styles and models copied and imitated by individuals may serve them well in their environments, but are frequently viewed as dysfunctional by the school and society.[276]

The ability of many individuals to function satisfactorily in social groups and to maintain dispositions, habits, and attitudes customarily associated with character and personality, is usually below expected levels set by the school. They are more likely than other children to be rejected by their peers; have fewer, less rigid controls over their impulses; have learned hostile and destructive patterns of behavior, and often seem unable to respond to traditional classroom instruction. Individuals imitate behavior techniques from their environments.[277]

---

[276] Carroll, 1993; W. Damon, *The Social World of the Child* (San Francisco, CA: Jossey Bass, 1997).

[277] G. R. Taylor, 1992; P. T. Ashton & R. B. Webb, *Making a difference: Teacher's sense of efficacy and student achievement* (White Plains, NY: Longman, 1986).

The importance and values of interpersonal skills instruction has been minimized in the schools. Mastering of these skills requires training and practice in order for children to interact appropriately with others. Interpersonal skills allow children to take appropriate social behaviors, understand individuals' responses to the behaviors, and respond appropriately to them. Lack of this development may lead to feelings of rejection and isolation in a classroom setting. There is also ample evidence to suggest that children's social difficulties may emanate from vastly different deficit areas. These deficit areas must be identified and remediated during the early years. Schools must design direct and immediate intervention programs that will permit individuals to experience success.[278]

Cognitive Behavior Modification

Social learning theory[279] has also influenced cognitive behavior modification. A major assumption of social learning theory is the notion that affective, cognitive, and behavior variables interact in the learning process. For example, the extent to which a child understands the cognitive concepts of place value will affect how well he or she performs the behavior of computing three-digit subtraction problems with regrouping (Refer to chapter 11 for concept learning strategies). Motivation and other affective variables also interact. In cognitive behavior modification, modeling is used as a primary means of instruction.

Research in social learning theory as well as in cognitive behavior modification supports the notion that modeling is very effective when used to teach children with disabilities. With cognitive behavior modification, students are asked not only to watch observable behaviors as the instructor performs the task, but also listen to the instructor's self-talk. In this way, the instructor is

---

[278] G. Brody, & Z. Stoneman, Social competencies in the developmental disabled: Some suggestions for research and training, *Mental Retardation,* 15 (1977), 41-43; Oswald & Nisbay, 1992; J. Ayers, Sensory *Integration Theory* (Los Angeles, CA: Psychological Services, 1972).

[279] Bandura, 1977.

modeling both observable behaviors and the unobservable thinking processes associated with those behaviors. Being able to model the unobservable thinking process is an important component for teaching such cognitive skills as verbal math problem solving, finding the main idea in a paragraph, editing written work, and solving social problems. In most instances, the person modeling is the teacher or a peer, but video puppets have also been used. Vaugh, Ridley and Bullock[280] used puppets as models for teaching interpersonal skills to young, aggressive children. The puppets were used to demonstrate appropriate social behaviors and strategies for solving interpersonal problems. Another effective cognitive behavior modification concept is self-verbalization, which is often used when teaching children with behavior problem. Strategies include teacher modeling, guided practice, and the gradual fading of teacher cueing. First, the teacher described and modeled self-verbalization. Then, the teacher provided external support and guidance as students attempted to apply the approach to problems.

Cognitive behavior modification is designed to actively involve students in learning. Michenbaum[281] characterized the student as a collaborator in learning. General guidelines to consider when using cognitive behavior modification (CBM) include:

1. Analyze the target behavior carefully
2. Determine if and what strategies the student is already using
3. Select strategy steps that are as similar as possible to the strategy steps used by problem solvers
4. Work with the student in developing the strategy steps
5. Teach the prerequisite skills

---

[280] S. R. Vaughn, C. A. Ridley & D. D. Bullock, Interpersonal problem solving skills training with aggressive young children, *Journal of Applied Developmental Psychology*, 5, (1984), 213-223.

[281] D. Meichenbaum, Teaching thinking: A cognitive behavior approach, in Meier, D. (1985). New age learning: From linear to geodesic, *Training and Development Journal*, (1983).

6. Teach the strategy steps using modeling, self-instruction, and self-regulation
7. Give explicit feedback
8. Teach strategy generalization
9. Help the students maintain the strategy

From its inception, social learning theory has served as a useful framework for the understanding of both normal and abnormal human behavior. A major contribution that has important implications for the modification of human behavior is the theory's distinction between learning and performance. In a now-classic series of experiments, Bandura and his associates teased apart the roles of observation and reinforcement in learning and were able to demonstrate that people learn through mere observation.

In a study of aggression, an adult model hit and kicked a life-size inflated clown doll, with children watching the attack in person or on a television screen. Other children watched the model perform some innocuous behavior. Later, the children were allowed to play in the room with the doll. All children who had witnessed the aggression, either in person or on television, viciously attacked the doll, while those who had observed the model's innocuous behavior did not display aggression towards the doll. Moreover, it was clearly shown that the children modeled their aggressive behaviors after the adult. This study accomplished its purpose by demonstrating that observational learning occurs in the absence of direct reinforcement.[282]

Self-Regulation of Behavior

According to Bandura,[283] "If actions were determined solely by external rewards and punishments, people would behave like weathervanes, constantly shifting in different directions to conform to the momentary influences impinging upon them." Self-regulation refers to the learner monitoring his or her thinking

---

[282] Bandura, Ross, & Ross, 1961.

[283] Bandura, 1986.

122

and actions through language mediation. When Meichenbaum,[284] developed his cognitive behavior modification training for the self-control of hyperactive children, he used Vygotsky's notions about how language affects socialization and the learning process. Vygotsky suggested that children become socialized when using verbal self-regulation. Children first use language to mediate their actions by overtly engaging in self-instruction and self-monitoring. Later, this language mediation becomes covert.[285]

Self-Observation

Studies have demonstrated that learning is enhanced when individuals have knowledge of and apply appropriate monitoring or executive strategies during the learning process. In order to influence their own actions, people need to monitor relevant aspects of their behaviors. Naturally, the behaviors that are monitored must be appropriate to the situation. Several factors influence whether self-observation will produce effective goal or standard setting and self-evaluation that will, in turn, lead to changes in behavior.[286]

Focusing on immediate behavior is more effective than monitoring the future effects of behavior. Another factor is whether an individual focuses on his or her successes or failures. Self-monitoring one's successes increase desired behavior, whereas observing one's failures causes little change or lowers performance. Helping students to pay more attention to their successes will increase their self-efficacy.[287]

---

[284] Meichenbaum, 1977.

[285] Vygotsky, 1978.

[286] Meichenbaum, 1977; Schunk, 1991; M. L. Yell, Cognitive behavior therapy, in T. J. Zirpoli and K. J. Melloy, *Behavior management application for teachers and parents* (Columbus, OH: MacMillan, 1993).

[287] R. Hamilton & E. Ghatala, *Learning and Instruction* (Houston, TX: McGraw- Hill, Inc., 1994).

Self-Efficacy

According to Bandura,[288] another factor that influences people's motivation to perform modeled activities is their perceived efficacy. "Self-efficacy" is an academic term that refers to how capable someone judges himself or herself to be in a given situation. It is a person's sense of AI can do it "or AI can not do it." In addition to its informative and motivational role, reinforcement, both direct and vicarious experiences, influence performance by its effects on self-efficacy. That is, seeing other people succeed or fail (or succeeding or failing oneself) affects a person's judgment of his or her own capabilities.

Perceptions of self-efficacy can have diverse effects on behavior, thought patterns, and emotional reactions. One's choice of activities and environments is influenced by one's perceived efficacy. Individuals tend to avoid tasks and situations which they believe exceed their capabilities, but they undertake tasks they feel capable of handling.[289] For example, students who do not view themselves as capable in math might attempt to avoid taking math classes. However, students with high self-efficacy for math will choose more math electives. Perceived efficacy influences the amount of effort people will expend and how long they will persist at a task in the face of difficulty.

One's perceived self-efficacy may or may not correspond to one's real self-efficacy. People may believe their self-efficacy is low when in reality it is high, and vice versa. The situation is best when one's aspirations are in line with one's capabilities. On the other hand, people who continually attempt to do things beyond their capabilities experience frustration and despair and may eventually give up on almost anything. On the other hand, if people with high self-efficacy do not adequately challenge themselves, their personal growth may be inhibited. The development of perceived self-efficacy and its impact on self-

---

[288] Bandura, 1995.

[289] Bandura, 1977.

124

regulated behavior are topics about which Bandura has been writing about extensively.[290]

Students with or without learning disabilities who believe they are capable of reaching a desired goal or of attaining a certain level of performance have a high level of perceived self-efficacy.[291] High self-efficacy in any given domain is important because it motivates future attempts at tasks in the same domain. For example, one motivation for a child with cerebral palsy to attempt tracing the letters of the alphabets is previous success in developing a functional pencil grip and successfully tracing horizontal and vertical lines. If the child's tracing letters improves, then self-efficacy in handwriting increases even more, which in turn, motivates future attempts to write. What if the tracing of letters goes badly? Self-efficacy in handwriting is likely to decline. Self-efficacy is determined in part by present attempts at learning and performance; it then affects future attempts at learning and performance.

Teachers can help students with learning and behavior problems identify and use appropriate internal evaluative standards by teaching them to set goals that are specific, proximal, and challenging. Specific goals clearly designate the type and amount of effort needed and provide unambiguous standards for judging performance. Specific goals are much more effective in directing behavior than global or general goals.[292] Proximal goals refer to immediate performance on tasks rather than to some distant future goal. Finally, goals that are effective in directing behavior are challenging rather than too easy or too difficult.

Teachers can model goal setting. In doing so a teacher can point out how he/she select attainable, yet challenging goals, describing how goals that are too

---

[290] Bandura, 1986.

[291] D. H. Schunk, Self-efficacy and academic motivation, *Educational Psychologists*, 26 (2) (1991), 206-222.

[292] Schunk, 1991.

easy and those that are unattainable can be impractical and frustrating. He/she can emphasize knowledge when setting goals and focus on setting self-improvement goals. Again, teachers must remember that only tasks that are challenging for the learner, but not so difficult that progress is impossible, are capable of providing information to students that increases self-efficacy.

Summary

Social learning theory was born into a climate in which two competing and diametrically opposed schools of thought dominated psychology. On the other hand, psychologist who advocated psychodynamic theories postulated that human behavior is governed by motivational forces operating in the form of largely unconscious needs, drives, and impulses. These impulse theories tended to give circular explanations, attributing behavior to inner causes that were inferred from the very behavior they were supposed to cause. They also tended to provide explanations after the fact, rather than predicting events, and had very limited empirical support.

On the other hand, there were various types of behavior theory that shifted the focus of the causal analysis from hypothetical internal determinants of behavior to external, publicly observable causes. Behaviorist were able to show that actions commonly attributed to inner causes could be produced, eliminated, and reinstated of the person's external environment. This led to the proposition that people's behavior is caused by factors residing in the environment.

Social learning theory presents a theory of human behavior that to some extent incorporates both viewpoints. According to Bandura, people are neither driven by inner force nor buffeted by environmental stimuli; instead, psychological functioning is best explained in terms of continuous reciprocal interaction and external causes. This assumption, termed "reciprocal determinism," became one of the dominant viewpoints in psychology.

An initial exposition of social learning theory was presented in Albert Bandura and Richard H. Walter's[293] text *Social Learning and Personality Development*. This formulation drew heavily on the procedures and principles of operant and classical conditioning. In his book *Principles of Behavior Modification*, Bandura placed much greater emphasis on symbolic events and self-regulatory processes. He argued that complex human behavior could not be satisfactorily explained by the narrow set of learning principles behaviorist had derived from animal studies. He incorporated principles derived from developmental, social, and cognitive psychology into social learning theory.

During the 1970s, psychology had grown increasingly cognitive. This development was reflected in Bandura's 1977 book, *Social Learning Theory*, which presented self-efficacy theory as the central mechanism through which people control their own behavior. Over the following decade, the influence of cognitive psychology on Bandura's[294] work grew stronger. In his book, *Social Foundation of Thought and Action: A Social Cognitive Theory*, he finally disavowed his roots in learning theory and renamed his approach "social cognitive theory." This theory accorded central roles to cognitive, vicarious, self reflective, and self-regulatory processes. Social learning/social cognitive theory became the dominant conceptual approach within the field of behavior therapy. It has provided the conceptual framework for numerous interventions for a wide variety of psychological disorders and probably will remain popular for a long time. In 1981, Bandura was honored with the Award for Distinguished Scientific Contribution to Psychology from the American Psychological Foundation in recognition for his work.

Social learning theories offer the school a common context through which environment, developmental sequence, and early experiences of individuals'

---

[293] Bandura & Walters, 1969.

[294] Bandura, 1986.

development can be understood and researched. These theories enabled educators to better understand how individuals think, how they feel about themselves, and how to become aware of factors in the environment precipitating cognitive and affective problems which may have some bearing on academic performance. The relationship between social learning theories and the academic performance of individuals are not well-established. Most research reported today, simply indicate that there is a causal relationship. There is a dire need to conduct empirical studies to determine to what degree social learning theories impact on the academic performance of these individuals.

Social learning theories appear to be an appropriate approach for integration skills for individuals. These theories provide teachers with a common language by which they can communicate about the effects of social learning theories on academic performance.

The study of social learning theories enables the school to better understand how individuals think about school-related processes and how they are likely to be feeling about themselves in relation to these processes. The school's understanding of both the cognitive and the affective characteristics of individuals with disabilities may be termed as "empathic." One way of showing empathy to children is through designing effective classroom environments that considers the cognitive and affect levels of the children.

Social development is a major area in which many individuals need assistance. They frequently have developed inappropriate interpersonal skills which are not accepted by the school. Inability to conform to expected social standards may result in unacceptable social skills, which are essential for developing personal relationships and accepting the role of authority figures.[295] Research findings by Hilliard, Butler, and Johnson[296] support the notion that the

---

[295] Taylor, 1992.

[296] Hilliard, 1989; Butler, 1989; Johnson, 1990.

culture plays a dominant role in shaping behavior. Children model and imitate behaviors from their environments. Innovative ways must be found by the schools to provide appropriate role models for individuals to imitate and copy.

Chapter 8

Cognitive Psychology

Overview

The study of cognition in psychology during the last four decades is more intense now than in any previous time. With the recognition that complex internal processing is involved in most learning and perception, a continual widening of the definition of cognition, and a number of examples are given in this chapter. From the examples, it will be clear how broad the current conception is. Currently, not only are all the major academic skills, ranging from reading to mathematics and science, included under cognition, but also much that is classically considered as part of perception. In fact it has become increasingly difficult to draw any sharp line between cognition and perception.[297]

From a theoretical standpoint there are many different approaches to cognition, but it is fair to say that none of them currently dominates the scene. As in the case of an exact definition of cognition, it is also not possible to give an exact definition or to delineate sharply the key theoretical concepts in the various approaches to cognitive theory. Without too much injustice, however, we can group the current theories can be grouped into four main classes, and the four main sections of this chapter are organized to represent each of the four main theoretical approaches.

In brief terms, the four approaches are: behavioral, developmental, information processing, or linguistic in orientation. The behavioral approach to cognition is typically represented by stimulus-response theorists like Estes, the developmental approach by Jean Piaget, and the information-processing approach

---

[297] Ormrod, 1999.

by Newell and Smith,[298] as well as current work in artificial intelligence. The linguistic approach has been most stimulated by Chomsky,[299] but the large literature on semantics derives not from the linguistic tradition of Chomsky and his colleagues, but rather from that of logicians and philosophers. Some attention will be given to both of these linguistic approaches.

Without attempting anything like an adequate or complete survey, we also indicate for these approaches some of the relevant studies directly concerned with the cognitive capacities of disabled children.

As we turned to these four theoretical approaches to cognition, it is important to emphasize that each is incomplete and unsatisfactory in several ways. There are some reasons of a real synthesis of theoretical ideas that have been emerging in psychology from a number of different viewpoints, but it is premature to indicate the lines of this synthesis. It is clear, however, that what once appeared as sharp conceptual differences between behavioral approaches on the one hand, and information-processing approaches on the other, has with time increasingly become less clear and less distinct. More is said about such a synthesis in the final section.

Behavioral Approach

The behavioral approach to cognition in the form of concept formation may be illustrated by the application of the simple all-or-none conditioning model. Bower and Estes[300] showed that a simple conditioning model could give an excellent account of paired-associate learning. In paired-associate experiments, the learner is shown, for example a nonsense syllable, and is asked to learn to

---

[298] A. Newell & H. A. Simon, *Human Problem Solving* (Englewood Cliffs, NJ: Prentice Hall, 1972).

[299] N. Chomsky, *Syntactic structure,* The Hauge: Moutan, 1957.

[300] G. H. Bower, Application of a model to paired-associate learning. *Psychometrika,* 26 (1961), 255-280; W. K. Estes, New developments in statistical behavior theory. Differential tests of axioms for associative learning, *Psychometrika,* 26, 73-84.

associate with it the response of pressing a left or right key. Given a list of, say, 20 nonsense syllables, half of them randomly assigned to the left key and half of them to the right key, the scientific problem is to give an exact account of the course of learning. The naive idea most of us have is that on each trial, with exposure to the stimulus and an indication of what is the correct response, learning will gradually occur. One traditional way of expressing this was the connection or response strength would gradually build up from trial to trial.

The experiments reported by Bower and Estes showed that in simple paired-associate learning the situation is somewhat different. The evidence is fairly clear that in the kind of paired-associate experiment just described the learner does not improve incrementally, but rather learns the association between a stimulus and responds on an all-or-none basis. There is no improvement in the probability of his or her making a correct response until he or she fully learns the association. The theory of such experiments can be stated rather explicitly within a classical stimulus-response framework. The only important concepts are those of conditioning a response to a stimulus and sampling the stimuli on a given trial, together with the reinforcement that serves as a correction procedure when incorrect responses are made or that informs the learner that a correct response has been made.[301]

In the Bower and Estes models, the two essential assumptions are these. First, until the single stimulus element is conditioned there is a constant guessing probability, p, that the learner responds correctly, c, that the single stimulus element will be conditioned to the correct response. The only change in this model in order to apply it to concept learning is that the concept rather than the single stimulus element is now that to which the correct response is conditioned.

In essence, according to Slavin,[302] in paired-associate learning, the student must associate response with each stimulus. Techniques to improve students'

---

[301] Ormrod, 1999.

[302] Slavin, 1999.

responses include imagery, the key word method, serial and free-recall learning, loci method, peg word method, and initial-letter strategies. For specific examples concerning the use of these paired-associate learning techniques, refer to Salvin.[303] Paired-associate learning involves learning a sequence of information in the correct order. The aforementioned strategies will aid students in associating with stimuli.

Developmental Approach

A major approach to cognition has been to describe in explicit terms the sequence of concept development in children from birth to adolescence.[304] Without question, the outstanding effort has been that of Piaget and his collaborators. The studies have ranged over most of the topics one would like to see included in a broad theory of cognition and have covered more conceptual ground than the behavioral approach just discussed. There are four examples, within the Piagetian developmental approach from major studies on the following concepts: the child's understanding of spatial concepts, including both two-and three-dimensional concepts; the development of geometrical concepts; the development of concepts of distance conservation, the spatial coordinate system, and the extensive and controversial studies on the concepts of conservation of mass, weight, and volume. Additional studies have been concerned with the development of number concepts and set concepts closely related to those of number concepts. For example, the notion of two sets being equivalent, that is, having the same cardinality. Still other studies have been devoted to the development of the concepts of causality and also of morality in children.

Those who want to get a deeper feeling for the Piagetian approach to cognition can look at either some of the many books of Piaget that have been

---

[303] Salvin, 1999.

[304] J. Piaget, The language and thought of the child (3rd ed.) (M. Gabain, Trans), (New York, NY: Humanities Press, 1959).

translated into English or at some of the excellent readings composed of shorter articles that have appeared in recent years. The book edited by Sigel and Hooper[305] provides an excellent survey and is recommended.

The enormous body of research studies generated by Piaget and his collaborators has given us an overview of the cognitive development of the child unequaled even approximately by any of the other approaches to cognition. The attempt has been to map out in broad terms the cognitive development along every major dimension of intellectual or perceptual skill. To a lesser extent, than one might expect, this conceptual apparatus and approach to cognition has not been extensively applied to disabled children. An example of work in this area is Woodward,[306] who considered one-to-one correspondence and equivalency of sets, as well as seriation and conservation of continuous quantity. She found that performance of retarded children whose chronological age was 12.9 was at about a level similar to an average normal child of from 4 to 7 years.

Granted that the developmental approach of Piaget has given by far the most extensive analysis of the whole range of cognitive concepts, it is natural to ask why this approach has not been uniformly adopted by most investigators and conceded to be the soundest approach to cognition. There are, I think, three reasons for reservations about the Piagetian approach to cognition. These reasons can be given and seriously held to without at the same time denigrating the great value of work that Piaget and his collaborators have done.

One objection to the developmental Piagetian approach to cognition is the lack of emphasis and attention given to language development. The linguistic approach emphasizes the overwhelming importance of language development for

---

[305] Sigel & Hooper, *Logical Thinking in Children Research Based on Piaget's Theory* (Holt, Rinehart & Wilson, 1969).

[306] Woodward, *Industrial Organizations: Theory and Practice* (London: Oxford University Press, 1961).

the cognitive development of a child, and its advocates find far too little attention paid to the problems of language development in the Piagetian viewpoint.

The second objection has been a methodological one by many experimental psychologists to the quality of the experimental data reported by Piaget and his collaborators. The standard objection has been that well-designed experiments have not been used as a basis for the conclusions drawn, but rather empirical methods have been based too much on anecdotal methods, or at the least, open-ended interviews in which children are verbally interrogated about their understanding of concepts and relevant cognitive tasks. This criticism is less valid than it was a decade ago, because much of the emphasis, especially on the part of American investigators following the Piaget line of development, has been on the careful design of experiments to test Piagetian concepts. There now exists a rather substantial literature of an experimentally sound character in the Piagetian tradition, and the reader will find current issues of journals like *Developmental Psychology* and the *Journal of Experimental Child Psychology* full of carefully designed experiments that clearly grow out of this tradition.

The third line of criticism of the Piagetian approach is the lack of clarity in the development of key concepts and the absence of sharply defined experimental tests of the key concepts. To illustrate the problem and to provide a comparison with the earlier discussion of all-or-none conditioning as a behavioral approach, we paraphrase and present briefly an analysis we have given elsewhere of Piaget's concept of stages.

We selected Piaget's concept of stages, because it is central too much of his work in development, and because it also has become increasingly important in developmental psycholinguistics. We hasten to add, however, that a similar analysis could be given of other key concepts. An instance of how Piaget uses the concept of stages can be gained from the following quotation, in which the analysis of three stages of multiple seriation is discussed in Piaget and Inhelder:[307]

"We shall distinguish three stages, corresponding to the usual three levels. During stage I, there are no seriations in the strict sense. The child's constructions are intermediate between classification and seriation. During stage II, there is seriation, but only according to one of the criteria, or else the child switches from one criterion to the other...Finally, during stage III (starting at 7-8 years), the child reaches a muliplicative arrangement based on the twofold seriation of the set of elements."

In this passage, as elsewhere in the writings of Piaget, there is little indication that matters could be otherwise--that development could be incremental and continuous and that stages may be an artificial device with no real scientific content. No one denies that children develop in some sequential fashion as they acquire new capacities and skills. The problem is in determining whether they proceed in stages or continuously. We could of course artificially and conventionally divide any period of incremental development and label it as a particular stage. In principle, the issue about stages versus incremental acquisition of concepts is exactly the issue faced by the behavioral approach in comparing the all-or-none conditioning model with the ordinary incremental model.

In other places, Piaget does comment on the question of the actual existence of stages, but he does not address the matter in ways that seem scientifically sound. Piaget[308] writes as follows:

"I now come to the big problem: the problem of the very existence of stages; do there exist steps in development or is complete continuity observed?...When we are faced macroscopically with a certain

[307] J. Piaget, Discussion in J. M. Tanner and B. Inhelder (Eds.), *Discussions on Child Development* (New York: International Universities Press, 1960).

[308] Piaget, 1960.

discontinuity we never know whether there do not exist small transformations which we do not manage to measure on our scale of approximation. In other words, continuity would depend fundamentally on a question of scale; for a certain scale of measurement we obtain discontinuity. Of course this argument is quite valid, because the very manner of defining continuity and discontinuity implies that these ideas remain fundamentally relative to the scale of measurement or observation. This, then, is the alternative which confronts us: either a basic continuity or else development by steps, which would allow use to speak of stages at least to our scale of approximation."

The confusion in this passage is in the introduction of the spurious issue of the scale of measurement. Obviously, this is an issue to be discussed in a refined analysis but, as the literature on all-or-none conditioning model versus incremental models shows, a perfectly good and sound prior investigation exists at a given level of measurement, namely, the level of standard experimental studies. What Piaget does not seem to recognize is the existence of a clear alternative and the necessity of testing for the presence or absence of this alternative in providing a more correct account of the sequential development that occurs in a child.

The discussion of stages is meant to indicate the tension that exists in any fair evaluation of the work of Piaget and his collaborators. On the other hand, they have without doubt contributed enormously to the current intense interest in cognition, especially in the cognitive development of children. Piaget and his collaborators have put the problem in a proper perspective by insisting on investigating not just a few skills and concepts, but the entire range that we intuitively expect and believe are part of the child's developing competence. On the other hand, both the theory and experimentation have often been loose and more suggestive than definitive. Methodological and theoretical criticisms are easy to formulate. Certainly, deeper clarification of both the experimental methodology and the theory is required before widespread applications to the critical problems of development in disabled children are extensively pursued.

Information-Processing Approach

The information-processing approach to cognition has been deeply influenced by related developments in computer science and the widespread impact of computers themselves since the early 1950s. A good example of any early influential article in this approach to cognition is Newell.[309] Feigenbaum and Feldman edited an influential book of the early 1960s.[310]

In broad terms, the difference between the information-processing approach and the developmental approach is Piaget's primary concern with the characterization of tasks and the sequence in which the child learns to solve these tasks; in contract, the information-processing approach has been concerned with the processing apparatus necessary to handle even the most elementary forms of cognition.

As the name suggests, the information-processing approach has been influenced by the organization of information processing in computers. There is concern that the major aspects of information processing that have been the focus of computer organization also be given attention in any conception of human processing. It is important not to be misunderstood on this point. Investigators like Mayer and Reisberg[311] are far too sophisticated to think that the present stage of computer development provides anything like an adequate model of human processing. Although they do not put it in so many words, it is probably fair to say that they would regard the problems of computer organization as indicating

---

[309] A. Newell & H. A. Simon, *Human Problem Solving* (Englewood Cliffs, NJ: Prentice Hall, 1972).

[310] E. A. Feigenbaum & J. Feldman, *Computer and Thought* (New York, NY: McGraw-Hill, 1963).

[311] R. Mayer, Learners as information processors: Legacies and Limitations of educational psychology's second metaphor, *Educational Psychology*, 31 (1996a), 151-161; D. Reisberg, *Cognition: Exploring the Science of the Mind.* (New York: W. W. Norton, 1977).

138

some of the necessary but not sufficient conditions for information processing in humans.

The major feature of the information-processing approach that differs from either the behavioral or developmental approach is the emphasis on the detailed steps a person or child takes in solving a concept, and the detailed analysis of the verbal protocol that can be obtained from him in the process of mastering a problem. The information-processing approach is like the developmental approach and is more like the behavioral approach in its emphasis on a highly detailed analysis of the structure and content of the protocol.

As is characteristic in other areas of psychology, the different approaches also tend to develop different types of tasks considered typical of cognition. The information-processing approach, especially in the work of Newell and Simon,[312] has been concerned with cryptarithimetic, simple logical inference, and the kind of problem solving that goes into complex games like chess.

The most characteristic and important feature of the information-processing approach has been the attempt to simulate in a computer program the detailed processing in which a human subject engages in problem solving. This has proven to be both a strength and weakness of this approach to cognition. It is a strength because of the effort to capture as much as possible the explicit details of the human subject's thought processes in mastering a cognitive problem; in this ambition it goes far beyond anything that has yet been attempted in the behavioral approach.

The weakness of the approach is methodological. It centers around the difficulty of evaluating whether or not the simulation, even at the level of individual subjects, provides a good match or not to the actual ongoing processing in the human subject. The complexity of the simulation raises new

---

[312] Newell & Simon, 1972.

methodological problems that do not arise in the same form in either the behavioral or developmental approaches to cognition.

Recently the broad spectrum of problems attacked under the heading of artificial intelligence by computer scientists has provided also a broader based approach to cognition than the particular approach of Newell and Simon.[313] It is not that the approach via artificial intelligence is in contradiction with that of Newell and Simon--it is that new components with a different emphasis have been added. The work of Marvin Minsky and Seymour Papert[314] has been especially influential in this development. They have taken this approach at a mathematical level in their book, *Perceptions*, and still more explicitly in their recent analysis of the close relation between artificial intelligence and the development of a child's intelligence. Perhaps the most characteristic feature of their recent work is the emphasis on a procedure or program on the one hand, and the process of debugging the procedure or the program on the other. The idea that learning a cognitive skill is primarily a matter of learning a procedure which itself might be broken into separate procedures, and that each of these separate procedures must go through a process of debugging, similar to debugging a computer program, is an important insight not previously exploited in any detail are far from clear. It is now a widespread belief that we must be able to conceptualize the internal programs that an organism uses in solving a conceptual or perceptual problem.

Today, researchers and psychologists have discovered that individuals do not just absorb information at face value, rather they do a great deal with the information they acquire, actively trying to organize and make sense of the information.[315] It is commonly agreed by most cognitive theorist that learning is a process of constructing knowledge from information an individual receives rather

---

[313] Newell & Simon, 1972.

[314] M. Minsky & S. Papert, *Perception* (Cambridge, MA: MIT Press, 1969).

[315] Ormrod, 1999.

than directly receiving information through the five senses.[316] Most of the theorists refer to constructing knowledge from information received as "constructivism" rather than the information processing theory. Individuals receive and react to information through individual and social constructivism. An example of individual constructivism may be found in Piaget's theory of cognitive structure, where a child constructs knowledge for oneself rather than absorbing it exactly as perceived. Social constructivism theories imply how individuals work as a team to make sense of their surroundings.

Linguistic Approach

An excellent expression of the linguistic approach to cognition is found in Chomsky.[317] At the outset, an important difference to be noted about the linguistic approach in contrast to the three other approaches discussed already is that the linguistic approach does not in principle propose to be a general theory of cognition, but rather it concentrates on that significant part of cognition that is language dependent or consists of language skills themselves. Linguistics like Chomsky consider the phenomenon of cognitive psychology and, consequently, believe that a large place should be occupied by the linguistic approach to cognition, even if it is not meant to encompass all cognitive phenomena.

Linguists and psycholinguists with a strong linguistic orientation have been insistent that none of the other approaches to cognition provides anything like an adequate detailed theory of language performance in either children or adults. Indeed, it is customary for linguists like Chomsky to insist that even their own theories offer only the barest beginning of an adequate approach to the analysis of language. Long ago, Aristotle defined man as a rational animal, but much is to be said for the viewpoint that man should rather be defined as a talking

---

[316] G. Leinhardt, 1994; Collins & Green, 1995; Marshall, 1992; R. Mayer, Learners as information processors: Legacies and Limitations of educational psychology's second metaphor, *Educational Psychology*, 31 (1996a), 151-161; Spiver, 1997.

[317] Chomsky, 1972.

animal. The linguistic approach to cognition insists upon the central place of language in the cognitive behavior of man and rightly denies the adequacy of any theory of cognition that cannot account for major aspects of language behavior.

The linguistic viewpoint has emphasized understanding the complex and sometimes bewildering grammar of spoken language. There is, however, another aspect of language with a long tradition of analysis, which is equally important from a cognitive standpoint. We have in mind the theory of meaning and reference, or what is usually termed the semantics of a language. This semantics tradition derives more from philosophy and logic than from linguistic. In support of this view, Houston[318] stated that different sentences many have the same meaning indicates the philosophical and logical view rather than the linguistic approach. Psycholinguists have recommended a procedure for finding out the sematic or the meaning of a sentence. Forster, Wanner and Maratsos[319] recommended that the sentence be divided into clauses; Foder, Bever, and Garrett support this view.[320] They articulated that after a sentence has been divided into clauses, its meaning can than be determined.

Methods that provide detailed descriptions of the grammatical and semantic structure of an individual's speech will continue to be developed. As this development continues, we will have a deeper understanding of cognition in the development of procedural grammars and semantics that yield not only a proper analysis of the structure of individual's speech, but also provide the necessary mechanisms for generating the speech, both in its grammatical and semantical feature.

[318] J. P. Houston, *Fundamentals of Learning and Memory* (3rd Ed.) (Orlando, FL: Harcourt Brace Jovanovich, 1986).

[319] K. Forster, Levels of process and the structure of the language processor, in W. E. Cooper and T. Walker (Eds.), *Sentence Processing* (Hillsdale, NJ: Erlbaum, 1979); E. Wanner, M. Maratsas, An ATN approach to comprehension, in M. Halle, J. Bresnan, and G. A. Miller (Eds.), Linguistic *Theory and Psychological Reality* (Cambridge, MA: MIT Press, 1978).

[320] J. A. Foder, T. G. Bever, & M. F. Garrett, *The Psychology of Language: An Introduction to Psycholinguistics and Generative Grammar* (New York, NY: McGraw-Hill, 1974).

Klein[321] voiced that language serves three important functions. It allows us to communicate with each other, it facilitates our thinking processes, and it enables us to recall information beyond the limits of our memory stores. The study of the meaning of language, called semantics, has shown that the same sentence can have different meanings and different sentences can have the same meaning.

A Comparison Between Cognitive and Behavioral Psychology

Most cognitive research has dealt with higher mental processes with humans, whereas behavioral research has centered its efforts on animal research. Standards for conducting studies with humans and animals differ significantly. Topics relevant to comprehension, understanding, memory, concept formation, and other higher mental processes cannot be successfully conducted using animals.

Another major difference between the two paradigms maybe in the major goals of the two approaches. Behaviorists attempt to establish relationships that exist between behavior and its antecedents as well as its consequences, where as cognitive theories attempt to make plausible and useful information about the processes that intervene between input and output. Additionally, Lefranscios[322] reflected that cognitive theories tend to be less ambitious in scope than behavior theories. He further voiced that there have been few attempts to build systematic inclusive cognitive theories that would explain all human learning and behavior. Emphasis in the last several decades has been on intensive research in specific areas, rather than on the construction of general systems.

---

[321] S. B. Klein, *Learning: Principles and Applications* (3rd ed.) (New York, NY: McGraw-Hill, Inc., 1996).

[322] G. R. Lefrancios, *Theories of Human Learning* (4th ed.) (Pacific Grove, CA: Brooks Cole Publishing Company, 2000).

Summary

In the behavioral approach, Estes[323] learning theory is applied to mental development. Suppes[324] shows how the simple all-or-none conditioning model applies to concept formation in children, and reviews Zeaman and House's application of an extension of this model for retarded children. Relative to handicaps, Suppes recommends a procedure not followed in practice to date, namely, estimation of parameters of the learning models for individual subjects, or for groups of subjects stratified according to mental age.

The developmental approach, dominated by Piaget,[325] has made considerable progress in describing the sequence of concept development in children, but this has not been applied extensively to disabled children. Suppes[326] advances three reasons for holding reservations about the viewpoint associated with Piaget, but none of the drawbacks is intrinsic to the approach. With work over time, it could prove highly fruitful in understanding the problems of development in disabled children.

The essence of the information-processing approach to cognition is a concern with the processing apparatus that appears to be necessary, and with the detailed analysis of the steps a child takes in attaining a concept. Newell and Simon[327] attempted to stimulate human information processing in a computer program, and Suppes touches on the strengths and weaknesses of this strategem. Minsky and Papert[328] suggest that formulating and debugging the separate

---

[323] W. K. Estes, New developments in statistical behavior theory. Differential tests of axioms for associative learning, *Psychometrika*, 26, 73-84.

[324] P. Suppes, Stimulus: Response theory of finite automata, *Journal of Mathematical Psychology*, 6 (1969), 327-355.

[325] Piaget, 1960.

[326] Suppes, 1969.

[327] Newell & Simon, 1972.

[328] Minsky & Papert, 1969.

procedures (subroutines) of a larger procedure (program) is the process people follow in solving a conceptual problem, and Suppes illustrated with some of his own work how an analysis along these lines might go. If through research in the years ahead analyses are made of the tasks disabled children should master, and the processes disabled children should follow, they also could contribute substantially to solving practical problems of instruction.

The linguistic approach focuses on what many consider to be the most important part of cognition, the part that is language dependent. Chomsky best represents the linguist's work on syntax; the contribution of philosophers and logicians to semantics was mainly by Tarski. As Suppes[329] pointed out, we should like a detailed account of both the grammar and meaning of speech of young children. He includes in this section a review of some studies of retarded and deaf children. He also picks up again the matter of sensory substitution, considered earlier by Sherrick, Harber, and Wickelgren, as he considers concept information in deaf children, and the possibility of using sign language to provide the equivalent of verbal instructions.

The major thrust of cognitive psychology has been to research and place emphasis on the perceptual and cognitive processes, whereas the behaviorists attempt to establish relationships that exist between behavior and its antecedents as well as its consequences. Individuals are prompted to use higher thinking processes to perceive, to arrive at understanding, to process information, and to solve problems. Both cognitive and behavioral theorists support the idea that learning should be studied objectively.

---

[329] P. Suppes, 1969.

Chapter 9

Impact of Early Cognitive Theorists

Overview

The preceding chapter established the relationship between cognitive psychology and cognitive theories of learning. In essence, cognitive psychology provided the framework for our present assumptions underlining cognitive learning theories. We alluded to the important work of Chomsky[330] in formulating our present understanding of cognitive theory. Works by Bruner[331] as well as countless others were instrumental in developing cognitive theory as a science.

By the early 1900s cognitive psychology was denouncing the S-R theory of learning and was formulating its own theory based upon cognitive psychology. The movement was lead by Tolman, Piaget, Vygotsky, and Gestalt psychologists. The impact and influence of their works today can be seen in shaping education reforms in educational practices.

Research in learning over the last two decades has given additional information on how children learn. A single paradigm based upon a behaviorist approach has shifted to include learning derived from the cognitive learning theory. According to Eggen and Kauchak[332] research in cognitive learning has led to improving our understanding of the social nature of learning, the importance of context on understanding, the need for domain-specific knowledge in higher-order

---

[330] Chomsky, 1957.

[331] J. S. Brunner, *The Process of Education* (Cambridge, MA: Harvard University Press, 1961); J. S. Brunner, *The act of discovery, Harvard Educational Review*, 31 (1961a), 21-32; J. S. Brunner, *The Process of Education* (Cambridge, MA: Harvard University Press, 1961b).

[332] P. Eggen, & D. Kauchak, *Strategies for Teachers: Teaching Content and Thinking Skills* (Needham Heights, MA: Allyn and Bacon, 1996).

146

thinking, expert-novice differences in thinking and problem solving, and the belief that learners construct their own understanding of the topics they study.

Edward C. Tolman

Tolman is considered to be a behaviorist, but his theory was basically cognitive. He believed that learning was internal and included a holistic view of learning. This concept was in contrast to the one advocated by behaviorists. Tolman's[333] theory was based upon a mechanistic view of learning. The theory attempted to emphasize and to understand the predictable nature of human behavior. Tolman adapted several ideas from behaviorists and, according to Ormrod,[334] postulated the following principles in his purposive behaviorism.

1. Behavior should be studied at a molar level.

   This view was in contrast to early behaviorists' beliefs. They attempted to reduce behavior to simple S-R responses. Tolman opposed the S-R view, he related that behaviors are too complex to be regulated to simple S-R reflexes and that a total approach must be used when analyzing behavior.

2. Learning can occur without reinforcement.

   Tolman opposed this view. His blocked-path study supported his theory that learning can occur without reinforcement.[335] This classical study involved three groups of rats that ran a different maze under different reinforcement conditions. Rats in Group I were reinforced with food each time they successfully ran the maze. Rats in Group II received no reinforcement for successfully completing the maze. Rats in Group III were not reinforced during the first 10 days, but were reinforced on the 11th day. The findings showed that the performance of the rats in group II and III improved even

---

[333] E. C. Tolman & C. H. Hovzik, Introduction and removal of reward and maze performance in rats, *University of California Publications in Psychology*, 4, 2 (1930), 57-275.

[334] Ormrod, 1999.

[335] Tolman, 1930.

though they did not receive reinforcement. Once the rats in group III began receiving reinforcements, their performance in the maze equaled and, in most cases, surpassed the performance of group I. Results suggest that reinforcement is not as important to learning as advocated by behaviorists and that organisms develop cognitive maps of their environments. A cognitive map may be defined as an internal organization of relationships between goals and behaviors.

3. Learning can occur without a change in behavior.

    Most behaviorists will adamantly denounce this statement. Tolman stated that learning can occur without a change in behavior. He defined this type of learning as latent learning. The Tolman and Honzik study, reported earlier, provide us with an example of latent learning. Rats in groups III and I must have equally learned the same amount during the first 10 days, even though their behaviors did not reflect such learning. In essence, the amounts of learning was not observed. Tolman proclaimed that reinforcement influences performance rather than learning, in that it increases the likelihood that learned behavior will be displayed.

4. Intervening variables must be considered.

    Variables such as drive, habit, strength, and incentive play critical roles in learning. All behavior has a purpose and all actions are directed toward the accomplishment of some goal. The intervening variable listed above contributed significantly to promoting or impeding learning.[336]

5. Behavior is purposive.

    Tolman supported the formulation of S-R connections provided that they are part of a process that produces a certain goal. He proposed that individuals' drives and activities are directed at achieving the goal. The behavior has a purpose, which is the achievement of the goal. According to Tolman, there

---

[336] Tolman.

are certain events in the environment that convey information relevant to achieving one's goals. Goals can only be successfully met only after one has mastered the events leading to rewards or punishment in one's environment. The anticipation of future rewards stimulates activities to guide our behavior toward achieving the goal. The role of punishment indicate negative activities which impede the achievement of goals. Tolman's theory implies that behavior has a purpose that is goal directed. Consequently, this theory of learning is frequently referred to as "purposive behaviorism."

6. Expectations affect Behavior.

When an organism learns that certain behaviors produce certain results, expectations are formed concerning the behaviors. The organism expects a particular action to lead to a designated goal. Individuals also expect specific outcomes to produce certain results. If goals are not achieved, individuals continue to search for that reward which will satisfy the goal. Tolman indicated the importance of knowledge gained through experience.

7. Learning results in an organized body of information.

Information is organized through what Tolman referred to as "cognitive maps." Tolman proposed that organisms develop "cognitive maps" of their environments by organizing information and knowing the location of them. The Tolman, Ritchie, and Kalish[337] experiment with rats gave some clarity to the term. Rats ran several times through a series of mazes. Data suggested that the rats learned how the mazes were arranged. Some of the entrances leading to some of the alleys leading to food was blocked, the rats had to choose other alleys to arrive at the food. The rats were able to locate the alley which was not blocked and provided a short cut to the food. According to Tolman, rats integrated their experiences into a body of information (cognitive maps) from which they figured out the shortest route to the food.

---

[337] C. E. Tolman, B. F. Ritchie, & D. Kalish, Studies in spatial learning: Orientation and the short-cut, *Journal of Experimental Psychology*, 36 (1946), 13-24.

Tolman's principal contribution to the development of psychological theory lies not so much in advances in knowledge and prediction made possible by his work, as is the fact that it represents a transition from behavioristic to more cognitive interpretations. It departs from behavioristic theories such as those of Skinner, Watson, and Guthrie, which rejected speculation about events that might intervene between stimuli and responses, by emphasizing the importance of cognitive variables such as expectancies.[338]

Classroom Application

Tolman suggested that our behavior is goal-oriented. We are motivated to reach specific goals and continue to strive until we obtain them. It is incumbent upon teachers to construct learning activities which will motivate the achievement of positive goals for children.

Jean Piaget

Jean Piaget's theory is basically cognitive and developmental. Much of Piaget's theory was based on the study of his own children. The method he developed to study his children was called the clinical method. He interviewed the children and used their questions for follow-up questions. Initially, the method did not receive much support because it was considered too subjective by theorists. However, today, the theory has stood the test of time and is considered a scientific approach for studying children. Piaget's work today, is considered the most comprehensive theory on intellectual development; it incorporates a variety of topics involving cognitive development. Papert[339] wrote that Piaget found the secrets of human learning and knowledge hidden behind the cute and seemingly illogical notions of children.

---

[338] Lefranscios, 1999.

[339] S. Papert, Jean Piaget: Child psychologist, *Time*, 100 (1999), 105-107.

Overview of Piaget's Contributions

According to Papert,[340] Piaget grew up near Lake Neuchatel in a quiet region of France known for its wines and watches. His father was a professor of medieval studies and his mother a strict Calvinist. He was a child prodigy who soon became interested in the scientific study of nature. At age 10, his observations led to questions that could be answered only by access to the university library. Piaget wrote and published a short note on the sighting of an albino sparrow in the hope that this would influence the librarian to stop treating him like a child. It worked. Piaget was launched on a path that would lead to his doctorate in zoology and a lifelong conviction that the way to understand anything is to understand how it evolves. Piaget published nearly 60 scholarly books, and in 1924, was appointed director of the International Bureau of Education. In 1955, he established the Center for Genetic Epistemology. In 1980, Piaget died in Geneva.

Piaget articulated that it is not until the growing child reaches the two operational stages that he or she begins to acquire the concepts of conservation. He interpreted the concepts of conservation to the idea that the mass of an objective remains constant no matter how much the form changes. He demonstrated this concept with the following example. A five-year-old is given two tumblers, each half-full of water. When asked, the child will agree that there is the same amount of water in each tumbler. However, if the water is poured from one glass into a tall narrow container, the child will reply that there is more water in the tall glass. The child, according to Piaget, has no concept of the conservation of matters. Most children develop this concept by the time he or she reaches his or her eighth birthday. This illustration demonstrates that knowledge can be described in terms of structures that change with development. Piaget advanced the concept of "scheme." He defined "scheme" as the basic

---

[340] Papert, 1999.

structure through which an individual's knowledge is mentally represented. As children develop mentally, physically, and socially, new schemes develop and old schemes are either integrated or modified into cognitive structures.[341]

As children develop, their movements become more complex and coordinated as they react with their environments. This process, according to Piaget, is called adaptation. Both assimilation involves modifying one's perception of the environment to fit a scheme. An individual must have an advanced knowledge of the condition to effectively use assimilation. According to Piaget, the sucking scheme permits infants to assimilate a nipple to the behavior of sucking. Accommodation involves modifying a scheme to fit the environment; in essence, accommodation involves a change in understanding. The integration of the two lead to adaptation. The balance between assimilation and accommodation is, according to Piaget, an equilibrium in which individuals can explain new events in terms of their existing schemes. When events cannot be explained in relationship to existing schemes, such events may create disequilibrium. Individuals must integrate their schemes in order to understand and explain conditions which create disequilibrium. The process from equilibrium to disequilibrium and back to equilibrium is referred to as equilibration, a process which leads to the balance between assimilation and accommodation.

Jean Piaget is credited with upsetting the world of developmental psychology, and has done more than any other theorist to challenge psychologists' belief in the stimulus-response theory concerning child psychology. He believed that reflexes and other automatic patterns of behavior had a minor role in the development of human intelligence. He postulated that only in the first few days of the infant's life that his or her behavior depends on automatic behavioral reaction. Initially, this view of infancy was radically opposed to current theoretical beliefs. His views sharply opposed the traditional behaviorist theory,

---

[341] Ormrod, 1999.

152

which maintained that man seeks to escape from stimulation and excitation, while his view maintained that the infant frequently and actively seeks stimulation. Today, Piaget's theory relevant to the aforementioned topic has stood the test of time. His child development theory has been scientifically validated.

According to Piaget's view of intelligence, the child passes through four major periods. These periods are sensory-motor, pre-operational, concrete, and formal operational. This theory maintains that all children go through these stages in an orderly sequence; however, some children can pass through the stages at different rates. Research findings by deRibaupierre and Rieben[342] support the above premise. Conclusions drawn by Crain[343] indicated that individuals may perform tasks with different stages at the same time, especially when they have mastered tasks in the formal stage. (Piaget's four stages of cognitive development have been well summarized in the professional literature. Our intent is to summarize the stages. The reader is advised to consult basic text in learning theory or cognitive development for additional details.)

Sensori-Motor Stage (Birth to Age 2)

During this stage, infants are exploring their world through the use of their senses and motor skills. Through interaction with the environment, infants achieve a major intellectual breakthrough. Children no longer believe that objects do not exist when they are out of sight. All infants have innate behavior called reflexes, such as sucking and grasping objects. From the basic reflexes, more complex behaviors develop to form advance schemes. Much of the learning during this stage is by trial and error. According to Piaget, by the end of the sensory motor stage, children have progressed from trial and error stages to a more planned approach to problem solving. Piaget further proclaimed that infants

---

[342] A. deRibaupierre & L. Rieben, Individuals and situational variability in cognitive development, *Educational Psychologist*, 30 (1), (1995), 5-14.

[343] W. C. Crain, *Theories of Development: Concepts and Applications* (Englewood Cliffs, NJ: Prentice Hall, 1985).

do not posses schemes that enable them to think about objects other than those directly in front of them. Children at this stage of development are unable to think critically because they lack the cognitive structures necessary for critical thinking. They are limited because they are in the learning by doing pre-operational stage (ages 2 to 7).

Language and concepts develop at a rapid rate during this stage. Children learn to use their cognitive abilities to form new mental schemes. This stage is characterized by thinking that is often illogical. An example of illogical thinking during this stage is children's reaction to a conversation of liquid problem. Children were given several size glasses with the same amount of water. Most children would pick the taller glass as having the most water.

According to Piaget, the children's thinking depends more on perception than logic during this state. During this stage, children develop cognitive structures which allow them to represent objects or events via symbols such as language, mental images, and gestures. Despite the accomplishments of this stage, Piaget emphasized that children in this stage of development are unable to solve many problems that are critical to logical reasoning. The thinking of children in this stage is rigid, inflexible, and strongly influenced by the effects of momentary experience.[344] A major limitation in children in the preoperational stage is that of egocentrism. Preoperational children are unaware of points of same way as they do. Piaget suggested that egocentrism is largely responsible for view other than their own, and they think everyone experiences the world in the rigidity and illogical nature of young children's thinking. Egocentric thinking is not reflective thought, which critically examines, rethinks, and restructures an aspect of the environment.

Another limitation of preoperational thinking is the problem of conservation, the idea that certain physical attributes of an object remain the same even though its external appearance changes. Preoperational children are easily

---

[344] L. E. Berk, *Child Development* (Boston, MA: Allyn and Bacon, 1991).

154

distracted by the concrete, perceptual appearance of objects, and often focus their attention on one detail of a situation to the neglect of other important features.[345]

The most important limitation of preoperational thought is its irreversibility. Reversibility, the main characteristic of logical operation, refers to the ability to mentally go through a series of reasonings or transformations in a problem and then reverse direction and return to the starting point.[346] Because children in this stage are incapable of reversible thinking, their reasoning about events often consists of collections of logically disconnected facts and contradictions. Children in this stage tend to provide explanations by linking together two events that occurred close in time and space, as if one caused the other. Children in this stage are less likely to use inductive or deductive reasoning.

Concrete Operations (Ages 7 to 11)

According to Piaget, this stage is a major turning point in cognitive development because children's thinking parallel adults. During this stage, children began to think logically about the conservation problem presented in the preoperation stage. Children can only apply their logical operations to concrete and observable objects and events. During this stage, children have problems dealing with abstract information. They cannot successfully distinguish between logic and reality. Seriation is an important task that children learn during this stage. The task involves arranging things in a logical order. To accomplish this task, children must be able to order and classify objects by some standard or criterion. During this stage, children can perform relatively well on a variety of problems that involve operational thinking like conservation, transitivity, and hierarchical classification as well as problems that require children to reason about spatial relationships. The accomplishment of this feat enables children to become more critical thinkers.

---

[345] Berk, 1991.

[346] Berk, 199.

Although thinking is much more adult-like that it was earlier, the stage of concrete operations suffers from one important limitation. Children in this stage can only think in an organized, logical fashion when dealing with concrete, tangible information they can directly perceive. Their mental operations do not work when applied to information that is abstract and hypothetical. Thoughts about abstract concepts such as force, acceleration, and inertia is beyond children in the concrete operational stage. The concrete operational approach does not address potential relationships that are not easily detected in the real world or that might not exist at all.[347]

Formal Operational Stage (Ages 11 to Adulthood)

During this stage, the child develops the ability to reason with abstract and hypothetical information; proportional thinking develops, which is essential to understanding scientific and mathematical reason, through which the child begins to understand the concept of proportion. The child has developed the skills to test hypotheses by holding selected variables constant. Children are also able to evaluate the logic and quality of their thought processes, and to make necessary corrections. In formal operations, children apply their logic directly to real objects. The abilities that make up formal operational thought, thinking abstractly, testing hypotheses, and forming concepts are critical to the learning of higher-order skills. According to Piaget, the formal operational stage brings cognitive development to a close.

Piaget is considered to be the giant in developmental psychology. His research refutes the behaviorists' view of learning. He believed that stimulus responses and other automatic patterns, advocated by behaviorists, have a minor role in the development of human intelligence. Piaget's theory of intellectual development involves four major periods of development in which the child passes through: (1) Sensory Motor, (2) Preoperational, (3) Concrete, and (4)

---

[347] Berk, 1991.

156

Formal operational. According to Piaget, these stages are limited by maturation. Certain physiological changes must be evident for children to complete tasks in certain stages.

Piaget's theory of cognitive development is very much related to critical thinking skills. Piaget suggested that the acquisition of knowledge is the result of interaction between the learner and the environment. Learning is, thus, facilitated by the child's acquisition of new skills and experiences.[348] It is these new skills and experiences, according to Piaget, that allows children to become progressively more capable of critical thinking. The Piagetian perspective would suggest that teaching critical thinking skills to very young children is not helpful because of their undeveloped cognitive structures.

Classroom Application

The impact of Piaget's theories of learning and education has been successfully summarized as follows by Berk:[349]

1. A focus on the process of children's thinking, not just its products. Educators must understand the processes employed by children to arrive at their answers and provide appropriate strategies based upon their cognitive functioning.

2. Recognition of the importance of children's self-initiated involvement in the learning process. Teachers should employ the discovery method in their classrooms.

3. A deep emphasis on practices geared toward making children think like adults. Piagetian-based education denounces this type of education. This teaching approach according to the theory may be worse than no teaching at all.

4. Acceptance of individual differences in development progression.

---

[348] L. E. Berk, Child *development (4th ed.)* (Boston, MA: Allyn and Bacon, 1997).

[349] Berk, 1977.

Teachers must recognize that, according to Piaget, all children go through the same developmental sequence, but they do so at different rates. Consequently, instructional strategies should be geared toward reaching the individual needs of children through individual and small group activities.

Lev Vygotsky

Vygotsky's theory according to Ormrod and Moll[350] lend support to the concept that natural properties as well as social relationships and constraints make possible the social construction of a child's higher psychological processes. The three major components of the Vygotskian theory are: (1) the internalization of auxiliary culture means, (2) the interpersonal or social process of mediation, and (3) the child's knowledge is formed with the zone of proximal development, a cognitive space defined by social relational boundaries.

Vygotsky supported the view that many learning and thinking processes have their beginnings in social interactions with others. According to Vygotsky, the process through which social activities evolve into internal mental activities is called "internalization." Internalizing one's behavior can change one's view towards a situation; it provides for an individual to look at a situation from different angles on their own, as well as improving one's interpersonal communication skills.

There are many tasks in which children cannot perform independently, but can perform with the assistance of others. This process is known as the zone of proximal development. Vygotsky indicated that children learn very little from performing tasks in which they can complete independently. Instead, they develop primarily by attempting tasks in collaboration with others.

One of the major tenets of Vygotsky's theory is that there is a functional relationship between the effects of the culture on cognitive development and

---

[350] Ormrod, 1999; I. Moll, The material and the social in Vgotsky's *Theory of Cognitive Development* (Clearinghouse on Teacher Education, ED 352-186, 1991).

biological growth.   Whereas the physical, biological, and neurological determinants are more readily understood and agreed upon, the impact of the culture determinants is not as easily understood. Cultural determinants include social processes which transform naturally through the mastery and use of culture signs.   In essence, the natural development of children's behavior form the biological conditions necessary to develop higher psychological processes. Culture, in turn, provides the conditions by which the higher psychological processes may be realized.

Classroom Application

The Vygotskian theory has several applications for classroom use.   One application is the framework for setting up cooperative learning arrangements in the classroom.   Another application is giving students more responsibility for their own learning, by actively involving them in the learning process as resources and group leaders.   The curriculum should be developmentally appropriate and include independent activities as well as performing activities with the assistance of others.

Gestalt Psychology

The Gestalt psychologists supported the importance of organizational processes in perception, learning, and problem solving.   They also believed that individual's were predisposed to organize information in particular ways.[351]   Max Wertheimer, Wolfgang Kohler, and Kurt Koffka were German psychologists who developed and field tested the theory.   The results of their experimentations assisted in advancing some basic concepts of the theory.

Wertheimer[352] is usually credited with starting the movement.   His experiment involved a description and analysis of an optical illusion known as the Phi Phenomenon. While riding a train, Wertheimer observed that when two lights

---

[351] Ormrod, 1999.

[352] M. Wertheimer, Experimentelle Studien, Uber das sehen von Bewegung. *Zeitschrift fur Psychologie*, 61, (1912), 161-265.

blink on and off in a sequential manner and rate, they often appeared to be one light moving back and forth. Based on this observation, Wertheimer concluded that perception of an experience is sometimes different from the experience itself. Wertheimer's experiment was instrumental in formulating one of the basic ideas and principles of Gestalt psychology: Perception is often different from reality. Gestalt psychologists supported the principle that human experience cannot be studied successfully in isolation. They advanced the concept that the whole is more than the sum of its parts. Consequently, a combination of elements must be evident to show a whole pattern.

Murray[353] provides additional information concerning the whole concept. He stated that the whole is different from the parts. He used music to clarify this concept. He related that when listening to music, the overall perception is not of isolated notes but rather of bars or passages. He further articulated that physical objects drive their identity not only from the parts that compose them but more from the manner in which these parts are combined.

Kohler's[354] research with chickens demonstrated the importance of the interrelationships among elements. This transposition experiment was conducted with hens using the following experimental procedures:

1. Hens were shown two sheets of gray paper, a light, and a dark shade.
2. Grain was placed on both sheets, but the hens were only permitted to feed from the dark gray sheet.
3. The experiment was changed; the hens were shown a sheet of paper the same shade in which they had previously fed, along with a sheet of an even darker shade.

---

[353] Murray, 1995.

[354] W. Kohler, *Gestalt Psychology* (New York, NY: Liveright, 1929).

The hens tended to go to the darker of the two sheets. The results tend to support that the hens had been conditioned to go to the dark shade because initially they were fed from the darker sheet.

Advocates of this theory believe that the organized structure and experience forms an imposing structure and organization on situations or conditions. Individuals tend to organize experiences in particular, similar, and predictable ways. The Gestalt psychologists advanced several principles to explain how individuals organize their experiences.

The first principle is the Law of Proximity. This law implies that individuals tend to perceive as a unit those things that are close together in space. The second principle is the Law of Similarity. This law states that individuals tend to perceive as a unit things that are similar to one another. The third principle is the Law of Closure. This law implies that individuals tend to fill in missing pieces to form a complete picture. The fourth principle is the Law of Pragnavz. This law proposes that individuals always organize their experiences as simply, concisely, systematically, and completely as possible.

Lefranscious[355] contended that insight is the cornerstone of Gestalt psychology. Basically, it means the perception of relationships among elements of a problem situation. In essence, it is the solution of a problem as a result of perceiving relationships among all of the situation. Insightful thinking requires a mental reorganization of problem elements and a recognition of the correctness of the new organization.

Classroom Application

Some of the principles advocated by Gestalt Psychologists have reference for classroom application. The theory addresses the role of perception in learning. How students interpret information can accelerate or impede their learning. Specific educational interventions are needed to improve the perception of

---

[355] Lefranscious, 1999.

children. Some children may learn best from using the whole method. Children employ different methods in organizing and structuring learning. Teachers should be apprised of this method and organize appropriate learning activities.

Summary

In this chapter we attempted to summarize the theories, in our opinion, which had the greatest reference for classroom use. The work of Tolman provided us with valuable information concerning goal-directed behaviors. The impact of Piaget's work is evident in schools today. His stages of development provided detailed information relevant to how children learn at different stages, and how the success of prior stages promotes the attainment of higher stages. The Vygotsky theory on the relationship between social skills and education achievement has been supported through research findings. The Gestalt theory is most remembered for its stance on the importance of organizational processes in learning and problem solving.

Most of these theories have denounced behaviorism and emphasize the mental processes in learning. They also believe that many aspects of learning may be unique to humans. Cognitive theorists believe that learning must be objectively studied and based upon scientific research. The theories also have some common threads associated with them, such as information processing, constructivism, developmental aspects, and contextual information. Additionally, these theories advocate the orderly and sequentially development of learning, for educators this implies that tasks must be mastered before high tasks can be achieved.

Chapter 10

Conceptual Learning

Frequently Used Cognitive Strategies and Procedures

The theories, as outlined in Chapters 8-10, encompass a wide range of factors and strategies concerning learning activities that educators can employ in facilitating learning in the classroom. They include the way in which the learner impact and perceive information, procedures, and strategies used to find solutions to problems. Learning consists of many processes. These cognitive processes, in our opinion, which will promote learning in the classroom and assist in closing the achievement gap, involves the following curriculum content and experiences associated with cognitive learning. They frequently include:

1. Concept Learning
2. Critical Thinking
3. Problem Solving
4. Holistic Learning, and
5. Reciprocal Teaching

No one strategy or approach will work for all children. Educators should assess and determine which approach works best for the individual learner.

Overview

A concept can be defined to be a disjunction of a variety of conjunctions or attributes that share one of more similarities.[356] Some concepts are easily defined by observable characteristics and are easily recalled. Thus, the printed word "dog," the sound of a dog barking, etc., can all elicit the same concept

---

[356] J. H. Flavell, P. H. Miller & S. A. Miller, *Cognitive development* (*3rd ed.*), (Upper Saddle River, NJ: Prentice Hall, 1993); H. J. Klaus-Meier, Conceptualizing in B. F. Jones and L. Idol (Eds.), *Dimensions of Thinking and Cognitive Instruction* (Hillsdale, NJ: Erlbaum, 1990).

representative. Similarly, the sight of a dog from various perspectives and the sight of dogs of different species with very different physical properties can all elicit the same general concept of a dog. It is hopeless to think that one can find some common set of physical attributes in all of the adequate cues for the concept "dog." Thus, it is erroneous to define concepts in a manner that requires abstraction of common properties.

Understanding concepts improves the thinking process. Klein[357] wrote that instead of separately labeling and categorizing each new object or event we encounter, we simply incorporate them into existing concepts. Concepts enable individuals to group objects or events that have common characteristics.

Compositions

Concepts are composed of attributes and rules. An attribute may be defined as any feature of an object or event that varies from one condition to another condition. Hair color, eye color, height, and weight are examples of attributes; they deviate from individual to individual. Attributes also have fixed values, such as the classification of cold and warm blood animals, using this principle, animals would be classified as cold or warm blood.

Concepts are generally classified as concrete and abstract.[358] Concrete concepts are easily recognized by common characteristics or traits; the example of the dog given earlier is an example. On the other hand, abstract concepts are difficult to conceptualize using common characteristics or traits. They are best described in terms of a formal definition. Gagne[359] used cousin as an example. There must be a formal definition of cousin in order to form a concept, simply by

---

[357] S. B. Klein, *Learning: Principles and Applications* (3rd ed.) (New York, NY: McGraw-Hill, Inc., 1996).

[358] E. A. Wasserman, C. L. DeVolder, & D. J. Coppage, Non-similarity based conceptualization in pigeons via secondary or mediated generalization, *Psychological Science*, 3 (1992), 374-379; E. D. Gagne, *The Cognitive Psychology of School Learning* (Boston, MA: Little Brown, 1985).

[359] Gagne, 1985.

looking at and observing cousin will not provide enough information to form a concept.

Theories of Concept Learning

Various theories of concept learning are based upon attributes and rules. It would probably be much too difficult by virtue of associative interference to associate sets of attributes one to another, without first chunking each set of attributes and defining a new internal representative to stand for the chunk. Refer to chapter 15 for additional information concerning chunking. For this reason, it seems likely that one stage in human concept learning is to chunk each set of attributes that constitutes a set of sufficient cues for the elicitation of the concept. After two or more chunks have been defined, if these chunks are sufficient cues for the elicitation of the same concept, then these chunks are associated to each other. This association of chunk is the second stage of the concept learning.

Prototype of a Concept

The more attributes a specific object share with a concept, the more the object exemplifies the concept. In support of this view, research by Rosch and Mervis[360] found that the five most typical members of the concept "furniture" had 13 attributes in common, whereas the five least typical members had only two (2) attributes in common. These researchers defined the "prototype" of a concept as the object that has the greatest number of attributes in common with other members of the concept. Once the prototype has been identified, the more an objective deviates from the prototype, the more different it will be to associate it as an example of the concept.

Rules and prototypes assist in defining the boundaries of concepts. According to Klein,[361] these rules determine whether differences between the prototype of a concept and another object mean that the other stimulus is less

---

[360] E. Rosch, Principles of categorization, in E. Rosch and B. Lloyd (Eds.), *Cognition and Categorization* (Hillsdale, NJ: Erlbaum, 1978).

[361] Klein, 1996.

typical of the concept or that it is an example of another concept. Sometimes boundaries of a concept are not clearly defined. An example of a boundary that has not been clearly defined is the difference between a river and a stream.[362]

Rules of Concepts

Concepts must have uniform rules that can be consistently applied to arrive at the same solution. Rules assist in this process by defining the objects and events which have particular characteristics of the concept.[363] The following illustration will assist in clarifying the above. The concept "dog" discussed earlier indicated the attributes employed to recognize a dog. Rules used to define concepts may range from very simple to complex. Only one attribute is needed to define a simple rule. On the other hand, a complex rule requires two or more attributes to define.

According to this theory, individuals should learn very specific concepts at first. Whereby "specific concepts" is meant, these are concepts which are elicited by only one or a few sets of cues. Only gradually would an individual learn all of the different sets of cues that are considered sufficient by adults to elicit the concept. The contrary argument often made is that individuals learn "overgeneralized" concepts to the right specific instances. Examples are cited that an individual may call every man "father." Klein[364] cited a number of examples that indicate that the overgeneralization position on concept learning is not correct and that individuals, in fact, learn much too specialized concepts at first.

---

[362] L. A. Zazdeh, K. S. Fu, K. M. Tanak, & M. Shimura, *Fuzzy sets and their applications to cognitive and decision processes* (New York, NY: Academic Press, 1975).

[363] L. E. Bourne, Jr., Learning and utilization of conceptual rules, in B. Kleinmuntz (Ed.), *Concepts and the Structures of Memory* (New York, NY: Wiley and Sons, 1967); D. H. Dodd, & R. M. White, *Cognition: Mental Structures and Processes* (Boston, MA: Allyn and Bacon, 1980); S. B. Klein, 1987.

[364] Klein, 1996.

However, the terms "specialized" and "overgeneralized" are usually not very clearly defined, so it is difficult to evaluate the present hypothesis with the previous findings. Usually, the terms "specialized" and "generalized" refer to logical generality, not psychological generality in the sense proposed here. Logical generality is a property of "dictionary definitions" of concepts. In this sense, the concept "dog" is more general than the concept "Saint Bernard dog" and less general than the concept "living thing." Clearly, the average individual learns the concept "dog" before he or she learns either of these two concepts. It is doubtful that any important psychological principle can be formulated regarding the degree of logical generality of concepts learned initially by individuals. With the currently proposed psychological definition of concepts as disjunctions of chunks, it is quite plausible that concepts develop increasing generality in the sense of having more and more chunk representatives associated to them.

Associative and Cognitive Processes

Other theoretical approaches to concept learning imply that it is both an associative and a cognitive process. According to Klein,[365] associative theory has both relevant and irrelevant attributes. The theory proposes that individuals associate a characteristic or attribute with the concept name as demonstrated earlier with the example of the "dog." Employing this theory, an individual should recognize that a stimulus is a member of a concept by determining whether or not it possesses that characteristics--cognitive approaches in concept learning involves a different approach than associative processes.

In cognitive processes, individuals confirm concepts by testing hypotheses. If hypotheses testing support the concept, the concept is deemed to be true. On the other hand, if hypotheses testing do not support the concept, other hypotheses should be generated until the concept is supported. It is assumed that the concept is true and can be tested using experimental conditions. Incorrect

---

[365] Klein, 1996.

168

results may be attributed to individuals not fully employing appropriate experimental conditions, or not testing different hypotheses to confirm the concept. Studies have shown that individuals can test more than one hypothesis at a time.[366] Several researchers have concluded that concept learning is a process of forming various hypotheses about the feature and rules that define a concept, and then employing methods and procedures to dispute or confirm the hypotheses.[367] For specific examples of confirming or rejecting concepts through hypotheses testing, refer to Klein and Ormrod.[368]

Classroom Applications

Concepts are learned by observations, experiences, and definitions. We alluded to this principle earlier in the chapter. The relationship between concept learning and transfer of learning has been well established providing that individuals have been trained and taught the concepts.[369] The researchers have indicated that we cannot assume that this association is automatic. Concepts and skills must be taught if individuals are expected to transfer learning to life situations. Practical application of the concept taught and the learning to be transferred must have a positive relationship. In essence, what is taught in school should have transferability for the life in society.

Children tend to understand some concepts better when they are related to other concepts in which they have knowledge. Concepts are also better learned

---

[366] M. Levine, Hypothesis behavior by humans during discrimination learning, *Journal of Experimental Psychology*, 71, (1996), 331-2338.

[367] J. S. Bruner, J. Goodnow, & G. Austin, *A Study of Thinking* (New York, NY: Wiley and Sons, 1956).

[368] Klein, 1996; Ormrod, 1999.

[369] G. D. Phye, Strategic transfer: A tool for academic problem solving, *Educational Psychology Review*, 4, 3 (1992), 93-421; M. Pressley, & L. Yokoi, Motion for a new trial on transfer, *Educational Researcher*, 23 (5), (1994), 36-38; E. A. Price, & M. P. Drisscoll, An inquiry into the spontaneous transfer of problem-solving skill, *Contemporary Educational Psychology*, 22 (4), 1997, 472-494; R. E. Mayer, & M. C. Wittrock, Problem-solving transfer, in D. C. Berlinear and R. C. Calfee (Eds.), *Handbook on Educational Psychology* (New York, NY: Macmillan, 1996).

when many concrete examples are provided.[370] Various amounts of abstraction can be infused once the concrete application is understood. Individuals also appear to understand concepts better when positive and negative examples are given simultaneously rather than sequentially.[371] In order to provide individuals with understanding concepts, Kinnick[372] stated that individuals understanding of a concept should be assessed by asking them to classify new examples of the concept. Another innovative approach that teachers may employ in developing individuals understanding of concepts is to ask them to make up their own examples and application of the concept under discussion.

Teaching concepts according to Tennyson and Park[373] involves extensive and skillful use of examples. They suggested that teachers follow the rules listed when presenting examples of concepts:

a. Order the example form easy to difficult.

b. Select examples that differ from one another.

c. Compare and contrast examples and non examples.

Slavin[374] wrote that teachers can use conceptual models to assist students in organizing and integrating information. Slavin's view is supported by research conducted by Hiebert, Wearne, & Taber, Mayer & Gallini, & Winn.[375] These

---

[370] V. Kinnick, The effect of concept teaching in preparing nursing students for clinical practice, *Journal of Nursing Education*, 29 (1990), 362-366.

[371] L. E. Bourne, Jr., D. R. Ekstrand, & R. L. Dominowski, *The Psychology of Thinking*. (Englewood Cliffs, NJ: Prentice Hall, 1971).

[372] V. Kinnick, The effect of concept teaching in preparing nursing students for clinical practice, *Journal of Nursing Education*, 29 (1990), 362-366.

[373] R. D. Tennyson, & O. Park, The teaching of concepts: A review of instructional design literature, *Review of Educational Research*, 50, 55-70, 1980.

[374] Slavin, 2000.

[375] J. Hiebert, D. Wearne, & S. Taber, Fourth graders' gradual construction of decimal fractions during instruction using different physical representations, *Elementary School Journal*, 9 (1991), 321-341; R. E. Mayer, & J. K. Gallini, When is an illustration worth ten thousand words? *Journal of Educational Psychology*, 82 (1990), 715-726; W. Winn, Learning from maps and diagrams, *Educational Psychology Review*, 3 (1991), 211-247.

researchers concluded that when models are part of the instructional sequence, not only do students learn more, but also they are better prepared to apply their learning to solve problems. Knowledge maps can be employed to teach a variety of content. A knowledge map can display the main concepts of an object and association between them. The values of using knowledge maps to teach concepts have proven to increase students' retention of content.[376]

Summary

A concept, throughout this chapter, has been defined as a group of objects that have common characteristics. The importance of rules, boundaries, and prototypes has also been articulated. Individuals can learn concepts by associating them with concrete objects initially and then being provided with more abstract forms. The importance of hypotheses testing was also addressed. We outlined specific strategies for testing hypotheses concerning attributes in concepts.

Concept learning is considered to be composed of two basic learning processes: chunking a set of attributes to define a new internal representative and association of chunks one to another. The first establishes a conjunction of attributes. The second establishes a disjunction of these conjunctions. This theory of concept learning and speculations regarding possible neural mechanisms are presented in more detail in Wickelgreen.[377]

It is possible that many individuals suffer, to a large extent, from an inability to form new concepts via deficits in the chunking process or deficits of the associative memory process. The simplest explanation might simply be that they have fewer free internal representatives available to become specified to stand for new concepts, but there are many alternative physiological difficulties

---

[376] R. H. Hall, M. A. Sidio-Hall, & C. B. Saling, *Spatially Directed Post Organization in Learning from Knowledge Maps.* Paper presented at the Annual Meeting of the American Educational Research Association, San Francisco, 1995.

[377] W. A. Wickelgren, Learned specification of concept neurons, *Bulletin of Mathematical Biophysics,* 31 (1969), 123-142.

that could impair concept learning. Whatever the reasons for this, the consequences for learning and memory of learning fewer concepts are that the encoding of anything one wishes to learn will be less distinctive from other materials coded into memory. This results in more retrieval and storage interference. For mentally retarded individuals, it may be very important to spend considerable time at the concept learning process, that is to say, learning the vocabulary in any area of knowledge, before proceeding to learn facts and principles involving those concepts. It could turn out that the learning of facts and principles would be almost normal in such an individual after sufficient time has been spent to teach him/her the basic concepts of the area.

Again, normal children learn many concepts that are later replaced by better concepts or are of no value to them in what they do later on. Although it is more costly and limits the choice of individuals with disabilities somewhat, to decide in advance exactly what concepts he or she should learn, this can greatly increase the efficiency of concept learning for a person with this type of disability.

Chapter 11

Critical Thinking and Problem Solving

Overview

Critical thinking is a complex of intellectual skills that are consciously, deliberately, and consistently applied by a thinker when he or she is confronted by a body of data from which a conclusion or solution must be derived, or by an argument of a third party who wishes the thinker to accept a predetermined interpretation, point of view, or conclusion.[378] In this sense, critical thinking is regarded in the broadest terms rather than narrowly, and it is though of as an intellectual process that is a natural, if sometimes unrefined, outgrowth of normal educational efforts. Therefore, occasions for critical thinking occur frequently rather than rarely, and in a large number of situations, not in a few narrowly defined special cases.

Critical thinking consists of two levels of intellectual skills in attempting to resolve problems. One level of skill focus, guidelines, and directs the process of critical thinking. The other set of skills is used by thinkers to resolve immediate problems. Thus, critical thinking results when the two levels of intellectual skills are working in concert to resolve problems.[379]

In the final analysis, critical thinking consists in the thinker deliberately and purposefully taking a series of actions to (a) understand the nature of the difficulty before him or her, (b) conduct an exhaustive surveillance of the information available that can be brought to bear on the difficulty (including an

---

[378] B. B. Hudgins, & S. Edelman, Children's self-directed critical thinking, *Journal of Educational Research*, 81 (1988), 262-273.

[379] J. N. French & C. Rhoder, *Teaching Thinking Skills* (New York, NY: Garland, 1992); L. E. Berk, *Child Development* (Boston, MA: Allyn and Bacon, 1991).

174

awareness of what information that is not available), and (c) possess one or more criteria against which the available information can be appropriately assessed.[380]

It was always believed that students would think if they could concentrate instruction on developing skills and strategies in the basic skill areas of reading, writing, and arithmetic as well as on disseminating knowledge in the content areas. There was an assumption that there was little need for providing instruction on thinking. Schools have placed little, if any, emphasis on enhancing thinking skills. As a result, over the past few decades, critical thinking among students has declined dramatically.[381] Declining test scores have been cited as evidence that students can perform well in dealing with note tasks but not with those demanding critical thoughts.[382] For example, Chipman and Segal[383] suggested that the results from the National Assessment of Educational Progress (NAEP) demonstrated that the problems in student writing lie in the thinking areas not the mechanics, the problems in reading in comprehension not decoding, and the problems in mathematics in solving problems not computing. Generally, basic skills in reading, math, writing, and science have improved, but students' ability to interpret, evaluate, make judgments, and form supportive arguments continue to decline.[384] According to Nickerson,[385] it is possible for a student to

---

[380] A. J. Binker, D. Martin, C. Vetrano, & H. Kreklau, *Critical Thinking Handbook* (Rohnert Park, CA: Center for Critical Thinking and Moral Critique 1990).

[381] A. Benderson, *Critical Thinking Focus* (Princeton, NJ: Educational Testing Service, 1984).

[382] B. F. Jones, Quality and equality through cognitive instruction, *Educational Leadership*, 47 (1990), 204-211; R. J. Marzano, *The Theoretical Framework for an Instructional Model of Higher Order Thinking Skills* (Denver, CO: Mid-Continent Regional Educational Lab, 1994).

[383] S. F. Chipman, & J. W. Segal, *Higher Cognitive Goals for Education: An Introduction* (Hillsdale, NJ: Lawrence Erlbaum Associates, 1995).

[384] Benderson, 1984.

[385] R. S. Nickerson, *Review of Research in Education* (Washington, DC: American Educational Research Association, 1991).

finish 12 years of education without becoming a competent thinker. Thus, it appears schools are producing adult citizens who lack critical thinking skills.

However, over the past few years, there has been an increasing interest in incorporating thinking instruction into the elementary and secondary curriculum. This interest has been expressed by professional organizations associated with the various academic disciplines as well as by organizations with a broad perspective such as the College Board.[386] While some states have incorporated the teaching of thinking skills into the overall curriculum, many more states have not incorporated critical thinking skills into the curriculum. Basically, other concerns have pressed for attention such as school safety, preparing for standardized tests, and negotiating teacher pay.

Principles and Components of Critical Thinking and Problem Solving Skills

There are several components or strategies associated with critical thinking and problem solving skills. The major strategies associated with the processes include generic skills, content specific skills, and content knowledge.

A major difference between problem solving and critical thinking is that critical thinking does not seem to involve a series of sequential steps. In critical thinking, the skills and strategies are not seen as part of a sequence, but rather as a group of skills and strategies chosen and used as needed by the particular task.[387] They can be used alone or in any combination.

In problem solving, students must employ a series of sequential steps. Strategies begin with a careful consideration of what problem needs to be solved, what resources and information are available, and how the problem can be graphically presented.[388] Following steps systematically and sequentially require

---

[386] Marzano, 1994.

[387] French & Rhoder, 1992.

[388] A. D. Katayama, & D. H. Robinson, *Study Effectiveness of Outlines and Graphic Organizer: How Much Information Should be Provided for Students to be Successful on Transfer Test?* Paper presented at the Annual Meeting of the American Educational Research Association, San Diego,

176

that some type of plan be developed. A plan developed by Branford and Stein[389] called IDEAL, appears to provide such a plan. The five steps in their plan include the following steps:

I Identify problems and opportunities.

D Define goals and represent the problem.

E Explore possible strategies.

A Anticipate outcomes and act.

L Look back and learn.

Research findings by Bransford & Stein, Martinez, and Mayer & Wittrock[390] agreed that by employing systematic and sequential steps for problem solving is a skill that can be taught and applied by children. Sternberg[391] related that most problems students face in school may require careful reading and some thought, but little creativity. This is a challenge to the schools to teach creative problem solving techniques. Creative problem solving techniques may be taught through, incubation, suspension, or judgment, appropriate climates, and analysis.[392] These authors have adequately defined and provided examples for each of the strategies; therefore, we will not attempt to repeat their findings, rather the reader is referred to their research.

1998; D. H. Robin, & K. A. Kiewra, Visual argument: Graphic organizers are superior to outlines in improving learning from text, *Journal of Educational Psychology*, 87, (1995), 455-467.

[389] J. D. Bransford, & B. S. Stein, *The Ideal Problem Solver* (2nd ed.) (New York, NY: W. H. Freeman, 1993).

[390] J. D. Bransford & B. S. Stein, 1993; M. E. Martinez, What is problem solving? *Phi Delta Kappan*, 70 (8), (1998), 605-609; R. E. Mayer, & M. C. Wittrock, 1996.

[391] R. L. Sternberg, Investing in creativity: Many happy returns, *Educational Leadership*, 53 (4), (1995), 80-84.

[392] B. K. Beyer, *Improving Student Thinking: A Comprehensive Approach* (Boston, MA: Allyn and Bacon, 1997); N. Frederiksen, Implications of cognitive theory for instruction in problem solving, *Review of Educational Research*, 54 (1984a), 363-407.

One set of generic skills, which is frequently included in a list of generic critical thinking skills, is that of reasoning.[393] The question of what is involved in reasoning has intrigued philosophers and psychologists for years. Nickerson[394] claimed that reasoning involve the production and evaluation of arguments, the making of inferences and the drawing of conclusions, the generation and testing of hypotheses. It requires deduction and induction, both analysis and synthesis, and both criticality and creativity. Nickerson[395] identified language, logic, inventiveness, knowledge, and truth as concepts closely related to reasoning. Beyer[396] articulated that reasoning is the "lubricant" in many critical thinking skills.

Closely allied to reasoning is the role of logic in critical thinking. Whether logic is considered part of critical thinking directly or a component of reasoning, the skills associated with logical thinking are frequently included in a generic list of skills.[397] Beyer[398] gave 10 mental operations that will aid critical thinking that is associated with logical principles. The list includes: determining the reliability of a source; the factual accuracy of a statement and the strength of an argument; distinguishing between verifiable facts and value claims, as well as between relevant and irrelevant information; and detecting bias, unstated

---

[393] A. Benderson, *Critical Thinking Focus* (Princeton, NJ: Educational Testing Service, 1984); D. Cannon, & M. Weinstein, Reasoning skills: An overview, *Journal of Philosophy for Children*, 6 (1985), 29-33.

[394] R. S. Nickerson, *Review of Research in Education* (Washington, DC: American Educational Research Association, 1991).

[395] Nickerson, 1991.

[396] B. K. Beyer, *Practical Strategies for the Teaching of Thinking* (Boston, MA: Allyn and Bacon, 1991).

[397] Benderson, 1984; Nickerson, 1996.

[398] Beyer, 1991.

assumptions, ambiguous arguments, and logical fallacies and inconsistencies in a line of reasoning.

While many approaches to critical thinking stress reasoning and/or a set of specific critical thinking skills, there is a growing recognition that critical thinking involves far more than reasoning and skills. There is increasing emphasis on the use of strategies in critical thinking. These strategies consist of cognitive, active, support, and metacognitive strategies.

Organization and reorganization of information and ideas is a critical cognitive strategy for thinking.[399] The use of organizational strategies help thinkers identify and clarify relationships among information and ideas, including linking new information to prior knowledge.

There are two active study strategies that are useful in developing critical thinking: self-questioning and summarizing. By asking themselves questions, thinkers are able to make themselves active in the learning process.[400] Wong[401] indicated that self-questioning could have three major purposes. It enables thinkers to become active participants, to engage in metacognitive processes, and to activate prior knowledge and to relate new information to it. Self-questioning fosters a spirit of problem solving which is essential to developing critical thinking skills.

Another active study strategy that is effective in developing critical thinking skills is summarizing information. In addition to being able to organize and reorganize information, and ask questions about the information, a thinker must be able to manage information in some usable manner. An effective way to

---

[399] B. Z. Presseisen, Avoiding battle at curriculum gulch: Teaching thinking and content, *Educational Leadership*, 45, (1988), 7-8.

[400] B. L. Wong, Self-questioning instructional research: A review, *Review of Educational Research*, 65, (1995), 227-268.

[401] Wong, 1995.

manage information is to summarize information so that the information needed to suit the thinker's purpose is available.

Support strategies have been cited as particularly significant in the promotion of critical thinking skills.[402] Support strategies involve fostering a positive attitude and strong motivation toward critical thinking and problem solving. A disposition toward higher-order thinking is frequently cited as a characteristics of a good thinker.[403] Nickerson[404] contended that a disposition toward thinking includes: fair-mindness, openness to evidence on any issue, respect for opinions that differ from one's own, inquisitiveness, a desire to be informed, and a tendency to reflect before acting.

Researchers and educators have found that critical thinkers use metacognitive knowledge and apply metacognitive strategies in a well planned, purposeful method through the critical thinking process. Metacognition is knowledge about and awareness of one's own thinking.[405] Metacognition involves knowledge of one's own capacity to think and remember knowledge of task variables, and knowledge of strategies.

While there is substantial support for the generic nature of critical and problem solving thinking skills, there is growing support for the notion that critical thinking skills and problem solving strategies are content specific. In essence, it is widely believed that there is a body of critical thinking and problem solving skills is applicable to every content area. However, there is some belief

---

[402] R. H. Ennis, *Developed Minds: A Resource Book for Teaching Thinking* (Virginia: Association for Supervision and Curriculum Development, 1985); R. H. Ennis, A logical basis for measuring critical thinking skills, *Educational Leadership*, 44, (1986), 44-48.

[403] Nickerson, 1991; D. F. Halpern, *Thinking Skills Instruction: Concepts and Techniques* (Washington, DC: National Education Association, 1987).

[404] Nickerson, 1991.

[405] C. R. McCormick, *Educational psychology: Learning, instruction, assessment* (New York, NY: Longman, 1997).

that how one thinks critically may be related to the specific material under consideration.[406] In this case, a thinker chooses the skills and problem solving strategies that are most appropriate for the task at hand. For example, in sorting through scientific data, there may be little need to distinguish between fact and opinion, but there is a great need to distinguish between relevant and irrelevant data. Basically, there is great controversy about whether critical thinking skills and problem solving strategies are generic or content-specific.

The need for appropriate and sufficient content knowledge is cited almost universally in relation to critical thinking.[407] Nickerson[408] implied that a thinker would not be able to reason effectively without some knowledge of the subject in question. In critically thinking and problem solving, however, a thinker must have more than a large storage of knowledge. They must also have the ability to evoke particular knowledge when needed and integrate information from various sources.[409] In addition, to fact, thinkers also need concepts and principles.[410] Basically, then, there is a kind of interdependency between critical thinking and problem solving. Critical thinking is essential in solving problems and on the other hand, problem solving is essential to critical thinking.[411]

Critical Thinking and Piaget's Theory of Cognitive Development

In his comprehensive theory of cognitive development, Piaget viewed the development of thinking as a special case of biological growth in general.

---

[406] Benderson, 1984.

[407] French & Rhoder, 1992.

[408] Nickerson, 1996.

[409] D. N. Perkins, R. Allen, & J. Hafner, *Thinking: the expanding frontier* (Pennsylvania: Franklin Press, 1993).

[410] R. J. Yinger, *New directions for teaching and learning: Fostering critical thinking* (San Francisco, CA: Jossey-Bass, 1990).

[411] R. S. Nickerson, D. N. Perkins, & E. E. Smith, *The Teaching of Thinking* (Hillsdale, NJ: Erlbaum, 1995).

Piaget's theory postulated that all children progress through four stages and that they do so in the same order: first the sensorimotor period, then the preoperational period, then the concrete period, and finally the formal operational period. Since chapter 9 has provided detailed information on the four stages, we will not repeat the information. The reader is referred to chapter 5 for specific information.

Classroom Applications

Marzano[412] summed up the value of developing critical thinking skills by stating that it is to enhance students' abilities to think critically, to make rational decisions about what to do or what to believe. Halpern[413] and Norris[414] support this view; they enumerated that learning to think critically requires practice. Teachers must provide classrooms that encourage exploration, discovery, acceptance of divergent ideas, free discussions, and posing questions to refute or validate information.

Research findings by Beyer[415] appears to be the strategies that teachers can employ in identifying critical thinking and problem solving skills that students should be exposed to as well as recognizing what strategies to use. He listed the following strategies:

   a. Distinguishing between verifiable facts and value claims.

   b. Distinguishing between relevant from irrelevant information, claims, or reasons.

   c. Determining the factual accuracy of a statement.

   d. Determining the credibility of a source.

   e. Identifying ambiguous claims or arguments.

---

[412] Marzano, 1990.

[413] Halpern, 1995.

[414] S. P. Norris, Synthesis of research on critical thinking, *Educational Leadership*, 42, (1985), 40-45.

[415] Beyer, 1998.

f. Identifying unstated assumptions.

g. Detecting bias.

h. Identifying logical fallacies.

i. Recognizing logical inconsistencies in line or reasoning.

j. Determining the strength of an argument or claim.

Beyer further elaborated that these strategies cannot be introduced in sequential steps, rather they should be based upon the cognitive development of the students. Teachers should teach students how to use the scientific method to solve problems by observing information, formulating hypotheses, testing hypotheses, interpreting data, presenting findings, and drawing conclusions.

While there is considerable information about critical thinking in general, the available research on critical thinking skills among school-aged children is quite limited. Soloff and Houtz[416] completed a design to measure the critical thinking ability in early elementary school students. In particular, the researchers assessed the subjects' ability at detecting bias. The subjects consisted of 102 students in a New York City elementary school, consisting of approximately an equal numbers of boys and girls, the sample incorporated students from kindergarten to grade four. The critical thinking test, developed by the researchers, contained short vignettes about two main characters. The tests were administered individually to each student. After hearing the story, the subjects were asked a series of 20 questions that assessed the subjects' ability, with differences becoming significant at grade four. No gender differences or interactions of gender by grade were found. The researchers concluded that critical thinking does begin to be seen at limited levels among the youngest age groups. However, in an earlier review of the literature, Norris[417] concluded that

---

[416] B. Soloff, & J. C. Houtz, Development of critical thinking among students in kindergarten through grade 4, *Perceptual and Motor Skills*, 73, (1991), 476–478.

[417] Norris, 1985.

critical thinking ability is not widespread among students. The author was unable to find recent literature to neither confirm nor disconfirm this statement.

Recent literature seems to suggest that instruction in critical thinking and problem solving skills can be beneficial. Hudgins and Edelman[418] experimented on the effects of training students in the use of critical thinking skills. Picking from three elementary schools in the same district, five experimental and two control groups consisting of a total of 39 fourth and fifth grades were formed. A test on critical thinking ability was initially given to the subjects to ensure that the subjects in both groups matched for critical thinking ability. All subjects were given a problem to solve in an individual interview. The subjects in the experimental group subsequently participated in a series of small group discussions in which they learned and applied critical thinking skills. All the subjects were again interviewed and asked to resolve the two problems aloud. The researchers found that subjects in the experimental group were more likely to apply the critical thinking and problem solving skills that they learned, used more available information, and produce a better quality answer.

Hudgins et al.[419] designed a study to determine if teaching critical thinking skills to children would benefit children in resolving scientific problems. The sample consisted of two dissimilar experimental groups and one control group. One experimental group learned critical thinking skills and was taught a specific scientific concept (e.g., the effects of gravity). The other experimental group learned about gravity under the direct supervision of their regular science classroom teacher, but did not learn critical thinking skills. The control group studied neither science nor critical thinking skills. The subjects consisted of 50

---

[418] Hudgins, & Edelman, 1988.

[419] B. B. Hudgins, M. R. Riesenmy, S. Mitchell, C. Klein, & V. Navarro, Teaching self-direction to enhance children's thinking in physical science, *Journal of Educational Research*, 88 (1994), 15-26.

St. Louis Catholic school students from grades four through six. All subjects were given a science information pre- and post-test. The researchers found that the two groups of experimental children did not differ significantly from each other on the science information test. In addition, the experimental groups scored higher on this test than the control group. The subjects were, also, interviewed separately and asked to solve a science problem involving the variables that affect the period of a pendulum and the motion of fallen bodies. As expected, the experimental group who was taught critical thinking skills outperformed both the control group and the experimental group who was not taught critical and problem solving thinking skills.

Riesenmy et al.[420] examined the degree to which children retain and transfer critical thinking skills after training. The research was conducted with 38 fourth and fifth grade students in a suburban St. Louis public school district. Twenty-eight students served as a control group in this study. The 38 subjects in the experimental group were randomly placed in small groups of four and trained in critical thinking skills through 12 discussion sessions. Each child in both the experimental and control groups were randomly placed in small groups of four and trained in critical thinking skills through 12 discussion sessions. Each child in both the experimental and control groups was individually tested before and after the training sessions for their ability to solve critical thinking problems. Post-tests were given either immediately after the conclusion of training sessions or 4 to 8 weeks afterwards. The results showed that the experimental children scored significantly better than control group children did in respect to retention of data. Specifically, the experimental group surpassed the control group children in the use of critical thinking skills, in the amount of information used, and the quality of their answers. The results also showed that experimental children did significantly better than the control group in respect to transfer problems.

---

[420] M. R. Riesenmy, S. Mitchell, B. B. Hudgins, & D. Ebel, Retention and transfer of children's self-directed critical thinking skills, *Journal of Educational Research*, 85, (1991), 14-25.

There is a scarcity measure concerning critical thinking ability among students. The available research, however, seems to suggest that students do not perform extremely well on the kinds of tasks that are used to indicate competence in critical thinking ability as measured by the Cornell Critical Thinking Test[421] and the Watson-Glaser Critical Thinking Appraisal.[422] In addition, there is evidence that students who are trained in critical thinking and problem solving skills do benefit from such training. Unfortunately, there are no studies available that provides evidence on the long-term impact of instruction in critical thinking. Moreover, there is little information available about what specifically makes students better thinkers and what specific ways they can still improve.[423]

Implications for Individuals with Disabilities

Some individuals with disabilities perform below expected levels in some academic areas, others perform at or above expected levels of achievements for age and grade. Disabilities may be specific to one or two competencies or to a cluster of closely related competencies, such as reading and writing.[424] Fortunately, some disabled students are of normal intelligence or above. Thus, it is possible that critical thinking skills may be beneficial to many disabled students.

Unfortunately, while programs in critical thinking skills have been initiated in regular curriculum programs, less attention has been paid to special education classrooms. In fact, until recently, learning activities in special education classrooms have been heavily influenced by the view that students with disabilities must be taught basic skills before any instruction in critical thinking

---

[421] R. H. Ennis, *Developed Minds: A Resource Book for Teaching Thinking* (Virginia: Association for Supervision and Curriculum Development, 1985).

[422] G. Watson, & E. M. Glaser, *Watson-Glaser Critical Thinking Appraisal, Forms A and B* (Cleveland, OH: Psychological Corporation, 1980).

[423] Norris, 1985.

[424] McCormick, 1997.

can be conducted. This tactic assumes that students with disabilities cannot benefit from instruction in reasoning until basic skills are mastered. However, research findings lend little support to this approach to instruction.[425] In the last few years, a new focus of special education research has emerged that seeks to develop and evaluate programs for teaching higher order thinking to disabled students. Research findings support the values of teaching higher order skills to children with disabilities. They profit significantly from such instruction.[426]

Analysis of some of the new approaches to instruction in higher order thinking with disabled students show that these students can not only reason with higher order skills, but also can outperform their nondisabled peers, depending upon the degree of disability, after receiving brief intervention programs in higher order thinking. Collins and Carnine[427] noted that students with disabilities in programs that emphasize higher order reasoning significantly improved their performance in argument construction to levels that equal that of students enrolled in logic course.[428]

Several of the current intervention programs for some disabled students have relied on teaching the concept of "sameness" or "analogical reasoning" as a base for promoting higher order thinking.[429] Such programs operate on the assumption that the brain searches for similarities and categorizes things based on

---

[425] B. Leshowitz, K. Jenkens, S. Heaton, & T. L. Bough, Fostering critical thinking skills in students with learning disabilities: An instructional program, *Journal of Learning Disabilities*, 26, (1993), 483-490.

[426] B. Means, & M. Knapp, Cognitive approaches to teaching advanced skills to educationally disadvantaged students, *Phi Delta Kappan*, 72 (1991), 282-289.

[427] Collins, M., & Carmine, D. Evaluating the field test revision process by comparing two versions of a reasoning skills CAI program, *Journal of Learning Disabilities*, 21 (1998), 375-379.

[428] Carmine, 1991.

[429] Carmine, 1991; B. Grossen, The fundamental skills of higher order thinking, *Journal of Learning Disabilities*, 24 (1991), 343-353

their common qualities. In this effort, Grossen[430] found that by using Euhler diagrams to facilitate understanding of the concept of "sameness," analyses of logic problems could be enhanced significantly. The trained subjects with average or above intelligence not only were more proficient at reasoning when using Euhler diagrams than their untrained peers with disabilities, but also performed at levels equal to those of normal college students and sophomore honor class students.

Although a major emphasis on the literature in higher order thinking for some disabled students has been on teaching basic operations of critical thinking, some questions have been devoted to using normative rules of reasoning and logic to promote critical reading skills. Darch and Kameenui[431] have argued that critical reading is closely related to the notion of critical thinking. They have proposed that critical reading relies heavily on the application of the following fundamental skills: (1) the ability to detect faulty information, (2) the ability to detect faculty causality, and (3) the ability to detect false testimonial. By using direct instruction, rather than discussion/working activity, they found that teaching skills have enhanced the critical reading skills of some disabled students, enabling them to distinguish between valid and invalid arguments.

Basically, some disabled students are less likely than normally achieving students to use strategies for performing academic tasks.[432] However, when taught various strategies such as critical thinking skills, most disabled students are able to carry out strategies to perform adequately on academic tasks.[433] Critical

---

[430] Grossen, 1991.

[431] C. Darch, & E. Kameenui, Teaching LD students' critical reasoning skills: A systematic replication, *Learning Disabilities Quarterly*, 10 (1987), 82-91.

[432] R. H. Bauer, Memory processes in children with learning disabilities, *Journal of Experimental Child Psychology*, 34 (1987a), 415-430.

[433] R. H. Bauer, Short-term memory in learning disabled and nondisabled children, *Bulletin of the Psychonomic Society*, 20 (1987b), 128-130.

188

thinking skills instruction for disabled students should include and provide content knowledge in the various academic areas, teaching the skills and strategies of critical thinking, and assisting these students in metacognitive processes.[434] As disabled students are taught critical thinking skills, not only can task-related performances increase, but also, these students can learn to attribute their performances to the use of the skills and strategies of critical thinking.[435] The long-term commitment of disabled students to the use of these new skills is increased when they understand that their performances improve because of their use.

Summary

For most people in education, it appears to be needless to ask why critical thinking is desirable. It is like asking why education is desirable. Philosophers of education argue that critical thinking is not just another educational option. Rather, it is an indispensable part of education because being able to think critically is a necessary condition for being educated, and because teaching with the spirit of critical thinking is the only way to satisfy the moral injunction of respect for individuals.[436] Thus, critical thinking is an educational idea.

Yet, critical thinking among American students is not widespread. It was once believed that the mere fact of imparting factual knowledge would facilitate higher order thinking among students. Unfortunately, research suggests that students do not posses the necessary skills that would indicate the ability to think critically. Students wind up graduating from high school and becoming adults who do not have the ability to think critically despite twelve or more years of schooling.

---

[434] French & Rhoder, 1992.

[435] J. G. Borkowski, M. Carr, E. A. Rellinger, & M. Pressley, *Dimensions of Thinking: Review of Research* (Hillsdale, NJ: Erlbaum, 1990).

[436] J. McPeck, *Critical thinking and education* (Oxford: Martin Robertson, 1991).

As a result, critical thinking is among the most debated subjects in education. Investigation of critical thinking processes, integration of critical thinking instruction into the curriculum, and the evaluation of students as critical thinkers has become a major focus in education in recent years. Nevertheless, there has not been a widespread movement to incorporate critical thinking skill instruction into the curriculum despite increasing emphasis on the need for critical thinking among students.

There is research available that suggests that instruction in critical and problem solving thinking can be beneficial, not only in academic areas, but in real life. However, research into this area is still quite limited. Moreover, such research has its own limitations. Thus, more studies are needed in the area of critical thinking skills, especially as it concerns disabled students.

Chapter 12

Holistic Learning and Education

Overview

The origin of holistic learning and education stems from a philosophy called "holism." The credit for this term goes to former South African Prime Minister General Jan Christian Smuts... "Smuts coined the term 'holism' from the Greek word 'Olos' (which means whole) in his epic book '*Holism in Evolution*' published in 1926."[437] Smuts is said to be before his time. He believed in an increasingly conscious universe, leading to more of a wholeness among various entities through interactions and interconnections.[438] These entities included spiritual, organic, and material wholes that should not be viewed in isolation of one another. The principles of holism direct these entities toward a higher sense of order. "Every facet of life is engaged in a lawful evolutionary pilgrimage toward greater unity and wholeness."

Although the term "holism" originated in 1926, A. S. Neill started Summerhill, an English school based upon the philosophy of holism, in 1921. Neill believed that children had more potential for learning when they had less adult influence. He believed that their individuality, uniqueness, and learning potential would emerge from being in an environment of love and freedom. Treating all students the same would be like producing robots.[439] Meier[440]

---

[437] B. Kun, Stop studying and start learning. *IT Review*, 2 (6), (1995), http://www.icon.co.za/-cogmotics/articles/stopstudying.htm

[438] L. Holdstock, *Excerpts from "Education for a new nation,"* Africa Transpersonal Association. (Reprinted with the permission of the author), (1987), http:/www.icon.co.za/-cogmotics/articles/new nation.htm.

[439] Holdstock, 1987.

192

supported Neill's philosophy stating, "Look at children. They learn holistically. That's why they are such accelerated learners...to children, the world is geodesic-- they plunge right into the whole of it." Even further support of this philosophy is given by Tarver,[441] who stated, "The holists contend that learning, if it is to be meaningful, must be a product of the learners constructions or discoveries; meaningful learning cannot be programmed in advance by either teachers or curriculum developers."

In 1968, George Leonard, an author on education and human potential discussed the connection between education and ecstasy. His research demonstrated that pleasure and fulfillment were at the heart of learning. Thus affirming that through human existence an individual seeks to fulfill human capacities, such as joy and freedom.[442] Taking a holistic approach to childhood education thus involves addressing the physical, emotional, psychological, and metaphysical needs and motivation of children.

Some of the pioneers of holistic education in the modern world include the Johann Pestalozzi, a Swiss humanitarian; Thoreau, Emerson, and Alcott, American Transcendentalists; Francis Parker and John Dewey, founders of progressive education; as well as Maria Montessori and Rudolf Steiner. Each of these pioneers contributed to the understanding that the purpose of education should be to "cultivate the moral, emotional, physical, psychological, and spiritual dimensions of the developing child.[443]

---

[440] D. Meier, New age learning: From linear to geodesic, *Training and Development Journal*, http://www.icon.co.za/cogmotics/articles/new age learning.htm, 1985.

[441] S. Tarver, Cognitive behavior modification, direct instruction and holistic approaches to the education of students with learning disabilities, *Journal of Learning Disabilities*, 19 (6), (1986), 368-375.

[442] J. P. Miller (ed.), & Y. Nakagawa, *Nurturing Our Wholeness: Perspectives on Spirituality in Education* (VT: Foundation for Educational Renewal, Inc., 2000).

[443] R. Miller, Holistic Education, Paths of Learning Resource Center, 2005. Retrieved January 30, 2007 from. http://www.infed.org/biblio/holisticeducation.htm.

Many times we shy away from the inclusion of a spiritual acknowledgement in the education process in order to uphold the separation of church and state. Another way to view the inclusion of spirituality or metaphysical concepts, as a part of a holistic framework, can be found in a form of holistic education called contemplative education, where the inner lives of teachers and students are viewed as vital aspects to effective teaching and learning. This awareness and integration of the spiritual inner realm of the human experience can be integrated into the education process without the teaching of religion in schools, but by manifesting the effects of our metaphysical practices in everyday teaching.

"Holistic education is based on the premise that each person finds identity, meaning, and purpose in life through connections to the community, to the natural world, and to spiritual values such as compassion and peace."[444] Holistic education seeks to stimulate and bring forth an intrinsic value of life and motivation for life-long learning. In holistic education, it is also understood that there is no one correct path to this awareness but that there are many paths of learning and a holistic education value for each of them. "What is appropriate for some children and adults, in some situations, and in some historical and social contexts, may not be best for others. The art of holistic education lies in its responsiveness to the diverse learning styles and needs of evolving human beings."[445] A holistic educator seeks to engage his or her teaching practice as opportunity for growth and learning for children as well as for him or herself and is open to the learning experience.

---

[444] R. Miller, 2005

[445] R. Miller, 2005.

Holistic Learning and Education Defined

There are numerous definitions of holistic learning and education. We will define those terms which have relevance for classroom application. Holdstock[446] wrote that defining holistic education is like trying to harness the full extent of education. Holdstock further stated that holistic education is multi-modal; it attempts to define everything about an individual in relation to environmental aspects associated with learning. Even our relatedness to inanimate matter and time is considered. It strives to complete that which is incomplete, to pay attention to those aspects of our humanness which have not received their proper or fair share of attention.

A similar view of holistic education is expressed by Miller,[447] who believed that the essence of holistic learning is conveyed in the following poem entitled, *"There was a child went forth,"* by Walt Whitman.

> There was a child went forth every day.
>
> And the first object he looked upon, that object he became,
>
> And that object became part of him for the day or
>
> a certain part of the day.
>
> Or for many years or stretching cycles of years.

In this poem, the child connects with his or her environment so that learning is deeply integrated. Holistic education goes beyond the existing curricula. It surpasses the three R's (reading, writing, and arithmetic), and the three L's (logic, language, and linearity) by asking previously unasked questions and making sure the inner self is not suffering from neglect.[448]

---

[446] Holdstock, 1987.

[447] J. J. Miller, Making connections through holistic learning, *Educational Leadership*, 56 (4), (1998, December and January), 46-48.

[448] Holdstock, 1987.

Holistic Learning and Education

A better understanding of holistic education can be achieved by a description of its theoretical framework, and its origin.   The theoretical framework for holistic education is that all aspects of a child's education must be connected in order for learning to be meaningful. If education is broken up into segments, which are then taught independently of one another, then concepts become disconnected and disjointed.   According to this theory, which was developed several decades ago, the material universe is seen as a dynamic web of interrelated events. None of the properties or any part of the web is fundamental; they all follow from the properties of the other parts, and the overall consistency of their inter-relatedness determines the structure of the entire web.[449]

Relationship to Theories of Learning

One does not have to research the topic of holistic learning very long before coming across the name Piaget. Many aspects of holistic learning are based on Piagetian theory.   Piaget believed that a child and his or her environment were interactive and that the mind was unable to separate itself from the social and physical world.[450] He believed that error and failure promoted understanding by transforming previously misunderstood concepts and that if this process were interrupted, it could totally disrupt the learning process.[451] He envisioned unstructured education.[452]

Vygotsky is another name that appears in research involving holistic education. "Vygotsky thought that social interaction with others provided the necessary scaffolding for construction of meaning." He supported Piaget's view

---

[449] Holdstock, 1987.

[450] B. Grobecker, Reconstructing the paradigm of learning disabilities: A holistic/constructivist implementation, *Learning Disability Quarterly*, 19 (1996), 179-200.

[451] C. Macinnis, Holistic and reductionist approaches in special education: Conflicts and common ground, *McGill Journal of Education*, 30 (1), (1995), 7-20.

[452] Tarver, 1986.

that development could not be separated from social and cultural activities.[453] This supports the holistic approaches of integration, cooperative learning, and interactive teaching.

Friedrich Froebel is another individual who deserves mention. In the 1840s, his philosophy of education for young children led to the founding of kindergarten, which literally meant a garden for children.[454] He advocated a nurturing child-centered approach to early childhood education, with emphasis on achievement and success. The process of learning, rather than what is learned, is emphasized.[455] This is one of the core values of holistic education.

Based on Piagetian theory, constructivism has recently become a trend in education. A theory of learning that describes the central role that learners' ever-transforming mental schemes play in their cognitive growth, constructivism powerfully informs educational practice. Advocates of constructivism believe that...equating lasting student learning with test results is folly.[456] By being so concerned with test outcomes, schools have begun to down-size their curricula to include test material, almost solely. This limits students' learning as well as teacher creativity. Students are programmed to memorize information and spit it out on a test so that their levels of knowledge can be assessed. These authors contended that the complexity of the curriculum, instructional methodology, student motivation, and student developmental readiness cannot be captured on a paper-and-pencil test.

---

[453] J. W. Santrock, *Life-span Development* (7th ed.) (McGraw-Hill Companies, Inc., 1999).

[454] Santrock, 1999.

[455] Santrock, 1999.

[456] J. G. Brooks, & M. G. Brooks, The courage to be constructivist *Educational Leadership*, 18-24, (1999, November).

Cobb, Yackel and Wood advanced an eloquent vision of constructivism related to mathematics.[457] They claimed that:

"Learning would be viewed as an active, constructive process in which students attempt to resolve problems that arise as they participated in the mathematical practices in the classroom. Such a view emphasizes that the learning-teaching process is interactive in nature and involves the implicit and explicit negotiation of mathematical meaning. In the course of these negotiations, the teacher and student elaborate the taken as shared mathematical reality that constitutes the basis for their on-going communication."

Pflaum[458] contended that construction is the dominant theory that underlies the technology movement. Many of the computer-based programs rely on principles associated with constructivism, involving computer activities that are behavior driven and provide immediate feedback, as well as create their own knowledge. On the other hand in constructivist theory, learners create their own knowledge, through exploration, questions, and discovery.

Constructivism, like holism, focuses not so much on what students learn, but on how they learn. It involves helping students internalize what they learn. By constructing mental structures, experiences are organized and further understanding is possible.[459] Since teachers have no way of knowing what mental structures exist within the mind of a particular child, it is important to vary

---

[457] P. Cobb, E. Yackel, & T. Wood, A constructivist alternative to the representational view of mind in mathematical education, *Journal of Research in Mathematical Education*, 23, (1992), p. 5.

[458] W. D. Pflaum, *The Technology Fix: The Promise and Reality of Computers in Our Schools,* (Alexandria, VA: Association for Supervision and Curriculum Development, 2004), p. 126.

[459] J. H. Holloway, Caution: Constructivism ahead, *Educational Leadership,* http://www.icon.co.za/-cogmotics/drbruce.htm, Dr. Bruce Copley (1999, November).

teaching methods. Five principles of constructivisim, as identified by Brooks and Brooks[460] are as follows:

1. Seek and value students' points of view.
2. Structure lessons to challenge students' suppositions.
3. Recognize that students must attach relevance to the curriculum.
4. Structure lessons around big ideas, not small bits of information.
5. Assess student learning in the context of daily classroom investigations, not as separate events.

Even though constructivism is a recent trend in education, it has its critics. The two most common criticisms are that it is too permissive and that it lacks vigor.

Components of Holistic Learning

According to Miller[461] three components that assist in holistic learning are balance, inclusion, and connection. Miller believes that a balance must exist between learning and assessment, so that one is not given more emphasis than the other. Focusing too much on test results distracts teachers from fostering the learning process, and vice versa. By inclusion, Miller means having students of different races and abilities working together, as well as balancing different types of learning, such as transmission, transaction, and transformational. Teachers who know how to balance a variety of teaching strategies will keep their students interest as well as promote their development.

Educators must find a balance between the various types of learning and learning styles that children bring to the classroom, such as individualized and group instruction, analytic thinking, intuitive thinking, content and process, learning, assessment, abstract learning, and concrete learning. To achieve holistic

---

[460] Brooks & Brooks, 1999.

[461] J. J. Miller, Making connections through holistic learning, *Educational Leadership*, 56 (4), (1998, December and January), 46-48.

learning in the classroom, educators need to balance instruction and assessment with learning.

Holistic education, in its truest sense, implies that all children are included in all activities in the classroom. To accommodate the diverse needs of children, teachers must employ various types of learning strategies. Miller[462] advocated three kinds of learning:

1. Transmission--one way flow of information from the teacher or the textbook to the student. The focus is on accumulating factual information and relevant basic skills.

2. Transaction--is characterized by greater interaction between student and teacher. Problem solving and developing cognitive skills are emphasized.

3. Transformational--the focus is on the total development of the child, intellectual, physical, emotional, aesthetic, moral, and spiritual development. Activities are designed to nurture all aspects of the students' development, such as storytelling and the arts.

4. Connection--the child connects with his or her environment so that learning is deeply integrated. Connections may occur between school subjects by integrating topics around a major theme. Connection learning also implies a degree of cooperation and collaboration with others as students participate in cooperative groups.

Holistic learning, to be effective, must include the integration of several theories of learning to promote learning. Educators should abstract from the major theories of learning discussed in previous chapters in the text and choose those aspects which will promote his or her instructional plans, and the needs and interests of the learners under his or her supervision.

---

[462] Miller, 1999.

Advocates for Holistic Learning Education

Holistic education has arisen out of a belief that traditional education does not work. The reason why it does not work is because our approach is based on Newtonian principles, knowledge is constructed by stacking building blocks upon a solid foundation.[463] This means that our knowledge is constructed piecemeal with the idea that the whole cannot be understood without first understanding each individual part. Advocates of holistic education believe that education should not be broken into pieces, with each piece being taught individually, because education is more than the sum of its parts.

Holistic thinkers believe that traditional education dulls the conscious, leads everyone down the same path, takes the meaning out of learning by teaching concepts in a disjointed way, forces people to conform, and robs people of their innovation, creativity, productivity, uniqueness, and potential.[464] Conventional education fills minds rather than opens them, kills creativity, and confuses knowledge with knowing and learning with studying." Kun[465] stated that it is clear that traditional Western educational policies and practices function at a level of efficiency and effectiveness that are far inferior to our biological, organizational, and technological systems.

Additionally, Meier[466] wrote that we are leaving the linear age of assembly line thinking and learning. Education's simulation of a factory, where there is uniformity of both process and output, is on its way out. Meier believed that we have entered a new age of learning, the geodesic age. It is an age that takes as its symbol the geodesic sphere--an interlocking network that suggests integration, interrelationship, and a sense of the whole. Geodesic relationships are mutual and

---

[463] Holdstock, 1987.

[464] Meier, 1985.

[465] Kun, 1995.

[466] Meier, 1985.

do not involve hierarchies. Everything is equal and everything exists and occurs simultaneously--just one whole, interdependent flow of energy.[467] Nobel Prize winner Ilya Prigogine supported this by stating that educational institutions are open systems that are self-organized and maintained by a continuous dynamic flow.[468]

The theory of the geodesic age falls under the umbrella of new age learning which seems to be interchangeable with holistic learning. The philosophy of new age learning or holistic learning deals with becoming whole. This is identical to holistic thinking, which emphasizes...contexts, relationships, and wholes.[469] Instead of studying parts that lead up to a whole, new-age learning involves beginning with the whole and branching out into parts. Some of the techniques involved in new-age learning are mind/body relaxation, mind-setting exercises, mental imagery, special music, embedded stimuli, positive paraconscious suggestion, and a host of other treatments.[470] One of the reasons why these techniques are thought to be effective is because of Prigogine's theory that...learning occurs more efficiently when the brain's fluctuations are augmented.[471]

A current leader in holistic education is Dr. Bruce Copley. Dr. Copley is a former university professor, based in South Africa, who turned writer and motivational speaker. After 20 years of teaching, Dr. Copley believed that a holistic approach was needed in education that he termed "Cogmotics." Cogmotics is said to be a revolutionary approach to learning, teaching, and training. The essence of this unique approach is to consciously stimulate and

---

[467] Meier, 1985.

[468] Holdstock, 1987.

[469] Kun, 1995.

[470] Meier, 1985.

[471] Holdstock, 1987.

integrate the mental, physical, spiritual, social, and emotional faculties within a safe, nurturing environment.[472] According to Kun,[473] cogmotics is widely considered to be the "missing link" in education. He used the following quote by Eric Butterworth, to capture the essence of Cogmotics:[474]

> "When the tie of learning that bind the human mind again and again and again are lost, and a person is introduced finally to himself, the real self that has no limitation, then the bells of heaven ring for joy and we are thrust forward into a grand rendezvous with life."

In support of the holistic philosophy, Myers and Hilliard[475] articulated that learning at the middle school level has focused too much on parts rather than wholes.   That is why they support the approaches of cooperative learning, literature-based reading, and holistic literacy.   These approaches involve identifying with the real life needs of the students. This leads us to a current trend in education today, whole language. Whole language is a holistic perspective on how language operates.[476]   Instead of breaking up the components of language (reading, writing, speaking, and listening) into separate parts, they are taught together as a whole. The connections in holistic learning involve those between school subjects, school members, the earth, and one's self. These connections lead to   links,   integrations,   discoveries,   collaborations,   cooperation,   respect, responsibility, and relationships.[477]

---

[472]   J.   H.   Holloway,   Caution: Constructivism   ahead,   *Educational   Leadership*, http://www.icon.co.za/cogmotics/drbruce.htm. Dr. Bruce Copley. 1999, November.

[473] Kun, 1995.

[474] Kun, 1995.

[475] R. D. Hilliard, & J. W. Myers, Holistic language learning at the middle level: Our last, best chance, *Childhood Education*, 73 (1997), 286-289.

[476] Hilliard, & Myers, 1997.

[477] J. J. Miller, 1998.

The learning environment for whole language is student-centered with the teacher acting as a facilitator. According to Schurr et al.,[478] three guidelines for creating this environment are:

1. Immerse students in reading, writing, speaking, and listening.

   --working on all these skills at once is more like real world experiences involving language

2. Create an environment that encourages students to take risks.

   --encouraging the interaction of ideas among students helps to make them feel secure

3. Focus on meaning.

   --emphasize clarity in all facets of language

Watson and Crowley[479] summarized nine holistic approaches, which are listed as helpful when implementing a whole language environment:

1. Find out what interests students and use that information to structure the curriculum.

   --enthusiasm + motivation = accomplishment

2. Read to students every day and/or tell them stories.

   --all literature comes from oral tradition

   --children learn to love literature by experiencing it

3. Provide young adolescents with the opportunities to write every day.

   --use topics of interest and vary activities

4. Encourage students to read "real" literature.

   --find books that appeal to students' interests

   --minimize the use of the "skills-focused" textbook

5. Take advantage of the social nature of reading and writing to promote

---

[478] S. Schurr, J. Thompson, & M. Thompson, *Teaching at the Middle Level: A Professional's Handbook* (Lexington, MA: D.C. Health, 1995).

[479] D. Watson, & P. Crowley, How can we implement a whole language approach? In C. Weaver (Ed.), *Reading Process and Practice* (Portsmouth, NH: Heinemann Educational Books, 1988).

paired and other cooperative learning activities.

--integrating several skills at once promotes learning of all skills involved

6. In addition to encouraging integrated reading, writing, speaking, and listening activities, encourage students to discuss the processes of reading, writing, speaking, and listening as well.

--discussion promotes clarity and reduces anxiety

7. Set the example where reading and writing are concerned.

--let students know that you read for pleasure and variety

8. Encourage parents to involve themselves in their children's education, particularly by setting an example for family literacy.

--this promotes the home-school connection

9. Use what works.

--be eclectic, use various, innovative approaches

Holistic approaches can also be applied to mathematics instruction. Instead of dividing math into its parts (numbers, problems, and concepts), and performing drills and exercises from workbooks, all of these skills can be taught interactively.[480] The teacher is once again a facilitator, guiding students through problem-solving activities. Learners develop complete understanding of the math concepts as they become proficient in the language of mathematics through verbal communication, paragraph answers, and written problems based on real-life situations. According to Archambeault,[481] there exists a phobia of math in our society. Individuals who may be intelligent in other areas of education exhibit deficits in the area of mathematics. One study by the National Research Council in 1989 reported that math anxiety is rooted in the belief that success in mathematics is dependent upon some sort of special ability, which most students

---

[480] B. Archambeault, Holistic mathematics instruction: Interactive problem solving and real life situations help learners understand math concepts, *Adult Learning, 5,* (1993), 21-23.

[481] B. Archambeault, 1993.

do not have.[482] It is believed that a holistic approach to teaching mathematics will reduce math anxiety and reduce the belief that math is such a foreign subject. This concept, similar to whole language, is called whole math and involves real-life, hands-on, interactive, problem solving learning experiences.

Archambeault[483] wrote there are a host of activities that can be included in a whole mathematics unit. Some of these include: shopping for groceries (using newspaper ads, preparing lists, calculating costs, comparing costs of different items, converting pounds to ounce, etc.); eating in a restaurant (ordering from menus, totaling bills, comparing costs of meals, writing menus); buying gasoline (using maps, estimating miles per gallon, calculating costs of gas, comparing costs of car to bus, recording speedometer readings and gas purchases); introducing fractions (using folded strips of paper to demonstrate halves, fourths, eighths, etc., comparing fractions to wholes, reducing, adding, and subtracting fractions); shopping by catalog (filling out order forms, calculating costs of items, discussing pros and cons of shopping by catalogs); and taking medicine (discussing ways of measuring medicines, comparing differences between tableware and measuring spoons, preparing charts showing when to take medicines, calculating numbers of doses and pills to be taken over a period). This is not even the complete list of ideas for whole math activities, proving that there are many creative, non-threatening ways to teach math so that it is relevant, interesting, and useful to learners. It is also interesting to note that most of the aspects of whole language are incorporated into whole math since it involves reading, writing, speaking, and listening. This supports the holistic viewpoint that learning is integrated and cannot be separated into parts. Everything is connected to everything else.

---

[482] Archambeault, 1993.

[483] Archambeault, 1993.

206

Although whole language is currently a widespread trend in schools around the country, it is not always welcomed by teachers with open arms. Ridley[484] identified four factors that appear to constrain teachers acceptance of whole language: (a) an orientation toward activities versus philosophy, (b) a resistance to change, (c) a lack of resources, and (d) concerns about accountability.[485]

Another reason why some teachers avoid holistic instruction is because it is often ambiguous and vague.[486] It has been said that holistic education has not been, and perhaps cannot be, the subject of formal evaluation. The pure holists contend that truly meaningful learning is too elusive to be measured; if that is the case, then there is no scientifically acceptable way to evaluate the approach.[487] Therein lies the problem with holistic education. If we do away with standardized tests because they reduce education to a listen-memorize-regurgitate[488] mind set, how will we know what our students know? Education cannot exist without some way of assessing student achievement. This view is in direct contrast to an article by Keefe[489] that states... "Only from a holistic perspective can assessment approach accuracy and validity." Keefe believes that assessment in holistic education is possible but that it takes time and that it should come from a variety of sources.

---

[484] L. Ridley, Enacting change in elementary school programs: Implementing a whole language perspective, *The Reading Teacher*, 43, (1990), 640-646.

[485] K. H. Au, & J. A. Scheu, Journey toward holistic instruction: Supporting teachers' growth, *The Reading Teacher, 49* (6), (1996), 468-477.

[486] Au & Scheu, 1996.

[487] S. Tarver, Cognitive behavior modification, direct instruction and holistic approaches to the education of students with learning disabilities, *Journal of Learning Disabilities*, 19 (6), (1986), 368-375.

[488] Kun, 1995.

[489] C. H. Keefe, Developing responsive IEPs through holistic assessment, *Intervention in School and Clinic*, 28 (1) (1992), 34-40.

Teaching Children with Disabilities

Aside from regular education, there has been a long time debate between the reductionist and constructivist (holistic) approaches in the field of special education. Reductionists believe that learning can be taught in parts that will eventually equal a whole. Learning is sequential, observable, and verifiable. The constructivists believed that learning is created by the learner. Learning is made meaningful through the application of new information to previous experiences. Practices in special education such as task analysis, specific skill training, and even the individualized education program (IEP)[490] are based on the reductionist approach to education.

The constructivists believed that the reductionist approach keeps students from learning because the elements being taught are not made into a whole that they can relate to. They believe that error is an important element of learning because it provides the teacher with some insight as to the students' thought processes. A rich learning environment should be provided that caters to the students' needs and interests, and skills should be taught when necessary to perform meaningful tasks.[491] Students should also have lots of opportunities to interact with others because social interaction helps to construct their knowledge. Students should have a say in what is taught, rules, expectations, and procedures.

Macinnis[492] States that there is some common ground between the reductionist and constructivist approaches in special education. Some examples from the book *Understanding Whole Language: From Principle to Practice*[493] are

---

[490] C. Macinnis, Holistic and reductionist approaches in special education: Conflicts and common ground, *McGill Journal of Education*, 30 (1), (1995), 7-20.

[491] Macinnis, 1995.

[492] Macinnis, 1995.

[493] C. Weaver (Ed.), *Reading Process and Practice* (Portsmouth, NH: Heinemann Educational Books, 1988).

direct teaching in the forms of teacher/students demonstrations, seizing "teachable moments," "authentic literacy events," and mini-lessons that take place during the holistic activity of whole language. Also, according to Macinnis,[494] a number of cognitive strategy theorists are moving away from the more reductionist approach to focus more on the work of Vygotsky and Piaget's constructivist concepts.

In an article by Tarver,[495] three approaches to the education of learning disabled students were compared: Cognitive Behavior Modification (CBM), Direct Instruction (DI), and Holistic. According to Tarver's research, the holistic approach received little or no support in comparison to the CBM and DI approaches. Several models based on the Piagetian theory of education, which were studied in Head Start and Follow Through Projects, produced little or no gains in areas such as basic skills, cognitive problem solving, and affective measures. According to Wagner and Stember,[496] the Piagetian theory...Lacked sufficient empirical support to serve, at present, as a basis for educational interventions...successively larger chunks of the theory are being undermined by new data.[497]

Grobecker[498] found that skill generalization in children with LD persists...because too much emphasis is placed on skill development and the information learned is not meaningful to the students. Generalizing is an abstract process that many LD students are not capable of. Grobecker continues to say that there are a number of adaptive strategies that can be used as students are

---

[494] Macinnis, 1995.

[495] Tarver, 1986.

[496] R. K. Wagner, & R. J. Stember, Alternative conceptions of intelligence and their implications for education, *Review of Educational Research*, 54 (2), (1984), 179-223.

[497] Tarver, 1986.

[498] B. Grobecker, Reconstructing the paradigm of learning disabilities: A holistic/constructivist implementation, *Learning Disability Quarterly*, 19 (1996), 179-200.

learning. Also, research conducted by Grobecker[499] indicates that active, strategic, learning behavior is advanced by honoring students' thinking processes, making contact with their unique thought structures, and encouraging self-reflection. Furthermore, children need to be engaged in meaningful problems within relevant learning contexts. Grobecker's article, "Reconstructing the Paradigm of Learning Disabilities: A Holistic/Constructivist Interpretation," is in support of a holistic approach to teaching learning disabled students.

Summary

It is evident from the research that a holistic approach to education is a controversial and much debated topic. The supporters of holistic education believe it is the only way to go with the future of education and those in opposition feel it is too vague and unstructured. Still others believe that success can be achieved through a combination of approaches used simultaneously. A combination of approaches seems to make the most sense, since the idea of reaching every student through the same technique is unrealistic.

To summarize, Miller[500] stated that, ..."In a way, holistic learning is a return to basics. It asks us to focus on what is ultimately important in life. It asks that we see our work as more than just preparing students to compete with one another. Although we still must teach skills to prepare students for the workplace, we need a broader vision of education that fosters the development of whole human beings."

---

[499] B. Grobecker, 1996.

[500] Miller, 1998.

Chapter 13

Reciprocal Teaching

Overview

Reciprocal teaching is a method which applies cognitive science to reading instruction. It is an instructional approach developed from research conducted by Palincsar and Klenk at the University of Michigan and Brown at the University of Illinois at Urbana Champaign. According to Palincsar and Klenk,[501] reciprocal teaching is an instructional procedure in which teachers and students take turns leading discussions about shared texts. The purpose of the discussions is to achieve joint understanding of the text through the flexible application of four comprehension strategies: prediction, clarification, summarization, and questions generation. These strategies are modeled by the teacher in the context of instruction, and the students practice the comprehension strategies in cooperative groups.

According to the developers, by using their prior knowledge and experiences in order to make predictions, the text becomes more meaningful and important to students.[502] By seeking clarification, students identify information important to understanding the text and rely on other members of the group to help them understand the key points. They also learn to reread the text to find

---

[501] A. S. Palincsar, & L. Klenk, Dialogues promoting reading comprehension, in B. Means, C. Chelemer, & M. S. Knapp (Eds.), Teaching *Advanced Skills to At-Risk Students,* (San Francisco, CA: Jossey-Bass, 1991).

[502] C. S. Englert, & A. S. Palincsar, Reconsidering instructional research in literacy from a sociocultural perspective, *Learning Disabilities Research and Practice*, 6 (1991), 225-229; L. M. Lysynchuk, M. Pressley, & N. J. Vye, Reciprocal teaching improves standardized reading-comprehension performance in poor comprehenders, *The Elementary School Journal*, 90 (5), (1990), 469-484; A. S., Palincsar, & A. L. Brown, Peer interaction in reading comprehension instruction, *Educational Psychologists*, 22 (1984), 231-253.

212

evidence for their understandings.[503] By generating questions, students establish ownership in the reading process. As students summarize, inaccuracies that cause misunderstandings become apparent and students are given explicit instructions in developing critical thinking skills. Teachers monitor the discussion and provide cognitive scaffolding. Brown, Palincsar, and Purcell[504] concluded that the strength of reciprocal teaching is that it focuses on reading to learn rather than learning to read.

Key Strategies

Reciprocal teaching. Is an instructional approach in which teachers and students take turns leading discussions about shared text. It is an interactive dialogue between the teacher and the students about content/materials that help students to learn how to become effective readers.[505]

The teacher first models the technique, providing practice time for students to take turns being the teacher, while the teacher monitors progress and provides feedback. When students are proficient at using the technique, it can be incorporated into cooperative learning activities. There are four steps involved in implementing the reciprocal teaching strategy: summarizing, questioning, clarifying, and predicting.[506] Each of these strategies help students to construct meaning from text and monitor their reading to ensure that they understand what they have read.

---

[503] Lysynchuk, Pressley, & Vye, 1990.

[504] A. L. Brown, A. S. Palincsar, & L. Purcell, Poor readers: Teach, Don't Label, The *School Achievement of Minority Children: New Perspectives* (Hillsdale, NJ: Lawrence Erlbaum Associates, Publishers, 1986).

[505] Brown & Palincsar, 1987; J. C. Campione, A. M. Shapiro, & A. L. Brown, Forms of transfer in a community of learners: Flexible learning and understanding, in A. McKeough, J. Lupant, & A. Marini (Eds.), Teaching *for Transfer: Fostering Generalization in Learning* (Mahwah, NJ: Erlbaum, 1995); B. Rosenshine, & C. Meister, Reciprocal teaching: A review of the research, *Review of Educational Research*, 64 (4), (1994), 479-530.

[506] Palincsar & Brown, 1984.

Summarizing. This strategy provides the student the opportunity to restate what they have read in their own words. They work to find the most important information in the text. Initially, their summaries may be of sentences or paragraphs, but should later focus on larger units of text.

Generating Questions. When students generate questions, they must first identify the kind of information that is significant enough that it could provide the substance for a question. In order to do this, they must identify significant information, pose questions related to this information, and check to make sure they can answer their own question.

Clarifying. When teaching students to clarify, their attention is called to the many reasons why text is difficult to understand; for example, new vocabulary, unclear reference words, and unfamiliar or difficult concepts. Recognizing these blocks to understanding, students may clarify or ask for clarification in order to make sense of the text.

Predicting. This strategy requires the reader to hypothesize about what the author might discuss next. This provides a purpose for the reading: to confirm or disapprove their hypothesis. An opportunity has been created for the students to link the new knowledge they will encounter in the text with the knowledge they already possess. It also facilitates the use of the text structure as students learn that headings, subheadings, and questions imbedded in the text are useful means of anticipating what might occur next.

The four strategies are used in a session where the discussion leader generates a question to which the group has to respond. The leader then summarizes the text and asks other members if they would like to elaborate upon or revise the summary. Clarifications are discussed. In preparation for moving on to the next portion of text, the groups generate predictions. The goal is to make flexible use of the strategies.

Introducing Reciprocal Thinking Strategies

When introducing the strategies to the students, in the initial stage, the teacher assumes primary responsibility for leading the dialogues and implementing the strategies. Through modeling, the teacher demonstrates how to use the strategies while reading the text. During guided practice, the teacher supports students by adjusting the demands of the task based on each student's level of proficiency. Eventually, the students learn to conduct the dialogues with little or no teacher assistance. The teacher assumes the role of a coach/facilitator by providing students with evaluative information regarding their performance and prompting them to higher levels of participation.[507]

Students should be taught in small heterogeneous groups to ensure that each student has ample opportunity to practice using the strategies while receiving feedback from other group members. The optimal group size is between six and eight students. Frequent guided practice is essential in helping students become more proficient in their use of the strategies.

The instructional materials selected should be appropriately based on certain criteria. The teacher should select material based on the student's reading/listening comprehension level. The material used should be sufficiently challenging. Incorporate text that is representative of the kinds of material students are expected to read in school, and on their level. Generally, students have been taught the Reciprocal Teaching procedure using expository of informational text. The story structure in narrative text lends itself quite well. Also, students are taught to use the four strategies incorporating the elements of story grammar (e.g., character, plot, problem, and solution).

There are no specific guidelines for a time frame. The first day of instruction is spent introducing the students to the four strategies. The length of each session will depend upon the age and the attention of the students, but will

---

[507] Slavin, 2000; Ormrod, 1999.

usually fall within the range of twenty to forty minutes per session. It is recommended that the initial instruction take place on consecutive days. After this point, instruction can be provided on alternate days if needed.

Instructional Uses of Reciprocal Teaching

The primary goal of reciprocal teaching is to improve the reading comprehension skills for students who have not benefited from traditional reading instructional methods. This is achieved by establishing a collaborative discourse in order to help students acquire strategies useful to construct meaning from texts.[508]

Content area texts have been found useful, especially at the middle school level. Palincsar and Klenk[509] explained that "shared texts contribute to the development of a learning community in which groups explore principles, ideas, themes, and concepts over time." They reported improved results of reciprocal teaching when using texts related by themes and/or concepts, for example, science concepts related to animal survival themes, such as adaptations, extinctions, and the use of camouflage and mimicry. They also explained that shared texts contribute to the development of a learning community in which groups explore principles, ideas, themes, and concepts over time.

The participants of reciprocal teaching vary according to reading ability. Reciprocal teaching is most compatible with classrooms that are social, interactive, and holistic in nature. To help students connect their personal background experiences with the text, reciprocal teaching can be used in diverse classrooms and communities. Research conducted by Palincsar and Klenk[510] illustrated that small groups of six to eight students work best using reciprocal teaching dialogue; on the other hand, middle school level teachers have used the

---

[508] Palincsar & Klenk, 1992.

[509] Palincsar & Klenk, 1992.

[510] Palincsar & Klenk, 1992.

reciprocal teaching dialogue with as many as seventeen students. Teachers have also trained students as tutors and have successfully monitored several groups led by the tutors. Reciprocal teaching has been used with students ranging in age from seven to adulthood. Reading levels and grade levels of students also varied.[511] Palincsar and Klenk[512] reported that since the beginning of the research program in reciprocal teaching in 1981, "nearly 300 middle school students and 400 first to third graders have participated." The early studies focused on students who were successful at decoding but scored poorly on tests of comprehension. The program was designed primarily for students considered at-risk for academic failure. Many of the participating students in the reciprocal teaching research program were identified as remedial or special education students. Later, studies were used to test the success of reciprocal teaching for students who were only learning to decode.[513] Studies have also considered the success of reciprocal teaching in content areas such as social studies and science. Many research replications have been conducted at the high school and junior college level.[514]

Teachers begin reciprocal teaching by reflecting on their current instructional strategies and activities that teach students' reading comprehension. Next, the theory supporting reciprocal teaching is introduced. Key theoretical elements include teachers modeling the strategies by thinking aloud and consciously striving to have students control the dialogue. All students are expected to participate and to develop skills at using the strategies and critical thinking. Variation exists in the amount of scaffolding the teacher must provide. Next, teachers watch tapes, examine transcripts of reciprocal teaching dialogues, and role playing. Teachers and researchers co-teach a lesson. After the formal

---

[511] Rosenshine & Meister, 1994.

[512] Palincsar & Klenk, 1991.

[513] Brown & Palincsar, 1986.

[514] Brown & Campione, 1991.

instruction, coaching is provided to teachers as they begin implementing reciprocal teaching.[515]

Research Findings

Palincsar and Klenk,[516] reported that the criterion for success was the attainment of an independent score of 75% to 85% correct on four out of five consecutively administered measures of comprehension, assessing recall of text, ability to draw inferences, ability to state the gist of material read, and application of knowledge acquired from the text to a novel situation. Using this criterion, approximately 80% of both the primary and middle school students using the reciprocal teaching strategies were judged successful following three months of instruction. Furthermore, these gains were maintained for up to six months to a year following instruction.

Palincsar and Brown[517] reported that "quantitative and qualitative analyses of transcripts showed substantial changes in the dialogue during the 20 instructional days." In addition, students improved their criterion-referenced test scores over a five-day period of reciprocal teaching while control students made no gains. Students improved in the writing of summaries, generating text-related questions, and identifying discrepancies in texts." Students who had been at the 20th percentile or below in social studies and science increased their scores in these subjects areas to or above the 50th percentile.

Reciprocal teaching, according to Rosenshine and Meister,[518] is dependent on quality of dialogue among participants. The quality of the dialogue can be determined through observation and by assessing the students' questions and summaries during the discussion. Standardized or experimenter-made tests,

---

[515] Palincsar & Klenk, 1992.

[516] Palincsar & Brown, 1986.

[517] Palincsar & Brown, 1986.

[518] Rosenshine & Meister, 1994.

multiple choice, short-answer, or summarizing essays also measure students' reading comprehension.

Palincsar and Brown[519] attributed success of reciprocal teaching to its interactive nature. Understanding the text and providing scaffolding (guided instruction), while the students acquire the skills, are important to the success of reciprocal teaching. Palincsar, Ransom, and Derber[520] cited the alignment of instructional strategies with assessment criteria as a major contributor to the success of reciprocal teaching.

Soto[521] attributed the success of reciprocal teaching to the social construction of knowledge. Students collaborate to construct the meaning of texts. Thus, this allows them to focus on information in texts that is meaningful to them and to use their diverse backgrounds and experiences to introduce multiple perspectives. In addition, through reciprocal teaching dialogues, teachers are better able to assess students' understandings of text and to utilize non-mainstream students' perspectives, to give merit in discussions, status differentiation based on ethnicity and home language is reduced.

Key Terms and Vocabulary List

Palincsar and Brown[522] have compiled an excellent list of terms and vocabulary in reciprocal teaching. The terms and vocabulary list can be easily applied in the classroom. They are as follows:

1. Inert knowledge: encapsulated information rarely accessed again unless you need it for an exam.

2. Theory change: paradigm shift, conceptual upheaval.

---

[519] Palincsar & Brown, 1986.

[520] A. S. Palincsar, K. Ransom, & S. Derber, Collaborative research and development of reciprocal teaching, *Educational Leadership*, 46 (4), (1989), 37-40.

[521] L. D. Soto, Enhancing the written medium for culturally diverse learners via reciprocal interaction, *Urban Review*, 21 (3), (1989), 145.

[522] Palincsar & Brown, 1984; 1989.

3.   Restructuring: modifying the knowledge base.

4.   Self-directed learning: conceptual development is inner directed and inner motivated.

5.   Social learning: conceptual development is other directed and has an intrinsically social genesis.

6.   Cooperative learning: an environment of group explanation and discussion, often with tasks or responsibilities divided up.

7.   Participant structures: interactive environments with agreed-upon rules for speaking, listening, and turn-taking.

8.   Thinking roles:

     Executive - design plans for action and suggests solutions.

     Skeptic - questions premises and plans.

     Instructor - takes on tasks of explanation and summarization for less-able group members.

     Record Keeper - keeps track of events that have passed.

     Conciliatator - resolves conflicts.

9.   Epistemic consideration: organize knowledge by defining the problem, isolating variables, referring to previous knowledge, and evaluation process.

10. Jigsaw method: children are divided into groups of 5 or 6. Each group is held responsible for a large body of knowledge, on which each member will be tested individually. Each member is assigned a topic area. SME's in the same topic area from different groups share information, then return to their groups and share that information with their group.

11. Elaboration: an explanation, a new proposition formed by linking old ones.

12. Preoperational thought: below 5 years old, children cannot comprehend concepts such as conservation of volume, conservation or spatial extent, perspective, etc.

13. Concrete operational thought: nonabstract thinking for kids 7 and up.

14. Intrapersonal function of language: language turned inward; the person

checks and demonstrates his ideas to a hypothetical opponent (internalized socialization); silent verbalization.

15. Zone of proximal development: the difference between potential and actual learning, between what a novice can do unaided versus in a supportive cooperative environment with an expert.

16. Proleptic teaching: group apprenticeship; novice participate in group activity before they are able to perform the task unaided.

17. Expert scaffolding: the expert provides support as needed, commensurate with the novice's expertise and the difficulty of the task, then removes it as the novice progresses.

18. Scaffolding structure: (usually individual) apprenticeship or mother/child: aid decreases as learner's skill increases, activity is shaped by the expert, scaffolding is internalized, expert doesn't verbalize.

19. Socratic dialogue: discovery learning, teacher probes for novel inferences and applications of knowledge by the student.

20. Tripartite teaching goals: facts, rules, and methods for deriving rules.

21. Knowledge-worrying activities: testing hypotheses.

22. Reciprocal teaching: an expert-led cooperative learning procedure involving 4 activities: questioning, clarifying, summarizing, predicting.

23. Heuristics: rules of thumb that evolve from experience.

24. Self-testing mechanisms: assess your own level of expertise: try to paraphrase some text; if you fail, you need to work on it.

25. Emergent skill: a skill that is partly learned.

Summary

The unique feature of reciprocal teaching is that the teacher and the students take turns leading a discussion that focuses on application of the four reading strategies. It also focuses on several different techniques used throughout teaching, modeling, scaffolding, direct instruction, and guided practice. Teachers should purposefully model their use of strategies so that students can emulate them. "Think Alouds" allow teachers to verbalize all their thoughts for students as they demonstrate skills or processes. Some key points to include in the think alouds are making predictions or show students how to develop hypotheses; describe visual images; share an analogy which links prior knowledge with new information; verbalize confusing points; and demonstrate fix-up strategies. These points should be identified by teachers so that students will realize how and when to use them. After several modeling experiences, students should practice using the strategy in pairs. Ultimately, students should work independently with the strategy, using a checklist to monitor usage of the critical points for Think Alouds.

Scaffolding is the process of providing strong teacher support and gradually removing it until students are working independently.[523] This instructional strategy is effective in helping students accelerate their learning. Scaffolding can be applied by sequence texts and through teacher modeling that gradually leads to students independence.

Palincsar, Ransom, and Derber[524] outlined strategies for mastering reciprocal teaching skills:

1. Make sure the strategies are overt, explicit, and concrete through modeling.
2. Link the strategies to the contexts in which they are to be used and teach the strategies as a functioning group, not in isolation.
3. Instruction must inform students. Students should be aware of what strategies work and where they should use particular strategies.
4. Have students to realize that strategies work no matter what their current level of performance.

---

[523] P. D. Pearson, Changing the face of reading comprehension instruction, *The Reading Teacher*, 38, (1985), 724-728; A. Collins, J. S. Brown, & S. E. Newman, *Cognitive Apprenticeship: Teaching the Craft of Reading, Writing, and Mathematics*, (Tech. Rep. No. 403), (Champaign: University of Urbana-Champaign, Center for the Study of Reading, 1987).

[524] Palincsar, Ransom, & Derber, 1998.

222

5.   Comprehension must be transferred from the teacher to the pupil. The teacher should slowly raise the demands made upon the students and then fade into the background. Students gradually take charge of their learning.

Teachers in Highland Park, Michigan, decided to implement reciprocal teaching as part of their reading instruction program at the elementary through high school levels,[525] and they were very well rewarded for their efforts. At the school level, dramatic improvements were observed on the Michigan assessment instrument in reading comprehension. At the faculty level, teachers themselves used reciprocal teaching on each other to enhance their proficiency in acquiring a second language (a goal for their staff development). Generally, research on using reciprocal teaching with children at-risk and children with disabilities has shown that it has increased their achievement.[526]

---

[525] C. Carter, Why reciprocal teaching? *Educational Leadership*, 54 (6), (1997), 64-68.

[526] M. Alfassi, Reading for meaning: The efficacy of reciprocal teaching in fostering reading comprehension in high school students in remedial reading classes, *American Educational Research Journal*, 35 (2) (1998), 309-332; Carter, 1997; Lysynchuk, Pressley, & Vye; Palincsar & Brown, 1984.

Chapter 14

Theory of Multiple Intelligence

Overview

Gardner[527] presented seven domains of abilities in his theory of multiple intelligences. They are: linguistic, spatial, logical-mathematical, interpersonal, intrapersonal, bodily-kinesthetic, and music intelligence. Recently, Gardner[528] added one and a half intelligence to the above domains. The eighth intelligence was named the naturalist and the half intelligence was called the moralist. The naturalist intelligence is involved with one's intelligence which is sensitive to the ecological environment, while the moralist intelligence is concerned with ethical issues. The seven intelligences will be summarized at this point.[529] Gardner described how to integrate the intelligences in the instructional process. They can be incorporated into any program as an alternative to any classroom assignment or learning center. (See Appendix A for examples and ways of integrating multiple intelligence into the instructional program).

The Seven Intelligences

The seven intelligences as described by Gardner[530] are:

Linguistic Intelligence. The capacity to use words effectively, whether orally (e.g., as a story teller, orator, or politician) or in writing (e.g., as a poet, playwright, editor, or journalist). This intelligence includes the ability to

---

[527] H. Gardner, *Frames of Mind: The Theory of Multiple Intelligences* (New York, NY: Basic Books, 1983; 1993a).

[528] H. Gardner, *Multiple Intelligences: The Theory in Practice* (New York, NY: Basic, 1993).

[529] T. Armstrong, *Multiple intelligences in the classroom* (Alexandria, VA: Association for Supervision and Curriculum development, 1994).

[530] Gardner, 1993.

manipulate the syntax or structure of language, the phonology or sounds of language, the semantics or meanings of language, and the pragmatic dimensions or practical uses of language. Some of these uses include rhetoric (using language to convince others to take a specific course of action), mnemonics (using language to remember information), explanation (using language to inform), and metalanguage (using language to talk about itself).

Logical-Mathematical Intelligence. The capacity to use numbers effectively (e.g., as a mathematician, tax accountant, or statistician) and to reason well (e.g., as a scientist, computer programmer, or logician). This intelligence includes sensitivity to logical patterns and relationships, statements and propositions (if-then, cause-effect), functions, and other related abstractions. The kinds of processes used in the service of logical-mathematical intelligence include: categorization, classification, inference, generalization, calculation, and hypothesis testing.

Spatial Intelligence. The ability to perceive the visual-spatial world accurately (e.g., as a hunter, scout, or guide) and to perform transformations upon those perceptions (e.g., as an interior decorator, architect, artist, or inventor). This intelligence involves sensitivity to color, line, shape, form, space, and the relationships that exist between these elements. It includes the capacity to visualize, to graphically represent visual or spatial ideas, and to orient oneself appropriately in a spatial matrix.

Bodily-Kinesthetic Intelligence. Expertise in using one's whole body to express ideas and feelings (e.g., as an actor, a mime, an athlete, or a dancer) and facilitate in using one's hands to produce or transform things (e.g., as a craftsperson, sculptor, mechanic, or surgeon). This intelligence includes specific physical skills such as coordination, balance, dexterity, strength, flexibility, and speed, as well as proprioceptive, tactile, and haptic capacities.

Musical Intelligence. The capacity to perceive (e.g., as a music aficionado), discriminate (e.g., as a music critic), transform (e.g., as a composer), and express (e.g., as a performer) musical forms. This intelligence includes sensitivity to the rhythm, pitch or melody, and timbre or tone color of a musical piece. One can have a figural or "top-down" understanding of music (global, intuitive), a formal or "bottom-up" understanding (analytic, technical), or both.

Interpersonal Intelligence. The ability to perceive and make distinctions in the moods, intentions, motivations, and feelings of other people. This can include sensitivity to facial expressions, voice, and gestures; the capacity for discriminating among many different kinds of interpersonal cues; and the ability to respond effectively to those cues in some pragmatic way (e.g., to influence a group of people to follow a certain line of action).

Intrapersonal Intelligence. Self-knowledge and the ability to act adaptively on the basis of that knowledge. This intelligence includes having an accurate picture of oneself (one's strengths and limitations); awareness of inner moods, intentions, motivations, temperaments, and desires; and the capacity for self-discipline, self-understanding, and self-esteem.

Identification of an Eighth Intelligence

Gardner[531] identified an eighth intelligence called the naturalist intelligence. This intelligence discriminated among living things, as well as sensitivity to other features of the natural world. Gardner further claimed that each pupil should be permitted to develop his/her optimal ability in the intellectual area of expertise. Refer to Appendix A for descriptions of the eight intelligences that can be used in instruction). A ninth intelligence, Moral, Spiritual, and Existential, are presently being researched; when validated, it will become one of the multiple intelligences.[532]

---

[531] Gardner, 1997.

[532] H. Gardner, *Intelligence Reframed: Multiple Intelligence for the 21st Century* (New York: Basic Books, 1999).

The Theoretical Basis for Multiple Intelligence Theory

Gardner[533] developed eight factors that each intelligence had to meet to be considered valid. They are as follows:

1.   Potential Isolation by Brain Damage

Through research with brain injured individuals, Gardner noted that all parts of the brain were not affected by the brain injury. Other parts of the brain not injured could perform other types of intelligences. He developed a system to show the brain structure for each intelligence, and ways intelligences can be demonstrated for each damaged neurological system.

2.   The Existence of Savants, Prodigies, and other Exceptional Individuals

Individuals with exceptionalities may have deficits in one or more areas of functions. Most exceptional individuals can function at high levels with other types of intelligences.

3.   A Distinctive Developmental History and a Definable Set of Expert "End State" Performances.

Each intelligence-based activity has its own developmental pattern which originates in early childhood and has its own peak of growth and inclination. Specific developmental stages for the various intelligences are not within the scope of this text. The reader is referred to Armstrong's *Multiple Intelligences in the Classroom.*[534]

4.   An Evolutionary History of Evolutionary Plausibility

Each of the seven intelligences must meet the test of having its roots deeply embedded in the evolution of human beings, and even earlier, in the evolution of other species.

5.   Support from Psychometric Findings

---

[533] Gardner, 1993.

[534] Armstrong, 1994.

Most theories of learning are based upon standardized measures of human ability, which is denounced by Gardner, however, he suggested that we review existing standardized tests for support of multiple intelligences. He indicated further that many standardized test include subtests similar to multiple intelligences. These sub-tests may assist in validating multiple intelligences.

6.   Support from Experimental Psychological Tasks

Psychological studies have shown the values of using specific skills to measure ability in various fields, but have failed to demonstrate how skills can be transferred to other areas. Certain individuals may be affluent readers but fail to transfer this knowledge in solving mathematical problems. Each of the cognitive skills listed are specific, and correlates with the principles of multiple intelligences, that is, individuals can demonstrate different levels of proficiency across the seven intelligences.

7.   An Identifiable Core Operation or Set of Operations

Each of the various types of intelligences has a set core of operations that derive the various activities under them. Refer to the description of the seven intelligences alluded to earlier in the chapter.

8.   Susceptibility to Encoding in a Symbol System

According to Gardner,[535] one of the best indicators of intelligent behavior is the capacity of human beings to use symbols. He articulated that each of the seven intelligences meets the criterion of being able to be symbolized.

Key Points in Multiple Intelligence Theory

Gardner[536] contended that there are four basic key points in his multiple intelligence theory. The four basic key points are listed as follows:

---

[535] Gardner, 1993a.

[536] Gardner, 1993a.

1.   Each person possesses all seven intelligences, however, they function differently from person to person depending upon environmental, genetic, and cultural factors.

Most individuals appear to fit one or more of these profiles, some are highly developed in some intelligences, others are moderately developed and are underdeveloped in intelligence.

2.   Most people can develop each intelligence to an adequate level of competency.

In spite of disabilities, Gardner[537] believed that all individuals have the capacity to develop all seven intelligences to acceptable levels if given the appropriate support.

3.   Intelligences usually work together in complex ways.

Intelligences, according to Gardner,[538] are always interacting with each other. To complete a simple task will involve the integration of several types of intelligences. An example may be a child riding a bike. The child will need bodily-kinesthetic intelligence to propel the bike, spatial intelligence to orient him or herself to the surroundings, and intrapersonal intelligences to believe that he or she can successfully control and guide the bike.

4.   There are many ways to be intelligent with each category.

A case and point presented was that a person may not be able to read, yet highly linguistic because he or she can tell a story or has a large vocabulary. Most intelligences can be demonstrated in a variety of ways.

The multiple intelligences theory is a cognitive model that seeks to describe how individuals use their intelligences to solve problems. Both learning styles and visual-auditory kinesthetic models have some similarities, but multiple intelligences are not specifically related to the senses. The multiple intelligences

---

[537] Gardner, 1993a.

[538] Gardner, 193a; 1999.

model are not regiment to one type of intelligence, they are multiple dimensional and integrative.

Assessing Student's Multiple Intelligences

There is no one best way for assessing multiple intelligences of children. Standardized tests appear to be limited in assessing the multiple intelligences. Authentic measures are criterion-referenced and compares past performances of students. According to individuals competent in the field, authentic measures of assessment probe students' understanding of material far more thoroughly than multiple choice or other standardized measures.[539] A survey for determining ones multiple-intelligences is located in Appendix B.

Observations

There are many types of authentic measures, the most commonly used type is observation. Teachers can observe and record children's behaviors in a variety of situations in the natural environment. These observations can serve as a source for documenting behaviors and comparing performances over a period of time.

Multiple Intelligences and Curriculum Development

Multiple intelligences can easily be infused throughout the curriculum by the teacher placing emphasis on the seven intelligences. It provides a system where teachers can experiment with various strategies and methods and determine which methods work best for diverse or disabled learners. Multiple intelligence strategies, such as promoting interpersonal skills may be introduced through cooperative learning. Whole language instruction may promote linguistic intelligence, playing music may promote music intelligence, drawing may promote spatial intelligences, role playing and dramatic activities may promote

---

[539] J. L. Herman, P. R. Aschbacker, & L. A. Winters, *Practical Guide to Alternative Assessment* (Alexandria, VA: Association for Supervision and Curriculum Development, 1992); D. P. Wolf, P. G. LeMahieu, & J. Fresh, Good measure: Assessment as a tool for educational reform, *Educational Leadership*, 49 (8), (1992), 8-13; V. A. Emia, A multiple intelligence inventory, *Educational Leadership*, 55 (1997), 47-50; Gardner, 1993a.

bodily-kinesthetic intelligence, and giving additional response time for students may promote intrapersonal intelligence.

Specific strategies for infusing multiple intelligences in curricula have been eloquently summarized by Armstrong.[540] The reader is referred to his work for specific details and implementation of the strategies. Innovative ways may be used to infuse multiple intelligences into the curriculum by the teacher relating or transferring information and resources from one intelligence to another. Other strategies to promote multiple intelligences may include integrating curriculum, learning stations, self-directed learning activities, students' projects, assessments, and community apprenticeship programs.[541]

Multiple Intelligences and Teaching Strategies

Multiple intelligences provide a wide avenue for teachers to employ in their instructional programs. A variety of strategies must be developed to meet the diverse needs of children.[542] There are a wide variety of strategies to employ in promoting multiple intelligences. Educators should feel free to experiment with other strategies.

1.   Linguistic Intelligence

Some recommended strategies include

- Reading
- Story Telling
- Brainstorming
- Tape Recording
- Journal Writing
- Playing Word Games

---

[540] Armstrong, 1994.

[541] Campbell, 1977.

[542] Armstrong, 1994.

- Publishing (takes many forms and may be ditto masters, photo copies), keyed into a word processor, and multi copies printed for distribution

2. Logical-Mathematical Intelligence

    Some recommended strategies include:

    - Experimenting
    - Calculations and Quantifications
    - Classification and Categorization
    - Socratic Questioning (teacher participates in dialogues with students to assist them in arriving at the correct answer)
    - Heuristics (finding analogies, separating, and proposing solutions to problems)
    - Science Thinking
    - Puzzles
    - Calculating

3. Spatial Intelligence

    Some recommended strategies include:

    - Designing
    - Visualization
    - Color Cues
    - Picture Metaphors (using one idea to refer to another, a picture metaphor expresses an idea in a visual image
    - Idea Sketching (drawing the key point, main idea, or central theme being taught)
    - Graphic Symbols (drawing graphic symbols to depict the concept taught)

4. Bodily-Kinesthetic Intelligence

    Some recommended strategies include:

    - Dancing

- Body Answers (children use their bodies as a medium of expression)
- The Classroom Theater (children dramatize or role play problems or materials to be learned)
- Kinesthetic Concepts (introducing children to concepts through physical illustrations or asking students to pantomime specific concepts)
- Hands-on Thinking (making and constructing objects with hands)

5. Musical Intelligence

Some recommended strategies include:

- Rhythms, Songs, Raps, and Chants
- Discographies (music selections that illustrate the content to be conveyed)
- Super Memory Music (designed to improve memory in other subjects through music)
- Musical Concepts (music tones can be used for expressing concepts in subject areas)
- Mood Music (create an emotional atmosphere for a particular lesson)

6. Interpersonal Intelligence

Some recommended strategies include:

- Leading
- Peer Sharing
- Organizing
- People Sculptures (students are brought together to collectively represent in physical form an idea or some specific learning goal)
- Mediating
- Cooperative Groups
- Relating
- Board Games

- Simulations (involves a group of people coming together to create a make believer environment)

7. Intrapersonal Intelligence

Some recommended strategies include:

- One-Minute Reflection Periods (students have frequent time outs for deep thinking)
- Mediating
- Personal Connections (weave students' personal experiences into the instructional program)
- Choice Time
- Feeling - Tone Moments (educators need to teach with feelings and to the emotions of students).
- Goal Setting Sessions (assisting students in setting realistic goals).

8. Naturalist Intelligence

Some recommended strategies are:

- Filed Trips to Locate Living Things
- Writing About Living Things
- Classifying Living Things
- Discussing the Habitat of Living Things
- Demonstrating How We Depend Upon Living Things
- Discussing How Living Things Depend Upon Each Other for Survival

Gardner[543] has advocated an assessment checklist for assessing multiple intelligences. The checklist shown on page 234 can be easily used by a wide-range of children.

---

[543] Gardner, 1993; 1999.

Checklist for Assessing Students' Multiple Intelligences

Name of Student: _____

Check items that apply:

Linguistic Intelligence

- _____writes better than average for age
- _____spins tall tales or tells jokes and stories
- _____has a good memory for names, places, dates, or trivia
- _____enjoys word games
- _____enjoys reading books
- _____spells words accurately (or if preschool, does developmental spelling that is advanced for age)
- _____appreciates nonsense rhymes, puns, tongue twisters
- _____enjoys listening to the spoken word (stories, commentary on the radio, talking books
- _____has a good vocabulary for age
- _____communicates to others in a highly verbal way

Other Linguistic Abilities:

Logical-Mathematical Intelligence

- _____asks a lot of questions about how things work
- _____enjoys working or playing with numbers
- _____enjoys math class (or if preschool, enjoys counting and doing other things with numbers)
- _____finds math and computer games interesting (of if no exposure to computers, enjoys other math or science games)
- _____enjoys playing chess, checkers, or other strategy games
- _____enjoys working on logic puzzles or brainteasers (or if preschool, enjoys hearing local nonsense)
- _____enjoys putting things in categories, hierarchies, or other logical patterns

- _____likes to do experiments in science class or in free play
- _____shows interest in science-related subjects
- _____does well on Piagetian-type assessments of logical thinking

Spatial Intelligence

- _____reports clear visual images
- _____reads maps, charts, and diagrams more easily than text (or if preschool, enjoys looking at more than text)
- _____daydreams a lot
- _____enjoys art activities
- _____good at drawings
- _____likes to view movies, slides, or other visual presentations
- _____enjoys doing puzzles, mazes, or similar visual activities
- _____builds interesting three-dimensional constructions (e.g., LEGO buildings)
- _____gets more out of pictures than words while reading
- _____doodles on workbooks, worksheets, or other materials

Other Spatial Abilities:

Bodily-Kinesthetic Intelligence

- _____excels in one or more sports (or if preschool, shows physical prowess advanced for age)
- _____moves, twitches, taps, or fidgets while seated for a long time in one spot
- _____cleverly mimics other people's gestures or mannerisms
- _____loves to take things apart and put them back together again
- _____puts his/her hands all over something he/she has just seen
- _____enjoys running, jumping, wrestling, or similar activities; or if older, will show these interests in a more "restrained" way (e.g., running to calls, jumping over a chair)

- _____shows skill in a craft (e.g., woodworking, sewing, mechanics) or good fine-motor coordinator in other ways
- _____has a dramatic way of expressing herself/himself
- _____reports different physical sensations while thinking or working
- _____enjoys working with clay or other tactile experiences (e.g., finger painting)

Other Bodily-Kinesthetic Abilities:

Musical Intelligence

- _____tells you when music sounds off-key or disturbing in some other way
- _____remembers melodies of songs
- _____had a good singing voice
- _____plays a musical instrument or sings in choir or other group (or if preschool, enjoys playing percussion instruments and/or singing in a group)
- _____has a rhythmic way of speaking and/or moving
- _____unconsciously hums to himself/herself
- _____taps rhythmically on the table or desk as he/she works
- _____sensitive to environmental noises (e.g., rain on the roof)
- _____responds favorably when a piece of music is put on
- _____sings songs that he/she has learned outside of the classroom

Other Musical Abilities:

Interpersonal Intelligence

- _____enjoys socializing with peers
- _____seems to be a natural leader
- _____gives advice to friends who have problems
- _____seems to be street-smart
- _____belongs to clubs, committees, organizations, or informal peer groups
- _____enjoys informally teaching other kids

- _____likes to play games with other kids
- _____has two or more close friends
- _____has a good sense of empathy or concern for others
- _____others seek out his/her company

Other Interpersonal Abilities:

Intrapersonal Intelligence

- _____displays a sense of independence or a strong will
- _____has a realistic sense of his/her abilities and weaknesses
- _____does well when left alone to play or study
- _____marches to the beat of a different drummer in his/her style of living and learning
- _____has an interest or hobby that he/she does not talk much about
- _____has a good sense of self-direction
- _____prefers working alone to working with others
- _____accurately expresses how he/she is feeling
- _____is able to learn from his/her failures and successes in life
- _____has good self-esteem

Other Intrapersonal Abilities:

Naturalist Intelligence

- _____talks a lot about favorite pets, or preferred spots in nature, during class sharing
- _____likes field trips in nature, to the zoo, or to a natural history museum
- _____shows sensitivity to natural formations (e.g., while walking outside with the class, will notice mountains, clouds; or if in an urban environment, may show this ability in sensitivity to popular culture "formations," such as sneakers or automobile styles)
- _____likes to water and tend to the plants in the classroom

238

- _____likes to hang around the gerbil cage, the aquarium, or the terrarium in class
- _____gets excited when studying about ecology, nature, plants, or animals
- _____speaks out in class for the rights of animals, or the preservation of planet earth
- _____enjoys doing nature projects, such as bird watching, butterfly or insect collections, tree study, or raising animals
- _____brings to school bugs, flowers, leaves, or other natural things to share with classmates or teachers
- _____does well in topics at school that involve living systems (e.g., biological topics in science, environmental issues in social studies)

Educators may employ creative ways for infusing multiple intelligences in the classroom by examining his or her instructional program and classroom management techniques and by changing instruction to meet the unique needs of the group. All of the multiple intelligences can be creatively used in the classroom by changing instructional procedures, structuring the classroom, arranging furniture, selecting appropriate resources and activities to support the various multiple intelligences. For opportunity for movement in the classroom, use music as an instructional medium, develop a sense of community, develop cooperative groups, and provide time for independent work. These activities can be incorporated under many of the multiple intelligences. Teachers are encouraged to experiment and use various methods to include the eight intelligences.

Integrating Multiple Intelligences With Learning Styles
and Brain-Based Research

Silver, Strong, and Perini[544] have advocated a method for integrating multiple intelligences with learning styles. Guild[545] proposed the same strategy by

---

[544] H. Silver, R. Strong, & M. Perini, Integrating learning styles and multiple intelligence, *Educational Leadership, 55* (1), (1997), 22-27.

integrating multiple intelligences with Brain-Based Researcher. Both of these models have applications for improved human learning.

Silver[546] and his associates developed a model showing how the learning style of a child can be matched with his or her strongest intelligence. The authors attempted to describe each of Gardner's intelligences with a set of learning styles. Samples of vocations and the particular intelligence associated with them were matched with a learning style profile.

Guild[547] proposed the multiple intelligences, learning styles, and brain-based research. She maintained that there are similarities and differences between multiple intelligences, learning styles, and brain-based learning. These fields are distinct and separate from one another in some ways, but practical in some instances in the classroom environment. It was further voiced that each of these theories projected a comprehensive approach to learning and teaching. Similarity in the three theories include the following: (1) Each of the theories is a reflective practitioner and decision maker, (2) The teacher is a reflective practitioner and decision maker, (3) The student is also a reflective practitioner, (4) The whole person is educated, (5) The curriculum has substance, depth, and quality, and (6) Each of the theories promotes diversity.

Some cautions to be aware of: (1) No theory is a panacea for solving all of the problems in education, (2) Simplistic application of the theories, and (3) None of the theories offer a cookbook approach to teaching.

The researchers concluded that both multiple intelligences, learning styles, and brain-based research can be integrated to form a functional model of human intelligence. The present models advocated appears feasible with additional

---

[545] P. B. Guild, Where do the learning theories overlap? *Educational Leadership*, 55 (1), (1977), 30-31.

[546] Silver, Strong, & M. Perini, 1997.

[547] Guild, 1977.

studies and experimentations conducted to validate the integration of multiple intelligences with learning styles and brain-based research.

The country of Bangladesh has made brain-based learning and multiple intelligences a national policy. A research team under the directions of Ellison and Rothenberger[548] observed classrooms and trained teachers in multiple ways of learning and multiple intelligence theory. Teacher trainers were involved in a number of self-reflective strategies and cooperative group activities. This experimental project may well serve as a model in Bangladesh for using multiple intelligences strategies and brain-based research.

Most teachers cannot associate a theory or theories or learning with their instructional program. Generally, their teaching strategies are not grounded in a theory.

Multiple Intelligences and Special Education

The comprehensiveness of multiple intelligences makes them amenable to children with disabilities. The theory considers children with disabilities as having strength in many of the multiple intelligences. In order for children with disabilities to demonstrate their skills in multiple intelligences, educators must use accommodations and alternative strategies to assist them to demonstrate their intelligences and to succeed in school.

The multiple intelligences theory does not subscribe to the deficit model used in special education; rather it supports eliminating labels. It does not endorse the use of standardized tests in assessment; rather, it supports the use of authentic assessment approaches. It does not support separation of children with disabilities from their normal peers, rather, it supports full inclusion. Finally, the multiple intelligences theory does not support separate tracks and instructional staff for children with disabilities; rather, it advocates establishing collaborative models that enable instructional staff to work together. Additionally, it provides a

---

[548] Silver, Strong, & Perini, 1997.

growth paradigm for assisting children with disabilities without considering their disabilities as impediments to using their multiple intelligences. The multiple intelligence theory has demonstrated how a child with a disability in one intelligence can frequently overcome the disability by using a more highly developed intelligence if appropriate alternatives are employed.[549]

Gardner[550] is not alone in supporting the values of multiple intelligences in teaching. Perkins'[551] research strongly supports Gardner's views. He identified three kinds of intelligences:

1. The fixed neurological intelligence which is associated with scores made on standardized tests of intelligence.

2. The intelligence of specialized knowledge and experiences acquired over time.

3. Early and prolong exposure to stimulating experiences in one's environment can promote their intelligence.

Perkins defined reflective intelligence as the ability to become aware of one's mental habits and transcend limited patterns of thinking. He further proclaimed that intelligence is not genetically fixed at birth and be enhanced through cultural and environmental enrichment.

Gardner[552] assessed intelligence as more than an IQ score because a high IQ, in the absence of production does not equate to intelligence. He support the definition, that intelligence is a biopsychological potential to process information that can be activated in a cultural setting to solve problems or create products that are of value in a culture.

---

[549] Gardner, 1983.

[550] Gardner, 1993, 1999.

[551] D. Perkins, *Outstanding IQ: The Emerging Science of Learnable Intelligence* (New York: The Free Press, 1995).

[552] Gardner, 1983.

242

Summary

There is nothing new relevant to multiple intelligences. Good teachers have employed the strategies for some time in their teaching by infusing thinking and mental processes with the curriculum. As indicated throughout the chapter, the multiple intelligences theory has many implications for curriculum development, teaching strategies, assessment, cultural diversity, ecological factors, classroom management, integrations with other theories, and computer applications. The use of the multiple intelligences theory has proven to be effective in promoting, motivating, and stimulating the many intelligences of learners. These intelligences can be nurtured and increased as well as work together or independently to promote learning.[553] The schools have not accepted this concept wholeheartedly. Adequate research, proving the values of the multiple intelligences theory, has been reported through this chapter. As with most research findings, the schools are usually decades behind implication. The time is now for endorsing and using Multiple Intelligences Theory (MI) to aid teachers in creating individualized, personalized, and culture relevant experiences for children.

In order to prepare students to use learning principles effectively, educators need to become knowledgeable about them. They need to be encouraged to study and learn how to transform learning theories into practice by infusing them into their instructional programs. Gardner[554] strongly advocated that students must be given opportunities to express the type of intelligence and cognitive styles that have strengths. Csikszentmihalyi's[555] viewpoint is similar to Gardner's.

---

[553] Gardner, 1999.

[554] Gardner, 1983; 1993; 1999.

[555] M. Cskszentimihaly, *Flow: The Psychology of Optimal Experiences* (New York: Harper and Row, 1990).

Chapter 15

Brain-Based Learning

Introduction

In ancient empires the roles and functions of the brain in learning was given much recognition in learning. It was believed that the brain, where ephemeral spirits roam, was indispensable. This belief dominated man's thinking until around the early part of the seventeenth century until a French philosopher Rene' Descantes conducted experiments with the brain. He codified the separation of conscious thought from the physical flesh of the brain. These experiments shed important information on the functions of the brain well into the present century. Another philosopher, Thomas Willis, expanded the work of Descantes. He was the first to suggest that the brain was the center of control for the body, but different parts of the brain controlled specific cognitive functions. However, a given mental task may involve a completed web of circuits which interact with other circuits throughout the brain. These early attempts to understand the working of the brain are responsible for our present understanding of brain functioning.[556]

In a more recent study, Polley and Heiser[557] experimented with how the brain responds to the intensity of sound. These researchers found that the brain of rats can be trained to learn alternate ways of processing changes in the loudness of sound. The discovery, they suggest, has potential for the treatment of hearing

---

[556] R. Shore, *Rethinking the brain: New insights into early development* (New York: Families and Work Institute, 1997); J. Shreeve, Beyond the brain, *National Geographic Society*, 207, (3), (2005, March), 2-31.

[557] D. B. Polley, & M. A. Heiser, Brain can be trained to produce sound in alternate ways, study shows. *Medical News Today*, (2004, December 16). [htt://www.medicalnewstoday.com/medicalnews.php?newsid=17695.

loss, autism, and other sensory disabilities in humans. It also gives clues, they infer, about the process of learning and the way we perceive the world. Experimentations over the centuries have shown that the brain responds to physical stimuli by converting them into electrical impulses that are processed by neurons in the area of the brain which controls the stimuli. Neurons fire faster or slower depending upon the intensity of the stimuli and the sense organ involved. This physiological change in the brain is similar to expanding a rubber band, and is referred to as "plasticity."

The implications of this study may provide strategies for training individuals with hearing impairments who cannot hear lower intensity sounds, but can hear well at higher levels. For example, children with autism may be assisted by specialists regulating the stimuli presented in the environment with a moderate stimulus.

The brain is a fascinating organ. It is composed of cells. The cells involved in learning are neurons and glial cells. A complete discussion of the anatomy of the brain is not within the scope of this chapter. Sprenger[558] provides detail information on the anatomy and the function of the brain. A brief summary on the structure of the brain is also provided for the reader information.

The brain accounts for only about 2 to 3 percent of body weight, but it uses 20 to 25% of the body's energy. It is encased in the skull and protected by cerebro-spinal fluid. The largest part of the brain is called the cerebrum. The cerebrum consists of two deeply wrinkled hemispheres of nerve tissue located in each hemisphere of the brain. Its major function is to control all conscious activities, such as memory, perception, problem solving and understanding meanings. At the back of the skull is the cerebellum. It consists of two hemispheres. It automatically controls and coordinates the muscles involved in such activities like riding a bicycle.

---

[558] M. Sprenger, *Learning and Memory: The Brain in Action* (Alexandria, VA: Association for Supervision and Curriculum Development, 1999).

The medulla controls involuntary muscle activity such as the beating of voluntary muscle activity in the body, such as learning to walk and riding a bicycle. The heart, the rate of breathing, stomach activities, swallowing and other vital body activities are controlled also by the medulla. The spinal cord extends downward from the medulla through the bony rings of the spinal column. Nerves that extend upward from the spinal cord to the brain pass through the medulla where they cross. Therefore, the left side of the brain controls the right side of the body, while the right side of the brain controls the left side of the body.

The human brain weights less than six pounds. It can store more information than all the libraries of the world. It communicates with itself through billions of neurons and their connections. All functions of the nervous system depend on the coordinated activities of individual neurons. The cells have a cell membrane, a nucleus, and other structures within the cell body. They differ significantly in size and shape. Research on learning and memory has shown that the brain uses discrete systems for different types of learning.

The basal ganglia and cerebellum, according to Damasio,[559] are critical for the acquisition of skills. For example, learning to ride a bicycle or play a musical instrument are functions of the basal ganglia. The hippocampus is integral to the learning of facts pertaining to such entities as people, places or events. The left hemisphere of the brain seems to be specialized for the representation of verbal material and right hemisphere of the brain specialized for a variety of nonverbal information processing (especially visual-spatial material). At the present time, it is certainly not clear how many different nonverbal modalities one ought to distinguish, nor is it clear how many verbal modalities or levels of a verbal modality one ought to distinguish. However, it is clear that many individuals suffer moderate to severe deficits in a particular modality, without showing any deficits, or even showing a partially compensating superiority, in other modalities

---

[559] A. R. Damasio, *Descarte's Error: Emotion, Reason, and the Human Brain* (New York, NY: Putnam Publishing, 1994), 3-19.

of functioning. Once facts are learned, the long-term memory of those facts relies on multicomponent brain systems, whose key parts are located in the vast brain expanses known as cerebral cortices.

Principles of Brain-Based Learning

Caine and Caine[560] have conducted extensive research in brain-based learning. They articulated that every human being has a virtually unlimited set of memory systems that are designed for programming and for the memorization of meaningless information. Individuals also have the need to place memories and experiences into wholes. Both memorization and integration are essential in the learning process. The authors also indicated that there are several principles associated with brain-based learning. They are:

1. The brain, a complex adaptive system, is self organized with functions that are both independent and inter independent.[561]

2. The brain is a social brain. The brain is capable of early interpersonal and social relationships that greatly advance or impede learning.

3. The search for meaning is innate. The search for meaning implies that the brain is attempting to make sense of our experiences. Development experiences are necessary for survival.

4. The search for meaning occurs through "patterning." Patterns may be innate or developed through interactions with individuals and their environments. The brain gives meaning and understanding to these patterns.

5. Emotions are critical to patterning. Emotions significantly influence learning. Social interactions are influenced by one's emotional tone. Emotions and learning are inseparable.

---

[560] R. N. Caine, & G. Caine, *Education on the Edge of Possibility* (Alexandria, VA: Association for Supervision and Curriculum Development, 1977).

[561] J. A. Kelso, *Dynamic Patterns: The Self-organization of Brain and Behavior* (Cambridge, MA: The MIT Press, 1995).

6. Every brain simultaneously perceives and creates parts and wholes. The brain is interdependent. Both hemispheres actively interact and reduce information to both parts and wholes.

7. Learning involves both focused attention and peripheral perception. The brain absorbs information when the individual is or is not paying attention to a task. Peripheral signals are also recorded and have significant importance on learning as well.

8. Learning always involves conscious and unconscious processes. Educators should be aware that the brain is constant at work with consciousness as well as unconscious experiences.

9. Consequently some learning may not occur immediately because the experiences have not been internalized.

10. We have at least two ways of organizing memory. O'Keefe and Nadel[562] indicated that we have two sets of memories, one for recalling meaningless and meaningful information. Information from these two sources are stored differently, meaning less experiences are motivated by reward and punishment, where meaningful experiences do not need rehearsal and allows for instant recall of experiences. The brain uses and integrates both approaches in learning.

11. Learning is developmental. The brain is constantly developing in childhood. In the early years, children expand their understanding of the world around them, storing the sights, smells, and tastes of various stimuli while learning about their environment and their relation with their peers. As a result of these experiences, their brains form millions of connections. At about 2, their brains begin to prime many of the excess connections in

---

[562] J. O'Keefe, & L. Nadel, *The Hippocampus as a Cognitive Map* (Oxford: Clarendon Press, 1978).

order to become more efficient.[563] Most of the development is shaped and molded by environmental influences. Children should be exposed to multiple experiences early in life to facilitate all aspects of learning.

12. Complex learning is enhanced by challenge and inhibited by threat. Teachers who employ strategies, which promotes a relaxed environment provide challenges rather than threats to students. Learning is expedited in a challenging and relaxed environment where students are safe to try, think, speculate and make mistakes.[564]

13. Every brain is uniquely organized. Genetic makeup and environmental influences determines to a significant degree how the brain is organized. The organization determines the various learning styles, talents and intelligence of individuals.

Educators should provide experiences that will promote all of the various principles that have been outlined. Duffy and Jonassen,[565] in support of the previous points, posit that learning is an active process in which meaning is developed on the basis of experiences. Similarly, Benson and Hunter[566] stated that humans do not passively encounter knowledge in the world; rather they generate meaning based upon what they choose to pay attention to. Attention is related to the meaning and purpose of the learning act.

The brain is constructed to deal with and adapt to changing elements in society. Educators must capture how the brain learns and program this knowledge

---

[563] Education Update. *How Teachers are Putting Brain Research to Use?* 47, 6, (2005), 103. Association of Supervision and Curriculum Development. Author.

[564] A. Kohn, *Punished by Rewards: The Trouble with Gold Stars, Incentive Plans, A's, Praise, and Other Bribes* (Boston, MA: Houghton Mifflin, 1993).

[565] T. M., Duffy, & A. D. Jonassen, *Constructivism and the Technology of Instruction: A Conversation* (Hillsdale, NJ: Lawrence Erlbaum, 1992).

[566] G. D. Benson, & W. J. Hunter, Chaos Theory: No strange attraction in teacher education, *Action in Teacher Education*, 14 (4), (1992), 61-67.

into instructional programs to promote self-directed learning activities for children.

Brain depicture, which every human being, is a virtually unlimited set of memory systems that are designed for programming and for the memorization of meaningless information, as well as placing memories and experiences into wholes. Both memorization and integration are critical in learning. Research by Caine and Caine[567] showed that teaching for memorization of meaningless facts usually induce downshifting. Downshifting is a response to a threat associated with fatigue or helplessness or both. Critical and high order thinking are impeded by downshifting.

The theory of brain-based learning projects children as active participants in the learning process. The teacher becomes the facilitator in guiding the learning activities of children. The instructional approach is changed from rote and information to one that is receptive, flexible, creative, and student centered. This theory advocates that students should be engaged in tasks that are meaningful to them and facilitate their interests.[568]

Brain-Based Research

Brain research is relatively new and scientists agree that much is unknown about this complex organ, the core of bodily functions. There is, also, little consensus regarding the impact of the research findings on education; but researchers agree that the possibilities are tremendous. Jensen[569] claimed that there are important implications for learning, memory, and training. Neuroscientists, researchers, and educators are conducting research on the function of the brain in an effort to combine the findings of the brain/mind field

---

[567] Caine & Caine, 1991; 1994a.

[568] Sprenger, 1999.

[569] E. Jensen, *Teaching with the Brain in Mind* (Alexandria, VA: Association for Supervision and Curriculum Development, 1998).

250

with other fields to diversify and strengthen the applications.[570] Neuroscience, though an important part of a larger puzzle, is not the only source of evidence. Neuroscience research combined with other fields like sociology, chemistry, anthropology, therapy, and others, offer powerful applications for education.

Important work in the area of neuropsychology, involving brain research, sheds light in better understanding of human brain functions. According to Turgi,[571] this work is so important that the United States' scientific community recognized the nineties as the "decade of the brain."

Sousa[572] wrote that upon birth, each child's brain produces trillions more neurons and synapses than one needs to make connections in the brain. Researchers have identified a family of brain chemicals called neurotransmitters, that either excite or inhibit nerve cells referred to as neuron. Neurons have branches called "dendrites" that receive electrical impulses, which are transmitted through a long fiber termed an axon. The synapse between the dendrites join the process together and release neurotransmitters, which stimulate the neurons to collect and carry information for processing through a complex and systematic route. New experiences and information are filtered, and then categorized contingent upon established brain structures as determined by prior knowledge and experience.[573]

Children are more adept at making new brain connections than are adults, and consequently, they integrate new experiences at an incredibly fast rate.[574]

---

[570] E. Jensen, *Brain-based Learning* (San Diego: Brain Store Incorporated, 2000).

[571] P. Turgi, Children's rights in America: The needs and the actions, *Journal of Humanistic Education and Development*, 31, (1992), 52-63.

[572] D. Sousa, *How the Brain Learns* (Reston, VA: National Association of Secondary School Principals, 1995).

[573] Sousa, 1995.

[574] J. Newberger, New brain development research: A wonderful window of opportunity to build public support for early childhood education, *Young Children*, 52 (1997), 4-9; C. Toepher, Jr.,

Consequently, a rich learning environment yields more complex brain pathways for organizing and connecting meaning to learning, social, and physical development. Opportunities of development learning occur when the brain demands certain types of input for stabilization of long-lasting structures in provision of organizational frameworks to retain future information. Commonly recognized milestones of motor development, emotional control, and vocabulary development are key indicators in sequentially formative development progression. A normally functioning brain has the learning readiness to receive and process the information necessary for each skill acquisition.

Thompson, Giedd, Woods, et al.[575] reported that optimization of brain connections occurs early in childhood as well as just before puberty. Although the brain of a 6-year-old child has grown to 95% of the adult brain size, size is not an important factor in the use of the brain cells that are produced. Because a second wave of brain cell production takes place just before puberty, it is important that young people are encouraged to take advantage of optimizing their brain activity by becoming involved in reading, physical activity, and musical skill development during elementary school age. Musicians and athletes are often most successful when they begin their training at a very young age; avid readers continue to read throughout adulthood. These are lasting activities that "wire" the brain for use later in life. It is also important to realize that drugs and alcohol have devastating effects on the brain connections in the pre-teen years when the brain is still in developmental stages.

The concept of brain-based learning is not without critics. They worry that so much is unknown about the brain and its function, that it is ludicrous to make assumptions based on presumptions rather than scientific evidence.

Curriculum design and neuropsychological development, *Journal of Research and Development in Education*, 15 (1982), 1-10.

[575] P. M. Thompson, J. N. Giedd, R. Woods, D. MacDonald, A. Evans, & A. Toga, Growth patterns in the developing brain detected by using continuum mechanical sensor maps. *Nature*, 404, (2000), 190-193.

252

Unfortunately, many of the myths about the brain are misinterpreted and misunderstood by individuals outside of the field. One of the most vocal critics is Bruer[576] who addressed the implications of the new brain research for educators in several significant publications, *The American School Board Journal*, 1993, February; *Educational Leadership*, 1997, March; *The School Administrator*, 1998, January; and *The NASSP Bulletin*, 1998, May.

Advocates are undaunted by the criticism. They suggest that although much has yet to be learned about the brain, what is known is helpful as the research continues to unfold new knowledge about the brain, its development, and its function. Sousa and Jensen[577] agree and summarized recent research, which has provided valuable information for educators to use in guiding learning activities.

Normal childhood experiences usually produce normal kids, and there are 'windows' of opportunity for development.[578] The most critical "windows" are those involved with our senses, the parent-infant emotional attunement, language learning, and non-distressed sense of safety. These "windows" are time-sensitive and cannot be recaptured. Developmental skills such as social, reading, music, and language have a much longer "sensitive" period and can be approached at a later time.[579] Jensen indicated that learning is strengthened in the brain through repetition and practice, but boredom weakens the process. Many factors influence learner success including parents, peers, genes, trauma, nutrition, and environment, but there is no way to quantify them. He summarizes that brain-based learning is not a panacea or a quick fix to solve all of education's problems,

---

[576] J. T. Bruer, Education and the brain: A bridge too far, *Educational Researcher*, 26 (8), 1997, 4-16.

[577] Sousa, 1995; Jensen, 2000.

[578] Jensen, 2000.

[579] Jensen, 2000.

but there are numerous examples of improved learning through the application of brain-based learning strategies.[580]

Research conducted by Bruer[581] concerning the role in learning for K-12 educators is not conclusive.

"However, we should be weary of claims that neuro-science has much to tell us about education, particularly if those claims derive from the neuroscience and education argument. The neuroscience and education argument attempts to link l learning, particularly early childhood learning with what neuroscience has discovered about neural development and synaptic change. Neuroscience has discovered a great deal about neurons and synapses but not nearly enough to guide educational practices. Currently, the span between brain and learning cannot support much of a load. Too many people marching in step across it could be dangerous."

Premised upon the above, Bruer[582] contended that learning, at the present, is better defended through the principles of cognitive psychology. Cognitive psychology provides the only firm ground that is presently connected between principles of learning and the brain. Several researchers, Sylwester[583] and Nuthall[584] support that learning is enhanced when a teacher identifies specific types of knowledge that are the focus of a unit or lesson. Application of this concept by teachers should include the following factors in involving instructional units for children's differences in the number of tasks.

---

[580] Jensen, 2000.

[581] Bruer, 1997, p. 15.

[582] Bruer, 1997.

[583] R. Sylwester, What the biology of the brain tell us about learning, *Educational Leadership*, 51 (4), (1993, December; 1994, January), 2226.

[584] G. Nuthall, The way students learn: Acquiring knowledge from an integrated science and social studies unit, *The Elementary School Journal*, 99 (4), (1999), 303-341.

254

Most brain-based education indicate a need for children to generate their own unique meaning regarding the content being learned. Hart[585] believed that teachers do not need to structure classroom tasks to facilitate meaning. He defended his view by stating:

"Since the brain is indisputably a multi-path, multi-modal apparatus the notion of mandatory sequences or even any fixed sequences is unsupported. Each of us learn in a personal, highly individual, mainly random way, always adding to, sorting out, and revising all the input from teachers or elsewhere--that we have had up to that point. That being the case, any group instruction that has been tightly, logically planned will have been wrongly planned for most of the group, (original emphasis) and will inevitably inhibit, prevent, or distort learning."[586]

Hart's[587] view of brain-based learning has gained wide spread support concerning the types of experiences that promote learning within children. These researchers concluded that the types of experiences teachers afford students should be varied and employ a variety of exposures that use their prior background of knowledge.[588] The reader is also referred to the following sources for additional strategies; Council for Exceptional Children and Appendix C.

---

[585] L. A. Hart, *Human Brain and Human Learning* (New York: Longman, 1983).

[586] Hart, 1983, p. 55.

[587] Hart, 1983.

[588] J. Barrell, Designing the invitational environment, in A. Costa (Ed.), *Developing minds: A resource book for teaching thinking* (3rd ed.) (Alexandria, VA: Association for Supervision and Curriculum Development, 2001); D. C. Hicks, Narrative discourse and classroom learning: An essay response to Eagan's "Narrative of learning: A voyage of implications." *Linguistic and Education*, 5 (1993), 127-148; B. J. Guzzetti, T. E. Snyder, & G. V. Glass, Promoting conceptual chance in science: A comparative meta-analysis of instructional interventions from reading education and science education, *Reading Research Quarterly*, 28 (2), (1993), 117-155.

Another view of learning principles is expressed by Hart, Caine and Caine, Campbell, and Druckman & Bjork,[589] articulated that structure is important when the psychology of "sameness" is recognized. Flavell[590] wrote that "to apply the term "structure" correctly, it appears that there must be, at a minimum, an ensemble of two or more elements together with one or more relationships inter-linking these elements." Learning is accelerated when the teacher present students with learning experiences that are similar enough to them to note the similarity between the known and unknown.

According to Piaget[591] learning requires multiple exposure to and complex interactions with knowledge as evident by the integration of new knowledge with existing knowledge (assimilation) and when existing knowledge structures are changed (accommodation). Piaget provided additional information on multiple exposure by revealing that multiple exposure to knowledge over time are necessary for assimilation, however, complex interaction with knowledge over time allows for more powerful accommodations.

The research of Anderson, Nuthall, and Rovee-Collier[592] was based upon Piaget's schema theory that provided another perspective on the importance of multiple exposures to and interaction with content. Accordingly, Anderson stated that "Schemata are the basic packets in which knowledge is stored in permanent

---

[589] Hart, 1993; Caine & Caine, 1991; J. Campbell, *Winston Churchill's Afternoon Nap* (New York: Simon & Schuster, 1986); D. Druckman, & R. A. Bjork (Eds.), *Constructivism and the Technology of Instruction: A Conversation* (Washington, DC: National Academy Press, 1994).

[590] J. H. Flavell, Stage related properties of cognitive development, *Cognitive Psychology*, 2 (1971), 421-453.1991, p. 443.

[591] Piaget, 1971.

[592] R. C. Anderson, Role of reader's scheme in comprehension, learning, and memory, in R. B. Ruddle, M. R. Ruddle, and H. Singer (Eds.), *Theoretical Models and Process of Reading (4th ed.)* (Newark: DE: International Reading Association, 1994); G. Nuthall, The way students learn: Acquiring knowledge from an integrated science and social studies unit, *The Elementary School Journal*, 99 (4), 1999; C. Rovee-Collier, Time window in cognitive development, *Developmental Psychology*, 31 (2), 1995.

memory." Rumelkart and Norman[593] present a view concerning schema development that is similar to Piaget's definition. They reported that schema development is synonymous with knowledge development. They divided the schema development into three types:

1. Tuning involves the gradual accumulation of knowledge over time and the expression of that knowledge in more parsimonious ways. Application of this schema for children will require the teacher to provide a variety of multiple exposures to the children to facilitate learning.

2. Restructuring involves reorganizing information or knowledge so that new insights might be generated from the reorganization. In achieving this schema teachers should not only expose children to multiple exposures but provide strategies to promote complex interactions to solve problems which can change their basic understandings of constructing new knowledge

Nuthall[594] contended that verbal, visual, and dramatic instruction can all be integrated in telling stories that can improve memory, and this does not require much preparation. Further, Nuthall[595] stated that other studies suggest that narratives provided powerful structures for the organization and storage of curriculum content in memory...stories often contain a rich variety of supplemental information, connect to personal experiences, and are integrated and held together by a familiar structure. Research findings by Barrell, Hicks, and Schank[596] support Nuthall's research.

---

[593] D. E. Rumelhart, & D. A. Norman, Accretion, tuning, and restructuring: Three modes of learning, in J. W. Colton & R. Klazky (Eds.) *Semanticfactors in cognition* (Hillsdale, NJ: Lawrence Erlbaum, 1981).

[594] G. Nuthall, The way students learn: Acquiring knowledge from an integrated science and social studies unit, *The Elementary School Journal*, 99 (4), (1999), 337.

[595] Nuthall, 1999.

[596] J. Barrell, Designing the invitational environment, in A. Costa (ed.), *Developing minds: A resource book for teaching thinking (3rd ed.)* (Alexandria, VA: Association for Supervision and Curriculum Development, 2001); D. C. Hicks, Narrative discourse and classroom learning: An essay response to Eagan's "Narrative of learning: A voyage of implications." *Linguistic and*

Several cognitive psychologists have voiced that learning is facilitated between two types of knowledge, declarative and procedural.[597] Declarative knowledge is based upon information, whereas procedural knowledge is knowledge of a skill or knowledge about the application of a process. In order for children to effectively employ procedural knowledge, they must learn to a level of automaticity with no thought or perceived effort. Consequently, teachers must provide practices using a variety of input modes. These input modes involve both direct and indirect experiences. They are designed to promote the mastery of learning through physical activity. Indirect experiences do not physically involve children. Activities including demonstrations, readings, observing, and listening contribute to (declarative or procedural) knowledge. Since many of the two experiences may be used interchangeable, teachers must determine which type will meet the needs of their classes.[598]

The brain is molded and reshaped by environmental forces acting upon it. As we interact with the world, the environmental forces become internalized, or mapped, in our brain. Zull[599] asserts that this process of brain rewiring continues throughout life. Research conducted by Draganski et al.[600] demonstrated how changes in the human brain affected learning. Young adults were exposed to several weeks of juggling three balls in the air. Results from MRI images of the

education, 5 (1993), 127-148; R. C. Schank, Tell me a story: A New Look at Real and Artificial Memory (New York: Charles Scribner and Sons, 1990).

[597] J. R. Anderson, Acquisition of cognitive skills, Psychology Review, 89, (1982), 369-406; P. M. Fitts, & M. I. Posner, Human Performance (Belmont, CA: Brooks Cole, 1967); D. LaBerge, & S. J. Samuels, Toward a theory of automatic information process in reading comprehension, Cognitive Psychology, 6 (1974), 293-323; J. R. Anderson, L. M. Reder, & H. A. Simon, Application and misapplications of cognitive psychology to mathematics education, unpublished paper, Carnegie Mellon University, 1995.

[598] G. Nutha; 1999; C. Rovee-Collier, Time window in cognitive development, Developmental Psychology, 31 (2), (1995) 147-169.

[599] J. E. Zull, The art of changing the brain, Educational Leadership, 62 (1), (2004), 68-69.

[600] B. Draganski, C. Gaser, V. Bush, G. Schuierer, U. Bogdahn, & A. Mary, Neuroplasticity: Changes in gray matter induced by training. Nature, 427 (6972), (2004), 311-312.

brain before and after the juggling experiment showed that learning to juggle generated increased activity in a part of the brain that controlled vision. When juggling was terminated, the brain activity, in the vision area returned to its normal state. Brain activity is increased with practice and repetition of experiences, especially in the early development stages.

By early childhood, a child's brain has reached 95% of its adult structure. Individuals are born equipped with most of the neurons their brain will ever have. Achievement of maximum brain-cell density occurs between the third and six month of gestation. Mahoney[601] revealed that preadolescence is another time for the acceleration of rapid brain growth. New connections are being made at a rapid rate as the brain reshapes itself. This rapid growth may be attributed to why some adolescents do not respond appropriately to the emotions of others because they are conscious of only about 5% of their cognitive activity. According to Maszak,[602] "most of our decisions, actions, emotions, and behaviors depend on the 95% of brain activity that goes beyond our conscious awareness." The author referred to these activities as part of the adaptive unconscious, where the brain integrates, controls, and directs automatic performances of the body.

Meltzoff[603] provided information relevant to brain related studies and implications for how children learn. The importance of modeling in shaping behavior was investigated. His research revealed that toddlers imitated the actions and behaviors they saw peers perform, and that they retained these behaviors and recalled them a day later. Retention and memory of language learning of babies were also explored. Data suggested that young babies can distinguish sounds from languages all over the world, but after six months they become culturally

---

[601] W. Mahoney, What was he thinking? *Prevention*, 56 (3), (2005), 159-165.

[602] M. S. Maszak, Mysteries of the mind, *U.S. News and World Report*, 138 (7), (2005), 57-58.

[603] A. Meltzoff, Learning how children learn from us, *Education Update*, 46 (4), 2 (Alexandria, VA: Association for supervision and Curriculum Development, 2004).

bound listeners and begin to lose that ability. Young children should be exposed to appropriate modeling techniques and be permitted to demonstrate them. These strategies can provide for the demonstration of appropriate skills in later life.

Brain Research in Adolescence

Ben Carson,[604] Director of Pediatric Neuro-Surgery at the Johns Hopkins Medical Institution in Baltimore, Maryland, is well known for his surgical skills in separating several sets of conjoined twins. In addressing a group of educators at a meeting of The Association for Supervision and Curriculum Development, 2004, he voiced that "young people are equipped with the most fabulous computer system in the universe--the human brain. And educators have the gift and responsibility to encourage adolescents to use their brains and their dreams. The intellect is there--all we need to do is give them the direction."

As in early childhood, the brains of adolescents undergo a second pruning phase, whittling away and fine-tuning cells, which are responsible for higher thinking and problem solving. The process continues until the early 20's and completes its transformation into the organ it will be and become throughout adulthood.[605]

In a recent *Time Magazine Supplement*[606] and a study conducted by Healy,[607] it was voiced that about the time the brain of adolescents switches from proliferating to pruning, the body experiences the hormonal assault of puberty. It is generally believed by psychologists that the intense, combustible emotions are attributed to the unpredictable behavior of teens to this biochemical on slaught. Research data support that parts of the brain responsible for receiving sensations

[604] B. A. Carson, A journey from the bottom of the class to brain surgeon, *Education Update*, 46 (4), 1 (Alexandria, VA: Association for Supervision and Curriculum Development, 2004), p. 1.

[605] *Education Update*, 2005.

[606] What make teens tick? *Time Magazine Supplement*, 53-59 (2004, May). Author.

[607] J. Healy, *Your Child's Growing Mind: A Practical Guide to Brain Development and Learning from Birth to Adolescence* (New York: Doubleday, 1994).

are heightened during puberty. However, the part of the brain responsible for making sound judgment are in the maturing stages. This may be attributed to the high rate of rule breaking, drug use, reckless risk taking, and sexual drives of adolescents. Educators and parents must recognize that many of these behaviors may be reduced, eliminated, or eradicated by employing techniques to motivate adolescents by modeling appropriate behaviors and rewarding them for making sound judgments.

With modeling and directions, the adolescent brain can be remodeled to counteract structural changes (see Appendix D). Parental involvement is crucial at this time. Some recommended strategies that parents can employ are:

1. Be assertive and involve the adolescent into low-conflict discussions where their opinions are respected, and they are given space to be self-reliant and strategies for resisting temptations

2. Adapt parenting skills as children become adolescents and their ability to reason improves. Good parenting can assist adolescents in coping with problems and making sound judgments.

3. Stay involved in the affairs of the teenagers by participating in school programs and spending time together.

4. Set systematic standards, such as study time, bed time, and structured extra curricular activities for adolescents, guiding them through decisions by using praise and reinforcement.

5. Employ the premack principle or change negative behaviors (for example: reduce drinking or the use of drugs by denying engagement or participating in some of the interest to the adolescents).

6. Assist adolescents in making up what the brain-structure lacks by practicing good parenting skills by being actively involved in affairs.

7. Adapt parental strategies based upon different situations.

8. Foster independence by providing psychological space to boast the self-image.

9. Give explanations for your decisions.[608]

In a recent Council of Exceptional Children publication[609] it was voiced that brain research is validating many good teaching practices and informs us about effective instructional practices that educators can employ and refine by providing functional and realistic practices for students. When students are provided with a variety of simulations, models, reinforcement, and enrichment, the brain builds additional neurociruits, which may improve synaptic connections and brain functioning.

Additionally, the research indicated that boys and girls process information differently. Boys tend to be right-brain dominant, more deductive, higher levels of stress, and more computer efficient. Girls tend to be left-brain dominant, inductive, and efficient senses. These differences imply that educators should provide activities for boys which stress spatial learning in math and science. Activities for girls should stress verbal skills. During middle childhood these differences become equated.

Implication of Neuro Science Research into the Curriculum

The correlation between brain research and pedagogy has not been well established. According to Wolfe and Brandt,[610] much experimentation will have to be conducted before brain research information can be taken into the classroom. However, educators have used research findings from neuroscience to infuse into the instructional program. Neuroscientific research has validated the following:

1. The brain changes physiologically as a result of experience. The environment in which a brain operates determines to a large degree the

---

[608] L. Steinberg, B. Brown, & S. M. Dornbush, *Beyond the classroom: Why school reforms have failed and what parents need to do* (New York: Simon and Schuster, 1996).

[609] Council for Exceptional Children. *Brain Research Shed New Light on Student Learning, Teaching Strategies, and Disabilities,* 10 (3), (2004), 1, 5, 7-10. Author.

[610] P. Wolfe, & R. Brandt, What do we know from brain research? *Educational Leadership,* 56 (3), (1998), 8-13.

functioning ability of that brain.[611] Appropriate development of the brain requires interaction between an individual's genetic inheritance and environmental influences.[612] Implications for educators are to provide an enriched environment to promote and stimulate intellectual growth.

2. That IQ is not fixed at birth was found by the research of Ramey & Ramey.[613] Therefore, intervention programs based on needs of impoverished children could improve intelligence. Their research findings indicated that the earlier the intervention the greater improvement in IQ was noted.

3. Some abilities are acquired more easily during certain sensitive or critical periods. Chugani[614] reported that during early years the brain over develops and has the ability to adapt and reorganize and develop some capacities at this stage more readily than in the years after puberty. If certain sensory motor functions are not stimulated at birth, the brain cells designed to interpret these functions will fail to develop and the cells controlling these functions are lost and the brain cells are diverted to other tasks during certain critical periods of brain development. During critical periods, factors such as pre-term birth,

---

[611] R. Kotulak, *Inside the Brain: Revolutionary Discoveries of How the Mind Works* (Kansas City, MO: Andrews and McMeely, 1996); W. T. Green, Experience-dependent sunaptogenesis as a plausible memory mechanism. In I. Gormezano and E. A. Wasserman (Eds.), Learning and memory: *The Behavioral Biological Substrates* (Hillsdale, NJ: Lawrence Erlbaum, 1992), pp. 209-299.

[612] M. Diamond, & J. Hopson, *Magic Trees of the Mind: How to Nurture Your Child's Intelligence, Creativity, and Healthy Emotions from Birth Through Adolescence* (New York, NY: Penguin Patnam, 1998).

[613] C. T. Ramey, & S. L. Ramey, 1996, Early interventions: Optimizing development for children with disabilities and risk conditions, in M. Wolraid (Ed.), *Disorders of development and learning: A Practical Guide to assessment and management (2nd ed.)* (Philadelphia, PA: Mosby, 1996).

[614] H. T. Chugani, *Functional Maturation of the Brain.* Paper presented at the Third Annual Brain Symposium, Berkeley, California, 1996.

maternal smoking, alcohol use, drug use in pregnancy, maternal and infant malnutrition, and post-birth lead poisoning or child abuse may make a significant impact on brain development.[615] The results pinpointed an urgent need to develop early intervention programs for at-risk parents and children that are adequately funded and managed by a competent staff.

4. Learning is strongly influenced by emotions as reported by Goleman, & LeDoux.[616] The authors summarized the importance of emotions in learning. Chemicals in the brain send negative and positive information to that part of the brain controlling the information. The information may be perceived as threatening or satisfying. If perceived as threatening, learning may be impeded; if perceived as satisfying, learning may be accelerated.

5. Attention is a prime factor in learning. Students must be exposed to strategies to promote attention. Educators should be aware of factors, which may impede or promote attention, such as diet, emotions, and hormones. Students should be taught the value of eating plenty of proteins and drinking an abundance of fluids, and limiting carbohydrates in large amounts.[617] Proteins will assist the brain in staying alert by providing the needed amino acid to produce the alertness neurotransmitters dopamine and norrepine phrine. Wurtman[618] articulated that the brain consists of about 80% water. Fluids are necessary to keep neuron connections strong. Excessive

---

[615] L. Newman, & S. L. Buka, Every *child a learner: Reducing risks of learning impairment during pregnancy and infancy* (Denver, CO: Education Commission of the States, 1997).

[616] D. Goleman, *Emotional Intelligence* (New York, NY: Banton Books, 1995); LeDoux, 1996.

[617] Jensen, 1998.

[618] J. J. Wurtman, *Managing Your Mind and Mood Through Food* (New York, NY: Perennial Library, 1986).

carbohydrates are calming. Limiting the intake of them assist in producing an alert state of the brain.

6. Semantic memory is associated with the memory of words. Sprenger[619] articulated that each learning experience should be organized to present a short chunk of information. The brain must process the information in some way after receiving the information. Specific strategies, such as graphic organizers, peer teaching, questioning strategies, summarizing, role playing, debates, outlining, time lines, practice tests, paraphrasing, and mnemonic devices may be used to assist students in building their semantic memories.

The brain can only receive data and information through the sensory perceptions. The brain categorizes non-language sensory perceptions in various sections of the brain. Lowery[620] wrote that human knowledge is stored in clusters and organized within the brain into systems that people use to interpret familiar situations and to reason about new ones. Construction in the brain depends upon such factors as interest, prior knowledge, and positive environmental influences. Learning is best facilitated through the introduction of concrete and manipulative objectives, the use of prior experiences and a gradual introduction of abstract symbols. New learning is basically a rearrangement of prior knowledge into new connections.[621] Curriculum innovation permits learners to construct their own patterns of learning through experimenting with various ideas and through the use of prior knowledge. Experimentation and practice reinforms the storage areas within the brain. If connections are not strengthened they will dissipate.[622]

[619] Sprenger, 1999.

[620] L. Lowery, How new science curriculums reflect brain research, *Educational Leadership*, 55 (3), (1999), 26-30.

[621] G. Cowley, & A. Underwood, Memory, *Newsweek*, 131 (24), (1998), 48-49, 51-54.

[622] M. Diamond., & J. Hopson, *Magic Trees of the Mind: How to Nurture Your Child's Intelligence, Creativity, and Healthy Emotions from Birth Through Adolescence* (New York, NY: Penguin Patnam, 1998).

Curriculum innovations must include strategies suited to the age range and development sequence of the learner, consider the interest, and emotional state of the individual, and determine his/her learning styles. Brain research can assist educators in understanding what promotes learning and to determine which teaching techniques, employing neuroscience research, can be integrated into the instructional program.

Brain-Based Models

Human behavior and learning are too complex to be regulated to one theory of learning. The behavioral-rational model, which principally dominates our thinking in education, is too limited. Brown & Moffett[623] remarked that this paradigm suggests that learning is neat, controllable, and programmable. It is grounded in empirical, behavioral notions of human learning, especially the idea that there is a discrete cause-effect linkage between teacher input and student output. Teaching is a one-size-fit-all process, in which students are passive recipients of information. Brain-base models are in contrast to behavioral-rational models. They support the notion that learning is open-ended, uncontrollable, greatly influenced by the learners' cognitive make-up, and dependent on the teacher's ability to assist diverse students to construct and draw meaning from learning experiences. The models recognize that learning is a complex and diverse process. The importance of emotions, feelings, relationships and human interactions combine to influence learning. The schools have failed to promote what Goleman[624] called "the emotional intelligence" of students and teachers. He summarized that emotional intelligence actually adds values to students classroom learning and teachers' professional learning. Educational change needs more depth. Brain-base models appear to provide educators with strategies to make the learner the center of the instructional process by promoting the whole child in the

---

[623] Brown & Moffett, 1999.

[624] Goleman, 1995.

learning process.   Some recommended resources that educators can use to facilitate learning may be found in Appendices E and F.

Principles of Learning Using Brain-Based Research

In promoting brain-base models, several researchers have advanced principles of learning, which educators can employ in promoting learning using brain-based research.

Principle 1.   Brown and Moffett[625] asserted that true learning comes from a fusion of head, heart, and body. The body reacts as a unified whole to promote learning; individuals are intellectually connected, emotionally engaged, and physically involved.

Principle 2.   Wheatley[626] indicated that research learning occurs in environments in which motivation is largely intrinsic rather than extrinsic. Learning cannot be confined into narrow roles. Learning activities must involve the whole child, and the integration of intellectual, emotional, and physical factors must be infused in the learning process.

Principle 3.   Innovative   schools   provide   brain   compatible   learning environments.[627] Innovative schools plan curriculum, instruction, and assessment that are integrated and stimulate the student in diverse ways of learning. They also recognize the importance of emotions in learning and develop strategies to enhance them.

Principle 4.   Innovative schools attend to the new findings in cognitive psychology and constructivist education. Brown & Moffett[628]

---

[625] Brown & Moffet,

[626] M. C. Wheatley, *Leadership and the New Science: Learning About Organization From an Orderly Universe* (San Francisco, CA: Berrett-Koehler, 1992).

[627] R. N. Caine, & G. Caine, *Making Connections: Teaching and the Human Brain* (Alexandria, VA: Association for Supervision and Curriculum Development, 1991).

[628] J. L. Brown, & C. A. Moffett, *The Hero's Journey* (Alexandria, VA: Association for Supervision and Curriculum Development, 1999).

related that innovated schools structure the learning process on the principle that knowledge is constructed, and that learning is a process of creating personal meaning from new information by relating it to prior knowledge and experience. Educators provide experiences for students to transfer information from one context to another. Transfer will not occur unless promoted by the teacher.

Principe 5. Above all, learning is strategic. Herman, Aschbacher, & Winters; Marzano[629] agreed that learning is goal directed and involves the learners assimilation of strategies associated with knowing when to use, adapt, and modify knowledge to manage one's learning process.

Principle 6. The Role of Learning Styles

The brain is a closed system; information can only enter the brain through the five senses. A multisensory experience will provide a better opportunity for attention. Different brains favor different sensory stimulation. Kinesthetic learners need more movement, auditory learners need to talk about the material, and visual learners need to see something concrete. Appropriate teaching styles will allow each of these kinds of learners to lock in on their learning.[630]

Teachers frequently find it difficult to assess an individual's learning style preference. Pupils learn through a variety of sensory channels and demonstrate individual patterns of sensory strengths and weaknesses. Educators should

---

[629] Herman, J. L., P. R. Aschbacker, & L. Winters, *A Practical Guide to Alternative Assessment* (Alexandria, VA: Association for Supervision and Curriculum Development, 1992); R. A. Marzano, *Different Kind of Classroom* (Alexandria, VA: Association for Supervision and Curriculum Development, 1992).

[630] C. P. Rose, & M. Nicholl, *Accelerated learning for the 21 century* (New York, NY: Delacourt Press, 1997).

268

capitalize on students learning styles in educating pupils. When preference or learning styles are not considered, classroom performance may be affected.[631]

Recognizing and understanding students' learning styles in the classroom is one critical factor associated with student outcomes. Indeed, in reality, it may be more important for instructors to have an understanding of the learning process and skill in facilitating individual and group learning than subject matter skill. For a brief summary of the various types of learning styles and their classroom implications refer to Taylor, 1997.

Summary

Brain research is not new. Neuroscientists have been experimenting with brain research for well over two decades. Ways of practically implementing these research findings into the classroom have been demonstrated to be effective in promoting learning. The brain is inseparable in the learning process. The more educators understand how to implement brain-based research strategies, the better they will meet the learning needs of pupils.

Brain and learning research provide educators with a mechanism for individualizing instruction for children from diverse cultural backgrounds by combining multiple intelligence, brain-based learning and learning styles, and infusing these theories with relevant cultural and sensory experiences in the curriculum. Integrating these strategies will permit educators to provide multifaceted, systematic, and environmentally rich resources for enhancing present and future academic success.[632]

It is of prime importance that educators consider and program enriched learning experiences into the curriculum which involves the personal and learning modalities of children, and permit students to demonstrate mastery through their

---

[631] S. Mason, & A. L. Egell, What does Amy like? Using a mini-reinforcer in Instructional activities, *Teaching Exceptional Children*, 28 (1995), 42-45; Taylor, 1998.

[632] F. R. Green, Brain and learning research: Implications for meeting the needs of diverse learners, *Education*, 119 (4), (1999). 682-687; Sylwester, 1993.

strongest modality. Additionally, mastery of learning may be demonstrated in individual and cooperative groups, around special topics, interests, games, dramatic play, artistic expressions, and stories. In demonstrating mastery, students should be permitted to explore, experiment, and pose questions relevant to the topic, lesson, or skill under investigation. Educators should provide an environment which promotes respect and acceptance of individual and cultural differences.

Chapter 16

Integrating Learning Styles Into The Curriculum

Introduction

The bell curve works well in establishing many normal distributions in school and society; however, it is the opinion of the authors that this statistical model does not represent the academic abilities of many minority children and should not be applied in instructing these learners. Rather the schools should be designed to plan and implement programs to promote learning based upon the development levels of the students, not upon prior developed standards. A comprehensive understanding of learning styles can assist educators in planning instructional programs for all students, including minorities, infusing information from learning styles into educating and referring them for service.

In support of the aforementioned, Griggs and Dunn's[633] research indicated that the learning styles of under-achieving students differ significantly from higher achievers. Many of the students in the low achieving group were from ethnic groups. Both groups showed increased test scores when they were taught and counseled. The authors concluded that teachers should not base their instruction solely on cultural groups but on learning styles of the children using diverse teaching strategies.

According to Griggs and Dunn,[634] students process and interpret new information in different ways. An understanding and use of learning styles will significantly enhance achievement and attitudes of children. The author summarized how children learn according to their visual, auditory, or kinesthetic

---

[633] S. Griggs, & R. Dunn, Hispanic-American students and learning style, *Emerging Librarian*, 23 (2), (1995), 11-14.

[634] Griggs & Dunn, 1995.

learning style. Additionally, there are several dimensions associated with learning styles.[635]

Children receive and order information differently and through a variety of dimensions and channels. Mason and Egell[636] implied that teachers frequently find it difficult to assess an individual's learning style preference. Making sense out of the word is a very real and active process. During early childhood, children master complex tasks according to their own schedules without formal training or intervention. The structured environment of the school appears to impede the personal learning styles of many exceptional individuals.

There is no one common definition of learning styles; however, researchers have considered learning styles from four dimensions: cognitive, affective, physiological, and psychological.

Cognitive Dimension

The cognitive dimension of learning styles refers to the different ways that children mentally perceive and order information and ideas. This process differs widely upon children, depending greatly upon the development structure of the brain and the influence of the environment situation.

Affective dimension refers to how students' personality traits--both social and emotional--affect their learning. This dimension refers to how the student feels about himself/herself and what way can be found to build his/her self-esteem. These research findings tend to indicate that learning styles are functions of both nature and nurture. Learning style development starts at a very early age.

Physiological Dimension

The physiological dimension of learning involves the interaction of the senses and the environment. There are several channels under the psychological

---

[635] G. R Taylor, *Using Human Learning Strategies in the Classroom* (Lanham, MD: Scarecrow Press, Inc., 2002).

[636] S. Mason & A. L. Egell, 1995.

dimension and they are: visual, auditory, tactile/kinesthetic, and a mixed combination of the five senses. The physiological dimension involves the senses and the environment. Does the student learn better through auditory, visual, or tactile/kinesthetic means? And how is he/she affected by such factors as light, temperature, and room design?

Evaluating Learning Styles

Pupils learn through a variety of sensory channels and have individual patterns of sensory strengths and weaknesses. Teachers should capitalize on using the learning styles of pupils in their academic programs. Exceptional individuals go through the same development sequence; however, due to developmental problems, some progress at a slower rate. Several aspects are recommended in considering factors characterizing a pupil's learning style:

1. The speed at which a pupil learns. This is an important aspect to consider. A pupil's learning rate is not as obvious as it may appear. Frequently, a learner's characteristics interfere with his/her natural learning rate. Although the learning rate is more observable than other characteristics, it does not necessarily relate to the quality of a learner's performance. Therefore, it is of prime importance for the teacher to know as much as possible about all of a learner's characteristics.

2. The techniques the pupil uses to organize materials he/she plans to learn. Individuals organize materials they expect to learn information from by remembering the broad ideas. These broad ideas trigger the details in the pupil's memory. This method of proceeding from the general to the specific is referred to as deductive style of organization. In utilizing inductive organization, the pupil may look at several items or objectives and form specific characteristics, and develop general principles or concepts. Knowing an exceptional individual's style of organization can

assist the teacher to effectively guide the learning process by presenting materials as close as possible to his/her preferred style of organization.[637]

3. The pupil's need for reinforcement and students in the learning situation. All learners need some structure and reinforcement to their learning, this process may be facilitated through a pupil's preferred channels of input and output.

4. Input involves using the five sensory channels--auditory, tactile, kinesthetic, olfactory, and gustatory. These stimuli are transmitted to the brain. In the brain, the sensory stimuli are organized into cognitive patterns referred to as perception. The input channel through which the person readily processes stimuli is referred to as his/her preferred mode of modality.

5. Similar differences are also evident in output which may be expressed verbally or non-verbally. Verbal output uses the fine motor activity of the speech mechanism to express oral language. Non-verbal output uses both fine and gross motor activities. Fine motor skills may include gesture and demonstration. Pupils usually prefer to express themselves through one of these outputs.

6. A pupil's preferred model of input is not necessarily his/her strongest acuity channel. Sometimes a pupil will transfer information received through one channel into another which he/she is more comfortable. This process is called internodal transfer. Failure to perform this task effectively may impede learning.

The differences in learning styles and patterns of some pupils almost assures rewarding educational achievement for successful completion of tasks. This is, unfortunately, not true for many exceptional individuals. The differences reflected in learning can cause interferences with the exceptional individual's

---

[637] Mason & Egell, 1995.

achievement. The educational environment of exceptional individuals is a critical factor. The early identification, assessment, and management of exceptional individual's learning differences by the teacher can prevent more serious learning problems from occurring.

Children display diverse skills in learning. This necessitates proven knowledge as well as sound theories for teaching. Some educators who are interested in the development of children often lack the necessary understanding of how children learn, what they are interested in, and how to put these two together. Due to wide individual differences among exceptional individuals, instructional techniques must vary. Individuals with exceptionalities need special attention; their teachers need special orientation to meet their special needs. The teacher must know what can be expected of them, and they try to adapt the activities to their capabilities.

It has been voiced that no activity provides a greater variety of opportunities for learning than creative dramatics. Children are given a rationale for creative dramatics with specific objectives and values, exercises in pantomime, improvisation, play structure, and procedures involved in preparing a play. Creative dramatics and play are not meant to be modes of learning styles, but rather, as more is discovered about learning and in particular the variety of ways certain exceptional individuals learn, they add immeasurable knowledge to the development of a theoretical construct for various types of learning styles. Equally important, these techniques may lead to the discovery of different learning styles at various developmental levels.[638]

In spite of the paucity of research studies in the area of learning styles, it is generally recognized that individuals learn through a variety of sensory channels and have individual patterns of sensory strengths and weaknesses. It then becomes tantamount to discover techniques for assessing the individual's sensory

---

[638] Taylor, 1998.

strengths and weaknesses, and to identify ways that materials can be presented to capitalize on sensory strengths and/or weaknesses. This does not mean that materials should be presented to the pupil via his/her preferred style, but it would mean that credit would be given for his/her strength (e.g., hearing) while he/she works to overcome his/her weakness (e.g., vision). Basic to the concept of learning styles is the recognition to initiate and sustain the learning process. Some exceptional individuals seem to have adequate sensory acuity, but are unable to utilize their sensory channels effectively.

A major concern of all education is to assist individuals in realizing their full learning potentialities. Educational services should be designed to take into account individual learning behavior and style. To be able to accomplish this task, it will be required that we know something about the pupil as a learner. The Maryland State Department of Education's Division of Instructional Television[639] has listed several ways to characterize a pupil's learning style: (1) the speed at which a pupil learns, (2) the techniques the pupil uses to organize materials he/she hopes to learn, (3) the pupil's need for reinforcement and structure in the learning situation, (4) the channels of input through which the pupil's mind proceeds, and (5) the channels of output through which the pupil best shows us how much he/she has learned.

The speed at which a pupil learns is important for individualizing instruction. Observations of the learner's characteristics will facilitate planning for his/her individual needs. A keen observer should be cognizant of the various ways an individual organizes materials. Some children learn best by proceeding from general to specific details, others from specific to general details. Knowing a pupil's style of organization can assist the teacher in individualizing his/her instruction. All learners need some structure and reinforcement in their learning. Pupils who have had successful experiences tend to repeat them. Proceeding

---

[639] Maryland State Department of Education, *Teaching Children With Special Needs* (Baltimore, MD: Division of Instructional Television, 1973).

from simple to complex, or from known to unknown principles provides opportunities for successful experiences for children.

The senses provide the only contact that any individual has with his/her environment. Sensory stimulations are received through the five sensory channels: auditory, visual, tactile, olfactory, and gustatory. These stimuli are organized into cognitive patterns called perceptions. Chapter 9 addressed cognitive patterns at length. The input channel through which the person readily processes stimuli is referred to as his/her preferred modality. The one through which he/she processes stimuli less readily is the weaker modality. Similar differences are also apparent in output which may be expressed verbally or non-verbally. Individuals usually prefer to express themselves through one of these channels.

A pupil's preferred mode of input is not necessarily related to his/her strongest acuity channel. Individuals with impaired vision may still process the vision stimuli they receive more efficiently than they do auditory stimuli. Sometimes a pupil will transfer information received through one channel into another with which he/she is more comfortable. This process is called intermodal transfer. An example of intermodal transfer might be the pupil who whispers each word as he/she reads it. The pupil is attempting to convert the visual stimuli (the printed word) into auditory stimuli (the whispering). Pupils differ in their ability to perform the intermodal transfer. For many exceptional individuals, failure to perform the intermodal transfer may hamper learning.

Many exceptional individuals might be using their preferred channels of input, which could be their weakest modality. Therefore, it is essential that the pupil's preferred mode of input and output be assessed. A variety of formal and informal techniques may be employed. Differentiation of instructional techniques based on assessment will improve the pupil's efficiency as a learner.

The following Tables (1, 2, and 3) have been prepared to provide some possible behaviors, assessment techniques, and instructional procedures to assist the teacher working with exceptional individuals. These tables describe three basic modalities: auditory, visual, and tactile kinesthetic. The olfactory and the gustatory modalities are not included in the tables because they constitute detailed medical and psychological insight that are outside the realm of education. Specific behaviors that are characteristic for auditory, visual, and tactile kinesthetic modalities are given, with suggestions.

Table 1

The Auditory Modality

Possible Behaviors Pupil who is strong auditorily may:		Possible Techniques The teacher may utilize these:		
SHOW THE FOLLOWING STRENGTHS	SHOW THE FOLLOWING WEAKNESS	FORMAL ASSSESSMENT TECHNIQUES	INFORMAL ASSESSMENT TECHNIQUES	INSTRUCTIONAL TECHNIQUES
Follow oral instructions very easily.	Lose place in activities.	Present statement verbally; ask pupil to repeat.	Overall pupil reading with the use of finger or pencil as a marker.	Reading: Stress phonetic analysis; avoid emphasis on sight vocabulary or fast reading. Allow pupils to use markers, fingers, etc., to keep their place.
Do well in tasks sequencing phonetic analysis. Appear brighter than tests show him/her to be.	Read word by word. Reverse words when reading. Make visual discrimination errors.	Tap auditory pattern beyond pupil's point vision. Ask pupil to repeat pattern.	Observe whether pupil whispers or barely produces sounds to correspond to his/her reading task.	Arithmetic: Provide audiotapes of story problems. Verbally explain arithmetic process as well as demonstrate.
Sequence speech sounds with facility.		Provide pupil with several words in a rhyming family. Ask pupil to add more words.	Observe pupil who has difficulty following purely visual directions.	
Perform well verbally.	Have difficulty with written work poor motor skill.	Present pupil with sounds produced out of his/her field of vision. Ask him/her if they are the same or different.		Generally: Utilize work sheets with large unhampered areas. Use lined wide-spaced paper. Allow for verbal rather than written responses.

Table 2

The Visual Modality

Possible Behaviors Pupil who is strong visually may:		Possible Techniques The teacher may utilize these:		
SHOW THE FOLLOWING STRENGTHS	SHOW THE FOLLOWING WEAKNESS	FORMAL ASSSESSMENT TECHNIQUES	INFORMAL ASSESSMENT TECHNIQUES	INSTRUCTIONAL TECHNIQUES
Possess good sight vocabulary.	Have difficulty with oral directions.	Give lists of words that sound alike. Ask pupil to indicate if they are the same or different.	Observer in tasks requiring sound discrimination, i.e., rhyming, sound blending.	Reading: Avoid phonetic emphasis, stress sight vocabulary; configuration, clues, context clues.
Demonstrate rapid reading skills.	Ask, "what are we suppose to do "immediately after oral instructions are given.	Ask pupil to follow specific instructions. Begin with one direction and continue with multiple instructions.	Observe pupil's sight vocabulary skills. Pupil should exhibit good sight vocabulary skills.	Arithmetic: Show examples of arithmetic function.
Skim reading materials. Read well from picture clues.	Appear confused with great deal of auditory stimuli.			Spelling: Avoid phonetic analysis; stress structural clues; configuration.
Follow visual diagrams and other visual instructions well. Score well on group tests.	Have difficulty discriminating between words with similar sounds.	Show pupil visually similar pictures. Ask him/her to indicate whether they are the same or different.	Observe to determine if the pupil performs better when he/she can see the stimulus.	Generally: Allow a pupil with strong auditory skills to act as another child's partner. Allow written rather than verbal responses.
Perform nonverbal tasks well. Identify and match objects easily.				

Table 3

The Tactile Kinesthetic Modality

Possible Behaviors Pupil who is strong tactile kinesthetically may:		Possible Techniques The teacher may utilize these:		
SHOW THE FOLLOWING STRENGTHS	SHOW THE FOLLOWING WEAKNESS	FORMAL ASSSESSMENT TECHNIQUES	INFORMAL ASSESSMENT TECHNIQUES	INSTRUCTIONAL TECHNIQUES
Exhibit good fine and gross motor balance.	Depends on the "guiding" modality or preferred modality since tactile kinesthetic is usually a secondary modality. Weaknesses may be in either the visual or auditory mode.	Ask pupil to walk balance bean or along a painted line. Set up obstacle course involving gross motor manipulation	Observe pupil in athletic tasks. Observe pupil in classroom space. Observe pupil's spacing of written work on a paper.	Reading: Stress the shape and structure of a word; use configuration clues, sandpaper letters; have pupil trace the letters and /or words. Arithmetic: Utilize objects in performing the arithmetic functions; provide buttons, packages of sticks, etc.
Exhibit good rhythmic movement. Demonstrate neat handwriting skills. Manipulate puzzles and other materials well. Identify and match objects easily.		Have pupil cut along straight, angled, and curved lines. Ask child to color find areas.	Observe pupil's selection of activities during free play, i.e., does he/she select puzzles or blocks as opposed to records or picture books.	Spelling: Have a pupil write the word in large movements, i.e., air, on newsprint, utilize manipulative letters to spell the word. Call pupils attention to the feel of the word in cursive to get feel of the whole word by following motion.

Note: Tables 1, 2, and 3 reprinted with permission of the Maryland State
Department of Education, Division of Instructional Television

The Relationship of Culture to Learning Style

Individuals from certain cultures have a preference for specific learning styles and this preference may effect classroom performance. Schools must also recognize that exceptional students from diverse backgrounds have a favored learning style which may affect academic performance. When teachers fail to accommodate students' favored learning style in their instructional delivery, they may not meet their individual's needs.[640]

Hilliard's[641] point of view supported the above analysis. He indicated that the lack of matching cultural and learning styles in teaching younger students is the explanation for low performance of culturally different minority group students. He contended that children, no matter what their styles, are failing primarily because of systematic inequities in the delivery of whatever pedagogical approach the teachers claim to master--not because students cannot learn from teachers whose styles do not match their own.

Guild[642] provided us with three cautions to observe when attempting to match learning styles with cultural styles:

1. Do students of the same culture have common learning styles? If so, how do we know? What are the implications for the instructional intervention and individual student learning? Care should be taken when matching learning and cultural styles; not to make generalizations about a particular group based upon culture and learning styles. An example would be to conclude that most exceptional individuals have the same traits as the targeted group.

---

[640] P. Guild, The cultural learning style connection, *Educational Leadership*, 51 (1994), 16-21.

[641] A. G. Hilliard, Teachers and cultural styles in a pluralistic society, *NEA Today*, 7:6: (1989), 65-69.

[642] Guild, 1994.

2. Caution should be taken in attempting to explain the achievement differences between exceptional individuals and their peers: this being especially true when academic differences are used to explain deficits.

3. There is some controversy between the relationship of learning and cultural styles due chiefly to philosophical beliefs and issues. Issues and philosophical beliefs, such as instructional equity versus educational equity and the major purpose of education, all combine to confuse the controversy. The relationship between the learning style and culture may prove to be divisive, especially as it relates to students in elementary and secondary schools. It may result in generalizations about culture and style and result in discrimination in treatment. It may be used as an excuse for student failure. There is also an implication that some styles are more valuable than others, even though learning styles can be neutral. If properly used, matching learning and cultural styles can be an effective tool for improving learning of exceptional individuals.

Visual Learning Style

Many children learn best when they can see information. High scores in this area denotes that they prefer textbooks over lectures and rely on lists, graphs, charts, pictures, notes, and taking notes. Significantly, a higher number of children rate this area higher than the auditory channel.

Haptic Learning Style

This is the high learning channel reported by children. In essence, most children prefer this style. Haptic students show a cluster of right-brained characteristics. They learn best from experimenting rather than from reading textbooks.

The combined scores in the three areas usually range from 10 to 30. Usually two areas will be close. Scores in the high 20s indicate that the student has satisfactorily developed all three channels and is able to use the modality that best fits the task. Scores below 20 indicate that the student has not yet developed a strong learning channel preference.

Usually students scoring in the 20s have great difficulty with school assignments because they do not have a clearly defined method for processing information. These students should be treated as haptic learners because the haptic style is much easier to develop than the others.

According to O'Brien,[643] the checklist will indicate areas of strengths and weaknesses in sensory acuity. Teachers can then adapt or modify their instructional program to include activities to support the strongest modality. Information from the checklist should be shared with the student. O'Brien[644] stated that, "All students benefit from knowing their learning styles, as well as how to use and manipulate them in the learning process."

Another well-known instrument for assessing learning styles is the Myers-Briggs Type Indicator. Learning styles are assessed from basic perceptual and judging traits. The Swassing-Barbe Modality Index assess auditory, visual, and tactile acuity by testing individuals in cognitive strengths, such as holistic and global learning in contrast to analytical, part, and the whole approach.[645]

These tests are culture and language specific. Individuals respond and interpret self-reporting instruments through their cultural experiences. The responses may be in conflict with established norms and yield conflicting results. Consequently, caution is needed when interpreting results, especially from exceptional individuals.

It appears to be psychologically sound that individuals should be introduced to new tasks through their strongest input channels and review tasks presented to the weak channels. The concept of learning styles holds great

---

[643] L. O'Brien, Learning styles: Make the student aware, *NASSP Bulletin* (October 1989), 85-89.

[644] O'Brien, 1989.

[645] Guild, 1994.

promises for facilitating the achievement of individuals. As further investigations are conducted in relationship to specific exceptional individuals, more will be discovered about sensory acuity and the inability of some individuals to use their sense modalities effectively. Some children are concrete learners, while others are abstract learners; others focus on global aspects of the problem, while others focus on specific points. Since schools traditionally give more weight to analytical approaches than to holistic approaches, the teacher who does not manifest analytical habits is at a decided disadvantage.[646]

Assessment Instruments

In assessment, the pupils preferred mode of input and output may be conducted through formal and informal techniques. A commonly used instrument is " The Learning Channel Preference Checklist." This checklist is divided into three major sections as outlined.

The Learning Channel Preference Checklist

The learning channel preference checklist is designed for assessing learning styles. Teachers can administer this checklist and follow up with interpretive discussions. Some modification and adaptation will be needed for exceptional individuals depending upon their disabilities.

Students are asked to rank each statement as it relates to them. There are no right or wrong answers. Students rate each item often (3), sometimes (2), and never (1), on three broad categories: visual, auditory, and haptic. The highest score indicates the preferred learning style in the aforementioned categories.

Auditory Learning Style

This is the least developed learning channel for most children, including exceptional individuals. Most children do not report this channel as their strongest, using the checklist.

---

[646] Hilliard, 1989.

The Relationship Between Learning and Instructional Styles

There is more indication that teachers choose instructional styles closely approximating their learning preferences. The key to the learning/instructional style theory is that students will learn more effectively through the use of their preference in learning styles.[647]

The matching of instructional style and learning style may also have implications for student achievement. The best way for schools to adapt to individual differences is to increase their effort by differentiated instructional techniques.[648] According to Hilliard,[649] learning styles and instructional styles matching may not be the only factor in student achievement. The reason younger students do not learn may not be because students cannot learn from their instructors with styles that do not match their learning styles. Additionally, he articulated there is not sufficient research or models to relate specific pedagogy to learning styles. Hilliard concluded by stating that a better perspective may be for teachers to provide sensitivity to learning styles in the instructional programs until appropriate instructional models are developed. A recommended model is proposed below.

A Proposed Model

The New Model lead to questions about how to motivate children for life long learning, how to improve self-esteem and discipline, how to awaken curiosity, and how not to be afraid to fail.[650] The new Model include (1) an example on context and learning how to learn, ask questions, how to pay attention to the right things, how to open and evaluate new concepts, and how to achieve access to information; (2) learning as a "process," a journey (both prior and new

---

[647] Hilliard, 1989.

[648] Guild, 1994.

[649] Hilliard, 1989.

[650] Taylor, 1994.

learning are legitimate); (3) an equalitarian structure where candor and dissent are permitted and autonomy is encouraged; (4) a relatively flexible structure with a belief that there are many ways to teach a given subject (e.g., classroom, workshops, field-based, independent learning); (5) a focus on self-image as the generator of performance; (6) inner experience is seen as a context for learning and exploration of feelings is encouraged; (7) guessing and divergent thinking are encouraged as a part of the creative proves; (8) a striving for whole-brain education, which augments and fuses rationality with holistic, nonlinear, and intuitive strategies; (9) labeling is used only in a minor prescriptive role and not as a fixed evaluation of the other; (10) a concern with the individual's performance in terms of potential and an interest in testing outer limits and transcending perceived limitations; (11) theoretical and abstract knowledge is heavily complemented by experiments and experiences, both in and out of classrooms (e.g., field trips, apprenticeships, demonstrations, visiting experts; (12) classrooms are designed with a concern for the environment of learning, varied and multi-leveled for the urban adult learner; (13) the encouragement of community input and even community control; (14) education is seen as a life-long process that may only be tangentially related to traditional educational settings; (15) the use of appropriate technology, with human relationships between teachers and learners being of primary importance; and (16) an environment where the teacher is also a learner who learns from students.

The New Model of learning implies a shift in consciousness, a new way of viewing the world and of carrying out education in that world. This new view or new consciousness seeks to transcend limits and unleash new creative energy for innovative activities intended to bring about constructive individual change and empowerments, as well as social change and community empowerment.[651]

---

[651] C. Ferguson, & J. Kamara, *Innovative approaches to education and community service: Model and Strategies for Change and Empowerment* (Boston, MA: University of Massachusetts, 1993).

These strategies appear to be more in tune with the learning and cultural styles of minority students. These strategies can be adapted and modified to meet the educational needs by implementing the following:

1. Develop or extend programs that emphasize a positive value through tutoring, mentoring, field experiences to city events, and involving parents.

2. Expand after school reading, math and language programs and establish prescriptive reading tabs at low performing schools

3. Develop collaborative mentoring programs to improve behavior, attendance, and conflict resolution in the schools in relationship with institutions of higher education and other community agencies. These programs may be held after school and on Saturdays.

4. Experiment with alternative approaches in teaching.

Implications For Education

By keying teaching and assessment techniques to the diverse ways people think and learn, teachers will be surprised at how much smarter their students get. Traditionally, teachers teach and assess students in ways that benefit those with certain learning styles, but place many other children at a marked disadvantage.

Exceptional individuals, as well as all individuals, favor a preferred style; however, they vary their styles, depending upon the situation. Teachers should be flexible in their teaching and use a variety of styles to assure all students' needs are met. Teachers are generally best at instructing children who match their own style of learning. Consequently, the more students differ from the cultural, socioeconomic, or ethical values of the teacher, the more likely the learning needs will not be met. Studies have shown that students receive higher grades and more favorable evaluations when their learning styles more closely match those of their teachers. Most students begin to experience success when they are permitted to pursue an interest in their preferred learning style. Educators should integrate and infuse available physical and human resources in the community by using a multisensory approach in their instructions

Summary

The preponderance of research on cultural and learning styles of all children has demonstrated the value of matching these two styles in order to facilitate the learning process. There is widespread belief that this matching can facilitate classroom instruction and provide all children, including exceptional individuals, with the skills necessary to succeed in learning, and when applied to educating them. However, there is little disagreement in professional literature concerning the relationships between learning and cultural styles and their impact on academic and social success in school.

Research conducted over the last decade has revealed certain learning patterns characteristic of certain exceptional and diverse groups.[652] Some cultural groups emphasize unique patterns and relationships. The implications for instructional intervention for these individuals should be self evident.

As indicated earlier, there is no universal agreement relevant to the application of cultural and learning styles to instruction. Some advocate that the application of cultural and learning styles to the instructional process will enable educators to be more sensitive toward cultural differences. Others maintain that to pinpoint cultural values will lead to stereotyping.[653] Another controversy revolves around cultural values. Other studies have shown that by significantly

---

[652] Hilliard, 1989; B. J. Shade, The influence of perceptual development on cognitive styles: Cross ethnic comparison, Early *Childhood Development and Care*, 51, (1989), 137-155; J. A. Vasques, *Cognitive style and academic achievement in cultural diversity and the schools: Consensus and controversy*, edited by J. Lynch, C. Modgil, and S. Modgil (London: Falconer Press, 1991); C. R. Bert, & M. Bert, *The Native American: An exceptionality in Education and Counseling*, ERIC, 351168, 1992; J. Hyum, & S. A., Fowler, Respect, cultural sensitivity, and communication, *Teaching Exceptional Children*, 28(1), 25-28.

[653] Guild, 1994.

increasing achievement, inequities in the delivery and instructional procedures are improved.[654]

A third controversy centers around how teachers operating from their own cultural and learning styles can successfully teach diverse and exceptional populations. Most of the research shows that the day-to-day rapport, caring teachers who provide opportunities for children to learn, are more valuable than matching teaching and learning styles.[655]

The major issue at hand in this controversy is not whether learning and cultural styles should be incorporated in the instructional plan for exceptional individuals, but whether using cultural and learning styles information will assist teachers in recognizing diversity and improve delivery of educational services for them.

---

[654] Hilliard, 1989; C. Bennett, Assessing teacher's abilities for educating multicultural students: The need for conceptual models in teacher education, in C. Heid (Ed.), *Multicultural education: Knowledge and perceptions* (Indianapolis, IN: University Center for Urban Education, 1988); C. Bennett, *Comprehensive Multicultural Education: Theory and practice* (Boston, MA: Allyn and Bacon, 1986).

[655] Taylor, 1992; Guild, 1994.

Chapter 17

A Proposed Model For Closing The Achievement Gap

Educational achievements of minority individuals have shown a steady decline in this country. Most of the decline has taking place in urban communities where an influx of minority individual resides. There are multiple reasons why these individuals are not achieving up to expected standards. Reasons for this lack of achievement may be attributed to the following that schools must face on a daily and regular basis: (1) political, (2) economic, (3) social, (4) technology, and (5) teacher preparation.[656]

Political

Politically, many diverse communities are deeply divided on policies involving the administration and structure of public schools. Legislatures associated with school improvement can unite the various diverse groups in the community by exerting control on funding and resources to support the schools and agencies associated with them, and collaboration between and among agencies serving the schools. Public officials' interventions are needed in setting up early intervention programs in order to offset some of the deprivations contributing to the achievement gap.[657] Political issues may incorporate principles from all of the learning theories in assessing and developing political views concerning governing the schools.

---

[656] F. M. Newmann, Beyond common sense in educational restructuring. The issue of content and linkage, Educational *Research, 22* (2), 4-22; Urban Education Project, The *Urban Learner Framework: An Overview* (Philadelphia, PA: Research for Better School, 1994); W. *A.* Williams, *Closing the Achievement Gap: A Vision for Changing Beliefs and Practices* (Alexandria, VA: Association for Supervision and Curriculum Development, 1996); Taylor, 2003.

[657] G. R. Taylor, *Parenting Skills and Collaborative Service for Students with Disabilities* (Lanham, MD: Scarecrow Press, 2004).

Economic

There have been major shifts in economical activity in the country during the last 19th and 21st centuries from industrial type employment to service type activities. As a result, many of the service type jobs were relocated into the suburbs due chiefly to the social and economical conditions in the cities, which resulted in massive exits from the central cities. This loss of tax base was chiefly related to decay in public schools within the cities and resulted in increasing the achievement gap.[658]

Schools serving minority individuals have traditionally been underfunded. The tax base has been significantly reduced due to the rate of exodus of taxpayers from the central cities. Median family income decreased as middle-income taxpayers left the central cities. This exodus left central cities with insufficient funds to operate the schools. Local, state, and federal agencies must contribute additional funds to make the schools safe, to provide additional resources, to advance technology, and to employ competent staff. It is the democratic right of all learners, including minorities, to be educated in safe schools, with adequate funding, and competent personnel. Economic conditions must be improved in central cities if the achievement gap is to be decreased. Integration of the three learning theories identified in the previous chapters will have relevance for addressing the economic issues confronted by the schools.

Social

Cultural and social values of minority learners may differ significantly from learners in the mainstream, because of a lack of cultural identity. Children's socioeconomic status should have no affect on how teachers judge their abilities to learn. Teachers who classify children into social class membership tend to show their prejudice toward selected groups of children. One

---

[658] G. R. Taylor, *Practical Applications of Social Learning Theories in Education for African-American Males* (Lanham, MD: University Press of America, 2003).

major condition for enhancing self-esteem in the classroom is the teacher's acceptance of the child. By accepting the child, the teacher indicates to the child that he/she is worthy of his/her attention and respect.

Another condition that promotes self-esteem is the presence of explicit limits in the classroom that are articulated early and are consistently enforced. Such limits should involve input from the children. They should participate in defining acceptable behavior, provide standards of conduct, and establish behavior expectations in the classroom and school. Standards and regulations are necessary for children to develop positive self-esteem because they set limits and expectations.[659]

Educators can abstract from theories of conditioning and social learning ways to improve negative behavior, or to promote positive behavior using rewards, reinforcement, modeling limitation, and observation are major principles in these theories. Techniques in these theories can be readily adaptive or modified to change behaviors in the classroom. Demonstration of appropriate behaviors can aid in closing the achievement gap by reducing inappropriate behavior. Refer to previous chapters for specific strategies to improve the social and cultural values of schools.

Meeting Standards

Standards for achievement are reflected in the core curriculum. Many minority and deprived learners cannot meet the expected standards due to test items not being correlated with the curriculum, test items did not reflect cultural values of the learners, or there was not enough instructional time for learners to master the content, there was insufficient time spent teaching critical thinking skills, and there was poor quality of instruction. In order to determine learners' strengths and weaknesses, valid and reliable assessment information is needed. Assessment should drive the instructional program. To achieve this end it must be valid and reliable.

---

[659] Taylor, 2004.

Assessment is a key component in education reforms. Achievement and the progress of children are judged based upon a set of local, state, or professional standards. A student's performance is measured in relationship to how well they meet standards. It was assumed that assessment provided sufficient data on how well students were performing in school. Recent data suggest that assessment has not provided sufficient information on what students know and can do relative to standards. To accurately determine strengths and weaknesses of students' multiple assessments, other than standardized tests, should be used, such as teacher made tests, criterion reference tests, and other informal tests to determine the achievement gap.[660] Principles from all of the learning theories discussed in Parts the previous chapters are recommended to develop effective assessment tools to evaluate the progress of children.

Teacher Preparation

Teacher preparation is an important factor in closing the achievement gap. Teachers must be specifically trained to teach minority and deprived learners to achieve stated standards. Teacher training programs in instructions of higher learning and in-service programs must alter their approach in educating teachers in instructing minority and deprived learners.[661]

Recommended strategies based on the above research include:

1. Teachers must be trained to assume responsibility for students' achievement. A first step would be to set high expectations for all students.

---

[660] G. R. Taylor, T. Phillips, & D. Joseph, *Assessment Strategies for Students with Disabilities* (Lewiston, NY: The Edwin Mellen Press, 2002).

[661] Taylor, 1997; 2003; E. Garcia, Language, culture, and education, in *Review of Research Education*, 19 (1993); C. Monteceinois, Multucultural teacher education for a culturally diverse teaching force, R. Marth (Ed.) In *Practicing What We Preach: Confronting Diversity in Teacher Education* (Albany, NY: Suny Press, 1995); B. Weiner, *Theories of Motivation: From Mechanisms to Cognition* (Chicago: Markham, 1972); K. Zeichner, & S. Melnick, *The Role of Community Field Experiences in Preparing Teachers for Cultural Diversity*. Paper presented at the Annual Meeting of the American Association of Colleges of Teacher Education (Chicago, IL: 1995).

2. Demonstrate to students that their contributions are valued and that they can achieve.

3. Consider diversity, languages, and cultures as strengths and infuse them within the instructional program.

4. Relate school experiences to home and community.

5. Become aware of one's cultural bias and develop techniques for objectively correcting them.

6. Provide information on how knowledge of learning styles can be employed in the classroom to minimize the achievement gap.

7. Demonstrate and model teaching strategies such as reciprocal teaching, conceptual learning, critical thinking, and problem solving. (Refer to chapters 11-14 for additional information).

8. Provide additional emphasis on community and parental involvement and classroom management techniques.

9. Implement an objective system of interviewing for admitting only those prospective learners who show a commitment for raising the academic level of all learners.

10. Provide prospective teacher observation and field experiences in diverse communities.

11. Establish consortiums for prospective teachers in multicultural education as part of the degree requirements.

12. Provide assistance for teachers to become highly qualified and certified.

13. Provide opportunities for teachers to observe excellent teaching during their practicum and student teaching experiences.

All of the learning theories summarized in the previous chapters can be incorporated in preparing teachers to instruct minority individuals in the content areas to develop knowledge bases needed to increase achievement.

296

Collaboration

Taylor[662] remarked that schools cannot effectively educate students without collaborating with parents and the community on a continuous basis. Effective collaborative strategies may include problem solving groups, discussion groups, and conferences. Participation and collaboration are impeded if educators do not view parents and community as competent. Research findings have shown that parental and community attitudes are difficult to accept by the school. Educators must find creative ways to assist some parents in changing their negative ways.[663] A collaborated effort must be made by local, state, and federal agencies to assist school systems in decreasing the achievement gap. The schools cannot bring significant improvement in closing the achievement gap unless there is strong professional and community support, with interagency collaboration.

Local Intervention

Collaboration and participation at local school districts may be improved if: (1) teachers accept and acknowledge parents' knowledge of their children's strengths and weaknesses; (2) provide a structure for parents and communities to express themselves, (3) provide opportunities for parents' participation with their children; (4) teaching parents about their rights under IDEA; (5) develop strategies for making parents welcome in the school, and (6) show empathy, not sympathy, to parents. These are a few strategies teachers can use.

---

[662] Taylor, 2004.

[663] L. Bank, J. H. Marlowe, J. B. Reid, G. R. Patterson, & M. R. Weinrott, A comparative evaluation of parent-training intervention for families of chronic delinquents, *Journal of Abnormal Child Psychology*, 19, (1991), 15-33.

State Intervention

State intervention is designed to set standards for collaboration to local school districts, to report on progress of schools in the state, and to provide assistance to schools that are not achieving standards. The state also develops and monitors policies, enforces federal regulations associated with collaboration, and regulates assessment strategies in local school districts. School buildings and construction are maintained by the state, as well as financial support to the districts.

Federal Intervention

One of the most effective federal programs is the Chapter I Program. The federal government has contributed billions of dollars to school systems to pay for individual services in the basic skills areas. These funds have had some impact on closing the gap; however; the impact has not significantly reduced the gap.[664] Collaboration on all fronts is needed to decrease the achievement gap. Each learning theory has specific principles to improve collaboration.

A Model for Closing The Achievement Gap

The achievement gap in school districts serving a large number of minority individuals is increasing. Factors and conditions responsible have been identified throughout the text. Data presented have shown that the achievement gap can be closed if school districts adhere to the following strategies:

1. Employ certified and qualified teachers.
2. Raise the tolerance levels of teachers.
3. Have teachers to set realistic expectations for students.
4. Increase parental and community involvement.
5. Equip the schools with state-of-art technology.
6. Choose unbiased tests to measure achievement.
7. Hold student to articulated standards.

---

[664] Commission on Chapter I. *Making Schools Work for Children in Poverty* (Washington, DC: American Association for Higher Education, 1992).

8. Use learning principles from each learning theory. [665]

The listed strategies cannot be successfully achieved in closing the achievement gap unless some objective system is developed for school systems to use. The proposed system involves using principles for learning theories to close the gap. The learning theories believed to be associated with classroom learning have been summarized in previous chapters.

Conditioning Theories

In summary, principles under conditioning theory may aid in closing the achievement gap by rewarding and reinforcing learners for high achievement and performance, evaluating and shaping behaviors, conditioning learners, motivating drill and practice, and reducing negative behavior. These theories indicate that processes governing behaviors are learned. Both the drives that initiate behavior and the specific behavior motivated by these drivers are learned through interactions with the environment. Conditioning and behaviorism have made significant impact upon learning and computer technology. When students are rewarded for learning, their achievement and learning increase.

Social Learning Theories

The role of social learning theories may assist in closing the achievement gap by having students to practice and demonstrate good modeling, observing and initiating appropriate social behavior, self-efficacy, social skills, and self-regulation. Social learning theories offer the school a common context through which environment, developmental sequence, and early experiences of individuals' development can be understood. These theories enable educators to better understand how individuals think, how they feel about themselves, and how to become aware of factors in the environment that may have some bearing on academic performance. There is a significant relationship between social skills interventions and academic achievement. Many social skill procedures, such as

---

[665] Taylor, 2004.

attending and positive interaction techniques, have been shown to increase academic performance.

Cognitive Theories

Cognitive learning has led to improving our understanding of the social nature of learning, the importance of context on understanding, the need for domain-specific knowledge in higher-order thinking, expert-novice differences in thinking and problem solving, and the belief that learners can be instructed to construct their own understanding of a topic. Variables such as drive, habits, and strengths have critical roles in learning. Learning is developmental and children must master each task before mastering advanced tasks. Learning is facilitated by the child's acquisition of new skills and experiences. How children interpret and receive information can accelerate or impede learning. Identifying and assessing learning styles are important in evaluating achievement.

Summary

Yancey and Saporito[666] articulated that the combined effects of concentrated poverty, cultural diversity, and isolation of deprived neighborhoods by race, ethnicity and socioeconomic status combine to widen the achievement gap. Educators must explore individualized approaches to educate learners. One teaching approach for all learners has proven ineffective. Achievement of all learners can be increased if cultural values are infused within the curriculum and expectations for learners are raised. Individuals tend to achieve at expected levels. Research findings have clearly shown that the achievement gap can be successfully closed if innovative and functional practices are used to assist minority learners to overcome the negative affects of their environments. The use of learning theories holds the promise for closing the achievement gap.[667] Much

---

[666] W. Yancey, & S. Saporito, *Urban Schools and Neighborhoods: A Handbook for Building an Ecological Database* (Philadelphia, PA: 1994).

[667] Taylor, 2004.

of the negative overtones can be reduced by involving learners in activities that appeal to their interests and real-life encounters, in assisting learners in recognizing the association of parts in formulating wholes.

Chapter 18

Some Concluding Remarks

The psychology of human learning and behavior is basically concerned with how learners learn under different situations. We clarified this concept in chapter 1 by indicating that learning is a change in performance through conditions of activity, practice, and experience. Many factors affect the learning process such as physical disability, biochemical factors, habits, attitudes, interests, social and emotional adjustments are to name but a few. Frequently, these factors must be modified in order to improve learning. Learning is a life long process and the permanent affects of it may not be immediately apparent, sometimes the affects of learning are latent. Many psychologists have contributed to the study of learning since the later part of the nineteenth century. Wundt is considered by many to be the father of psychology. Other psychologists such as Pavlov, Thorndike, Watson, Tolman, Skinner, and Bandura made their impact on the field of learning theory during this time frame. The major impact of their works is addressed in chapters 3, 4, and 5.

Contrasting Views in Learning Theory

The two major views of learning are expressed by behavioristic and cognitive psychologists. Views expressed by these psychologists are diametrically opposite to each other. According to behavioristic psychologists, learning theory is based upon observable behaviors reinforced with rewards. In their views, the mind has limited applications in human behavior and learning. Behaviorists believe that their principles can be applied to all organisms. Cognitive psychologists refer to these views of learning chiefly among them are Tolman, Piaget, Vygotsky, and Gestalt Psychology, an overview of these theorists may be found in chapter 11. According to their theory learning is too complex to

302

be regulated to stimuli responses behavior. They advocated that human behavior involves processes such as problem solving, decision-making, perceptions, information processing, attitudes, emotions, judgment, memory and motivation. Cognitive models emphasis these unobservable mental processes as assessing how individuals learn. [668]

Both of the major theories of learning support the role of memory and motivation in learning. However, cognitive models tend to emphasize these traits more than behavioral models. Behavioral models tend to limit memory in learning. On the other hand cognitive models tend to minimize the notion that students learn only because they are rewarded, reinforced or punished. Memory models reflex the cognitive view of learning more than the behaviorist models. Both major theories have strategies that educators may employ. (Refer to chapters 2, 4, 9, 11, 12, 13, and 14)

The major two learning theories remained separate until the mid-twentieth century. It was the work of Bandura[669] that combined the two theories. He integrated the models by combining environmental and cognitive factors in studying human behavior through observation and modeling techniques. (Refer to chapter 5 for details on Bandura's Social Learning Theory).

Importance of Learning Theories to Educational Practices

Theories overviewed in this text have covered several decades of experimentation. It should be readily concluded from this text that no one learning theory is comprehensive enough to cover all aspects of human learning and behavior. Theories can bias our understanding of learning by producing research findings in conflict with our beliefs. Individually, each theory has made

---

[668] A. Amsel, Behaviorism, Neobehaviorism, and Cognitivism in Learning Theory: Historical and Contemporary Perspective (Hillsdale, NJ: Erlbaum, 1989); A. Newell, Unified Theories of Cognition (Cambridge, MA: Harvard University Press, 1990); L. M. Thomas, Comparing Theories of Child Development (3rd ed.), (Belmont, CA: Wadsworth, 1992); Thomas, 1996.

[669] Bandura, 1977.

its contribution to learning. Collectively, the importance of theories in educational practices may be summed up as follows:

1. Theories provide us with information relevant to the learning process by reporting research studies that can be applied to instructional procedures in the classroom.

2. Theories assist educators in determining areas of the curriculum that should be investigated. The introduction of new and innovative strategies is usually based upon some theoretical concept; educators should test these concepts and discover practical ways of applying the theory in the classroom through action research methods.

3. Educators can apply information from learning theories to design learning environments to facilitate learning. This is particularly important for arranging learning environments for specific types of disabilities and behaviors displayed by children with disabilities.

Commonalties Among Learning Theories

Most learning activities proceed from the simple to the complex, from the known to the unknown, and from the concrete to the abstract. Some of the learning theories outlined and discussed in this text follow the aforementioned principles. Real and concrete experiences, which have practical application to the real world, should be the foundation for developing educational units. A preponderance of theories in both behavioristic and cognitive learning theories supports this view. Learning experiences should move from the concrete to various levels of abstractions.

Motivation is viewed as important by most learning theories. Motivation is important in the learning process. Without motivation, learning will not precede in an orderly and systematically manner. Students who are motivated appear to perform better academically. They generally have higher activity levels, are goal directed, and are persistent in completing assigned or designated tests. Educators should be aware of the values of motivation in learning.

Ormrod, Baddeley & Hitch, Hergenhahn & Olsen[670] have outlined strategies that educators can apply in improving extrinsic and intrinsic motivation in students.

Sprenger[671] wrote that brain research is not new but the application to instruction use in the classroom is. Sprenger further stated that there are hundreds of theories on brain research, but they are not applicable to practical application in the classroom. Presently, neuroscientists are exploring ways to apply brain research to the classroom. We have captured this research in chapter 15.

Learning, brain research, and memory are integral components linked together. The various types of memories explained in chapter 16 work in conjunction with the brain. Neuroscientists have discovered that there are storage areas in the brain, which control the various memory functions. According to Sprenger,[672] research has shown that memory lanes begin in specific brain areas. These lanes contain the file in which memory is stored. Educators may employ memory strategies outlined in chapter 16 to assist students in the learning and memory process.

Requirement of An Adequate Theory of Learning for Teachers

According to Lindren,[673] if a theory of learning is to aid educators in becoming effective teachers, it must accomplish the following:

1. It must help us understand all processes of human learning. It also applies to the entire range of skills, concepts, attitudes, habits, and personality traits that may be acquired by the human organism. It is one view that no one learning

---

[670] Ormrod, 1999; A. D. Baddeley, & G. J. Hitch, Working memory in G. Bower (Ed.), *The Psychology of Learning and Motivation* (New York, NY: Academic Press, 1974); B. R. Hergenhahn, & M. H. Olson, *An Introduction to Theories of Learning* (5th ed.) (New Jersey: Prentice Hall, 1997).

[671] M. Sprenger, *Learning and Memory: The Brain in Action* (Alexandria, VA: Association for Supervision and Curriculum Development, 1999).

[672] Sprenger, 1999.

[673] Lindren, 1987.

theory is comprehensive enough to cover all of the aforementioned processes. Consequently, educators must abstract from several learning theories those processes which best fit the individual needs for his/her class.

2. It must extend our understanding of the conditions or forces that stimulate inhibit or affect learning in any way. Not only must the learner's attitudes be considered, but also parental attitudes, social class, and emotional climate of the school and classroom should be considered important by behaviorist theories. We have addressed the importance of attitudes, social factors and mental processes in chapter 7. Educators must infuse cognitive factors in their instructional programs in order to facilitate learning.

3. It must enable us to make reasonably accurate predictions about the outcome of learning activity. A learning theory is useful only to the extent that it enables us to make an accurate prediction about learning. Most learning theories are concerned with success, few consider factors associated with failure. Both factors must be considered in the classroom. Educators need to know factors associated with success as well as failure so that effective instruction strategies can be conducted.

4. It must be a source of hypotheses, clues, and concepts that we can use to become more effective teachers. An adequate theory of learning should be dependable with ideas and insights that provide a base for a variety of approaches to the solution of the teaching-learning process. Learning theories should provide educators with a variety of approaches for those who have failed to promote learning in students.

5. It must be a source of hypotheses about learning that can be tested through classroom experimentation and research, thus extending our understanding of the teaching-learning process. Classroom experimentation and other kinds of research offer the means whereby ideas about learning and new techniques can be tested as to their validity and practicality. Educators should consider the classroom as a learning laboratory where experiments with various type

strategies, methods, theoretical constructs and theories are conducted to validate effective teaching and classroom management techniques.

Some Predictions

The cognitive strategies outlined in chapters 11-14 were considered by behaviorists to be subjective and outside of the scope of empirical research. Today, theories and hypothesis testing have shown that these strategies have deepened our understanding of human learning and behavior. Cognitive theories and strategies have stood the test of time, and it is projected that empirical research will continue to validate the importance of these processes.

Traditional theories used to differentiate and define human behavior will become more marginalized and unified and describe ways in which human behavior will be described as flexible and interactive, rather than separate theories. The field of neuroscience will have a significant impact on unifying theories of learning by providing new research and information about the mind and learning.

Appendix A

Descriptions of the Eight Intelligences

AUTHOR STUDY/Chris Van Allsburg by Linda H. Lord

Logical-mathematical Intelligence

Knowledge	Van Allsburg uses the formula "What if....What then?" when creating his stories. List five "What...." scenarios that might be used for his next book.
Comprehension	Van Allsburg has written fifteen children's books. On a timeline, put them in order by publication date.
Application	In Ben's Dream, Ben takes an imaginary trip around the world. Using the monuments Ben sees and information in the back of the book, trace his trip on a world map and compute the number of miles he traveled.
Analysis	Walter (Just A Dream) wishes he could visit the future. Using the computer program "SIM City 2000, make a diagram of a city of the future.
Synthesis	On graph paper, create a topiary garden based on that of Abdul Gasazi. (The Garden of Abdul Gasazi).
Evaluation	On a scale of 1-10, rank Van Allsburg's books in terms of artistic appeal.

Linguistic Intelligence

Knowledge	Research Chris Van Allsburg using books and the Internet. Write five new facts you learned about the author/ illustrator.
Comprehension	You are a newspaper reporter assigned to interview Alan Mitz (The Garden of Abdul Gasazi). Paraphrase his comments and rewrite the interview as it will appear in the paper.

308

*Application
Write a moral that <u>relates</u> to the adventures of the Two Bad Ants.

Analysis
<u>Examine</u> the picture on the cover of The Stranger. Develop your own plot built around this illustration.

Synthesis
<u>Revise</u> the board games found in Jumanji and Zathura, to create one based on a theme of your choice.

Evaluation
The author's work had been described as "surrealistic fantasy." Read at least five of his books and <u>decide</u> if this is an appropriate description.*

Bodily-kinesthetic Intelligence

Knowledge
Using the box of objects, <u>locate</u> those that could represent Van Allsburg's stories. Place them on the table and <u>tell</u> about them.

Comprehension
Use sock puppets to <u>interpret</u> the actions of the crew in *The Wretched Stone*.

Application
<u>Construct</u> the letters of the alphabet *(The Z Was Zapped)* using pipe cleaners.

Analysis
Make a pipe cleaner broom *(The Widow's Broom)*. Manipulate this to <u>infer</u> which movements of the human body can be duplicated by the broom.

Synthesis
Using clay, <u>sculpt</u> a model of three of the landmarks in *Ben's Dream*.

Evaluation
The ants *(Two Bad Ants)* carried "crystals" back to the Queen. Simulate this by getting on all fours and trying to carry a large box. <u>In your opinion</u>, is it possible for real ants to accomplish this task?

---

* Linda H. Lord, Using *Literacy Centers to Differentiate Instruction*. IRA Convention, REO, May 2-6, 2004.

Spatial Intelligence

Knowledge	Using the black and white photos from *Ben's Dream,* label each of the monuments shown.
Comprehension	Assemble the pieces of a puzzle to depict a scene or cover from one of Van Allsburg's books.
Application	You are riding on the "Polar Express." Draw what you see as you look out the window.
Analysis	Analyze the line drawings of the town of River bend *(Bad Day at Riverbend).* See if you can differentiate the various buildings that would be found in a small town in the Old West.
Synthesis	Create a story quilt that shows the many jungle animals *(Jumanji)* in their habitats.
Evaluation	Visualize the world of the future. Evaluate the world as described by Van Allsburg *(Just a Dream).* Do you agree or disagree with his description?

Musical Intelligence

Knowledge	Identify by clapping, the number of syllables in the phrase: "Bibot is the richest man on earth." *(The Sweetest Fig).*
Comprehension	Paraphrase the story *The Wreck of the Zephyr* and put it in the form of a haiku poem.
Application	Using the text from The Z was Zapped, add a familiar tune to make a song that a first grader would sing.
Analysis	Listen to the sounds of several different bells. Look at the picture of the bell in The Polar Express and infer which sound would represent that particular type of bell.
Synthesis	Compose a song based on the book *Zathura.* This should be sung to the tune of "Twinkle, Twinkle Little Star".
Evaluation	You are the musical director for the film version of *The Wretched Stone.* Select the music you feel best suits the mood in the beginning of the voyage, the period when the

stone was onboard the "Rita Anne" and the rescue of the crew.

Interpersonal Intelligence

Knowledge

Identify the theme in *The Widow's Broom* and work with a group to list other stories that have the same theme.

Comprehension

Since the main character in *The Stranger* never spoke, retell in your own words how he felt when he woke up in Farmer Bailey's home.

Application

Fritz the dog has appeared in most of Van Allsburg's books. In a character journal, interpret Fritz's reactions to finding himself in so many different settings.

Analysis

Van Allsburg moves the reader through many emotions in each of his books. Compare the feelings he creates in *The Stranger* to those in *The Sweetest Fig.*

Synthesis

Work with a small group to create a Reader's Theater script for *The Wretched Stone*. Be sure to capture the emotions of the crew before and after they encountered the "stone".

Evaluation

Your literature circle group has just read *The Stranger*. As you discuss the story, give your opinion on the symbolism of the "stranger".

Intrapersonal Intelligence

Knowledge

In *The Polar Express,* the sound of the bell can be heard only by one who believes in Christmas. Tell how you would react if you were put in the boy's place.

Comprehension

In your journal, describe what you feel and think as you ride through Riverbend *(Bad Day at Riverbend).*

Application

Chris Van Allsburg was making a statement about conservation of our natural resources in *Just a Dream.* Amili: his predictions of the future world to your life and give examples of what you will do to protect the air and water in your community.

Analysis	Van Allsburg started his career as a sculptor. <u>Analyze</u> the illustrations in his books for evidence of this three-dimensional quality.
Synthesis	<u>Plan</u> a trip around the world, such as that in *Ben's Dream,* that would allow you to visit the monuments that you find most interesting.
Evaluation	After seeing the movie *Jumanji,* you felt compelled to <u>compose</u> a letter to the editor of your local paper voicing your views on animal rights. Put your thoughts on paper.

Naturalist Intelligence

Knowledge	In <u>Two Bad Ants</u>, the text and illustrations are from the ant's perspective. <u>Identify</u> each kitchen item that becomes a part of their adventure.
Comprehension	Observe an ant farm. <u>Describe</u> their activity in a daily journal.
Application	<u>Paint a picture</u> of a forest using the detail and use of perspective that Van Allsburg incorporates in his books.
Analysis	<u>Examine</u> the effects pollution has on the water animals in your area *(Just a Dream)*. Determine which factors have the most affect on wild life and find or organize a group that focuses on finding a solution to the problem.
Synthesis	The adventure in *Two Bad Ants* took place in a kitchen. Move the setting outdoors and <u>suggest</u> a sequel. Create illustrations from the ants' perspective.
Evaluation	Chris Van Allsburg has been nominated to receive a commendation from "Greenpeace." You have been chosen to <u>evaluate</u> the message in <u>Just a Dream</u> and give your recommendation to the committee.

Appendix B

Multiple Intelligence Survey

© 199 Walter McKenzie, The One and Only Surfaquarium
http://surfaquarium.com/MI/inventory.htm

Part I

Complete each section by placing a "1" next to each statement you feel accurately describes you. If you do not identify with a statement, leave the space provided blank. Then total the column in each section.

Section 1
_____ I enjoy categorizing things by common traits
_____ Ecological issues are important to me
_____ Hiking and camping are enjoyable activities
_____ I enjoy working on a garden
_____ I believe preserving our National Parks is important
_____ Putting things in hierarchies makes sense to me
_____ Animals are important in my life
_____ My home has a recycling system in place
_____ I enjoy studying biology, botany and/or zoology
_____ I spend a great deal of time outdoors

_____ TOTAL for Section 1

Section 2
_____ I easily pick up on patterns
_____ I focus in on noise and sounds
_____ Moving to a beat is easy for me
_____ I've always been interested n playing an instrument
_____ The cadence of poetry intrigues me
_____ I remember things by putting them in a rhyme
_____ Concentration is difficult while listening to a radio or television
_____ I enjoy many kinds of music
_____ Musicals are more interesting than dramatic plays
_____ Remembering song lyrics is easy for me

_____ TOTAL for Section 2

314

Section 3

_____ I keep my things neat and orderly
_____ Step-by-step directions are a big help
_____ Solving problems comes easily to me
_____ I get easily frustrated with disorganized people
_____ I can complete calculations quickly in my head
_____ Puzzles requiring reasoning are fun
_____ I can't begin an assignment until all my questions are answered
_____ Structure helps me be successful
_____ I find working on a computer spreadsheet or database rewarding
_____ Things have to make sense to me or I am dissatisfied

_____ TOTAL for Section 3

Section 4

_____ It is important to see my role in the "big picture" of things
_____ I enjoy discussing questions about life
_____ Religion is important to me
_____ I enjoy viewing art masterpieces
_____ Relaxation and meditation exercises are rewarding
_____ I like visiting breathtaking sites in nature
_____ I enjoy reading ancient and modern philosophers
_____ Learning new things is easier when I understand their value
_____ I wonder if there are other forms of intelligent life in the universe
_____ Studying history and ancient culture helps give me perspective

_____ TOTAL for Section 4

Section 5

_____ I learn best interacting with others
_____ The more the merrier
_____ Study groups are very productive for me
_____ I enjoy chat rooms
_____ Participating in politics is important
_____ Television and radio talk shows are enjoyable
_____ I am a "team player"
_____ I dislike working alone
_____ Clubs and extracurricular activities are fun
_____ I pay attention to social issues and causes

_____ TOTAL for Section 5

Section 6

_____ I enjoy making things with my hands

_____ Sitting still for long periods of time is difficult for me
_____ I enjoy outdoor games and sports
_____ I value non-verbal communication such as sign language
_____ A fit body is important for a fit mind
_____ Arts and crafts are enjoyable pastimes
_____ Expression through dance is beautiful
_____ I like working with tools
_____ I live an active lifestyle
_____ I learn by doing

_____ TOTAL for Section 6

Section 7
_____ I enjoy reading all kinds of materials
_____ Taking notes helps me remember and understand
_____ I faithfully contact friends through letters and/or e-mail
_____ It is easy for me to explain my ideas to others
_____ I keep a journal
_____ Word puzzles like crosswords and jumbles are fun
_____ I write for pleasure
_____ I enjoy playing with words like puns, anagrams and spoonerisms
_____ Foreign languages interest me
_____ Debates and public speaking are activities I like to participate in

_____ TOTAL for Section 7

Section 8
_____ I am keenly aware of my moral beliefs
_____ I learn best when I have an emotional attachment to the subject
_____ Fairness is important to me
_____ My attitude effects how I learn
_____ Social justice issues concern me
_____ Working alone can be just as productive as working in a group
_____ I need to know why I should do something before I agree to do it
_____ When I believe in something I will give 100% effort to it
_____ I like to be involved in causes that help others
_____ I am willing to protest or sign a petition to right a wrong

_____ TOTAL for Section 8

Section 9
_____ I can imagine ideas in my mind
_____ Rearranging a room is fun for me
_____ I enjoy creating art using varied media

316

_____ I remember well using graphic organizers
_____ Performance art can be very gratifying
_____ Spreadsheets are great for making charts, graphs and tables
_____ Three dimensional puzzles bring me much enjoyment
_____ Music videos are very stimulating
_____ I can recall things in mental pictures
_____ I am good at reading maps and blueprints

_____ TOTAL for Section 9

Part II

Now carry forward your total from each section and multiply by 10 below:

Section	Total Forward	Multiply	Score
1		X 10	
2		X 10	
3		X 10	
4		X 10	
5		X 10	
6		X 10	
7		X 10	
8		X 10	
9		X 10	

Part III

Now plot your scores on the bar graph provided:

100									
90									
80									
70									
60									
50									
40									
30									
20									
10									
0	Sec 1	Sec 2	Sec 3	Sec 4	Sec 5	Sec 6	Sec 7	Sec 8	Sec 9

Part IV

Now determine your intelligence profile!

Key:

Section 1 – This reflects your Naturalist strength
Section 1 – This suggests your Musical strength
Section 1 – This indicates your Logical strength
Section 1 – This illustrates your Existential strength
Section 1 – This shows your Interpersonal strength
Section 1 – This tells your Kinesthetic strength
Section 1 – This indicates your Verbal strength
Section 1 – This reflects your Intrapersonal strength
Section 1 – This suggests your Visual strength

318

Remember:
- Everyone has all the intelligences!
- You can strengthen an intelligence!
- This inventory is meant as a snapshot in time – it can change!
  M.I. is meant to empower, not label people!

Appendix C

Using Brain Research to Impact Instruction for ALL Learners

Presenter: Dr. Andrea F. Rosenblatt
Barry University, Miami Shores, Florida

1. Introduction and interactive experience

2. What recent brain research tells us about how we learn

3. Using the implications of this research with ALL learners, especially those from urban settings

4. Suggested brain compatible strategies and classroom environments to be used with all learners

5. Using multiple resources and putting it all together

6. Where do we go from here?

7. Question and answer session[*]

---

[*] Source: Andrea Rosenblatt, (2004). Using Brain Research to Impact Instruction for all learners. International Reading Association, 49 Annual Convention, Teaching the world to Read, Reno-Tahoe, Nevada

USING BRAIN RESEARCH TO IMPACT INSTRUCTION FOR ALL LEARNERS

ELEMENTS OF A BRAIN-COMPATIBLE CLASSROOM AND THEIR IMPLICATIONS FOR INSTRUCTION

1. Absence of Threat

☐ Focus on avoiding threatening situations, where the student is intent on survival, not learning.

☐ Develop personal connections with students.

☐ Assist the school in creating a community of learners through cross-level activities.

☐ Provide students with clear expectations, both academically and behaviorally, and opportunities for risk-taking.

2. Meaningful Content

☐ Create opportunities to link new learning experiences with prior knowledge.

☐ Establish relevance for the material to be learned.

☐ Provide real-life, hands-on experiences both in the classroom and out.

3. Choices

☐ Allow opportunities for students to select a topic, book, or use of a multiple intelligence to display learning, which provides a feeling of some control.

☐ Give chances for students to take ownership of their learning.

4. Adequate Time

☐ Provide opportunities for students to reflect on their learning.

☐ Create multiple learning situations for students to be immersed in information, experiences, and practical applications of new knowledge.

☐ Give students new information using different times of the day and days of the week.

5. Enriched Environment

☐ Display learning resources throughout the room.

☐ Change materials often, because the brain seeks to be continuously challenged, and novelty is critical.

☐ Locate lessons in different environments inside and outside the classroom.

☐ Allow students to have water at their desks.

☐ Use background music and live animals and plants to enrich, where possible.

☐ Design learning units that uses many modalities to enrich and provide a greater chance for retention.

☐ Create opportunities for students to work in natural light and air.

6. Collaboration

☐ Provide opportunities for interaction among students, because the human brain is a social communicative brain.

☐ Teach and model cooperative and collaborative skills.

☐ Use a variety of groupings.

7. Immediate Feedback

☐ Make provisions for students to receive immediate feedback from differing people, including other students and themselves.

☐ Select types of feedback carefully. Rewards and punishments can be stressors.

☐   Provide rubrics, models, and scaffolding to help guide the students and prepare them for assessments and feedback.

8. Mastery, Memory, and Application

☐   Guide students, through brain-based practices, to help them master important skills and strategies.

☐   Emphasize the importance of a strong knowledge base and then have students apply this knowledge in meaningful situations.

☐   Elicit strong emotions, which will enhance memory.

☐   Embed skills and strategies into stories, enhancing memory and relevance for the learner.

☐   Identify students' background knowledge for the topics and then provide needed information and experiences.

Appendix D

Brain Research In Adolescence

Much research has been on the adolescent brain in recent years.

During the teen years, the brain does not grow in size, but it changes. Between age 16 and 20:

* the brain development so that the adolescents are more able to control what they do;

* this brain development allows adolescents to gain better control over their emotions;

* the brain develops so that adolescents became better at planning and understanding abstract concepts, like philosophy.

Adolescents can make choices that will affect their brain development.

* When a teenager concentrates on math, music, sports, or other activities that require thinking, new circuits can form in the brain.

* When a teenager chooses passive, non-thinking activities and just "hang out" or watches a lot of television, the brain will make circuits for this kind of activity.

So, adolescents' decisions about how to make their brains "work" will affect the way their brain develops. To carry out the work of the brain, during adolescence and throughout life, one needs a good supply of oxygen (from exercise) and protein (from body). By improving cardiovascular health, one can increase the flow of oxygen-rich blood to the brain. This has been shown to improve brain function.[*]

---

[*] Sources: Franklin Institute: http://www.fi.edu/brain. Neuroscience for Kids: http://www.faculty.washington.edu/chuldre/neurok.html; PBS: http://www.pbs.org/wgbh/pages/frontline/shows/teenbrain/work/anatomy.html Connors, C. Keith, Ph.D., Feeding the Brain, Plenum Press, New York, 1989. Restak, Richard, M.D. The Secret Life of the Brain, The Dana Press and Joseph Henry Press, Washington, DC, 20001.

Appendix E

Resource Materials on Brain-Based Learning

Videos

The Brain and Learning. (1998). Alexandria, VA: ASCD. #498062H01

The Brain and Reading. (1999). Alexandria, VA: ASCD. #499207H01

Audiotapes

The Brain, the Mind, and the Classroom. (1997). Alexandria, VA: ASCD. Incorporating brain research into curriculum and instruction. (Presented at the ASCD Annual Conference – March 1998). Alexandria, VA: ASCD.

Grangaard. (1998). *Brain-Based Learning: Practical Applications to the Classroom.* (Presented at the ASCD Annual Conference –March 1998). Alexandria, VA: ASCD.

Jensen, E. (1997). *Links Between Diversity Training and Brain Research.* (Presented at the ASCD Annual Conference – March 1997). Alexandria, VA: ASCD.

Nolan, M. & Howerton, L. (1998). *A Brain-based Model of Learning Styles.* Alexandria, VA: ASCD.

Raebeck, B. (1998). *Building Brain-based Schools.* (Presented at the ASCD Annual Conference – March 1998). Alexandria, VA: ASCD.

Sorgen, M. (1998). *Creating a Brain-friendly Classroom.* Alexandria, VA: ASCD.

Websites

The Brain Store (Eric Jensen): www.brainstore.com

The Children's Literature Web Guide: http://ucalgary.ca/~dkbrown/

The Cinderella Project:
http://www.dept.usm.edu/~engdept/cinderella/cinderella.htmt

Mindware: Brainy Toys for Kids of All Ages: www.mindwareonline.com

National Institutes of Health (Lots of good research information): www.nih.gov

Neuroscience for Kids:
http://www.faculty.washington.edu/chudler/neurok.html

Sapolsky, Robert M. Ph.D. Stress: www.Sfn.org/nas/summaries/Sapolsky.html

Society of Neuroscience: www.sfn.org

Whole Brain Atlas. Anatomy of the Brain, CATs, MRIs, etc.:
www.med.harvard.edu/AANLIB

APPENDIX F

The National Center for Teaching Thinking

"All Students Can Be Good Thinkers"

Welcome

We would like to welcome you to the website of the National Center for Thinking (NCTT), a service organization for educators with business offices located in, Massachusetts, USA. NCTT is dedicated to providing programs of excellence for K-12 schools and colleges on teaching and assessing skillful thinking. NCTT offers custom–designed long term staff development programs, special courses, workshops, and a summer institute (usually held the first full week of July after the 4th of July holidays). It draws upon a staff distinguished in the field from the USA and abroad.

THIS WEBSITE PROVIDES YOU WITH

- Information about specified activities conducted by NCTT during the next year.
- A means of registering for these activities electronically.
- Articles and sample lessons written by NCTT consultants and reflecting the work of NCTT trained teachers.
- A list of resources available via this website from NCTT on teaching thinking. It is our conviction at NCTT that all students can be taught in ways that bring out their natural capabilities as quality thinkers. We are dedicated to sharing with educators around the world examples of means and methods of doing so, and to helping educators implement these in their classrooms, courses, and programs. If you are one of these educators we invite you to explore this website. If you wish to contact us directly we

will do our best to speak to your specific needs what we provide here. Our email address is info@nctt.net.

Appendix G

Imaging Study Reveals Brain Function of Poor Readers Can Improve

A brain imaging study has shown that, after they overcome their reading disability, the brains of formerly poor readers begin to function like the brains of good readers, showing increased activity in a part of the brain that recognizes words. The study appears in the May 1 *Biological Psychiatry* and was funded by the National Institute of Child Health and Human Development (NICHD), one of the National Institutes of Health. "These images show that effective reading instruction not only improves reading ability, but actually changes the brain's functioning so that it can perform reading tasks more efficiently," said Duane Alexander, M.D., Director of the NICHD. The research team was led by Bennett Shaywitz, M.D., and Sally Shaywitz, M.D., of Yale University, in Syracuse, New York; Vanderbilt University, in Nashville, Tennessee; and the NICHD.

According to Dr. Sally Shaywitz, the results show that "Teaching matters and good teaching can change the brain in a way that has the potential to benefit struggling readers. Along with testing the children's reading ability, the researchers used functional magnetic resonance imaging (fMRI), a sophisticated brain imaging technology, to observe the children's brain functioning as they read.

In all, 77 children between the ages of 6 and about 9 and ½ took part in the study. Of these, 49 had difficulty reading, and 29 children were good readers. Of the 49 poor readers, 12 received the standard instruction in reading that was available through their school systems. The remaining 37 were enrolled in an intensive reading program based on instruction in phonemic awareness and phonics.

In the study, the 37 poor readers in the intensive reading program outpaced the 12 poor readers in the standard instruction groups, making strong gains in three measures of reading skill: accuracy, fluency, and comprehension. These gains were still apparent when the children were tested again a year later. Moreover, fMRI scans showed that the brains of the 37 formerly poor readers began functioning like the brains of good readers. Specifically, the poor readers showed increased activity in an area of the brain that recognized words instantly without first having to decipher them.

The intensive reading program the 37 children took had strong components in phonemic awareness and phonics. Phonemic awareness refers to the ability to identify phonemes, the individual sounds that make up spoken words. The word "bag," for example, is made up of three such elemental units of speech, which can be represented as bbb, aaa, and ggg. The brain strings together the 40 phonemes making up the English language to produce hundreds and thousands of words. In speech, this process is unconscious and automatic.

Beginning in the 1970's, NICHD-funded researchers learned that developing a conscious awareness of the smaller sounds in words was essential to mastering the next step in learning to read, phonics. Phonics refers to the ability to match spoken phonemes to the individual letters of the alphabet that represent them. Once children master phonics, the NICHD-funded studies showed, they could make sense of words they haven't seen before, without first having to memorize them. Further NICHD-supported research found that instruction in phonemic awareness was an essential part of a comprehensive program in reading instruction that could help most poor readers overcome their disability.

In the 1900's, the Shaywitzes had used fMRI to learn that reading ability resides in the brain's left half, or hemisphere. Within the hemisphere, three brain regions work together to control reading. In the left front of the brain, one area recognizes phonemes. Further back, another brain area "maps" phonemes to the letters that represent them. Still another brain area serves as a kind of long-term storage system. Once a word is learned, this brain region recognizes it automatically, without first having to decipher it phonetically.

Poor readers, the researchers had learned in the earlier studies, have difficulty accessing this automatic recognition center. Instead, they rely almost exclusively on the phoneme center and the mapping center. Each time poor readers see a word, they must puzzle over it, as if they were seeing it for the first time.

In the current study, the researchers discovered that, as the 37 poor readers progressed through their instruction program, their brains began to function more like the brains of good readers. Specifically, the brains of these children showed increased activation in the automatic recognition center.

"This study represents the fruition of decades of NICHD-supported reading research," said G. Reid Lyon, Ph.D., Chief of NICHD's Child Development and Behavior Branch. "The findings show that the brain systems involved in reading respond to effective reading instruction."

The NICHD is part of the National Institutes of Health (NIH), the biomedical research arm of the federal government. NIH is an agency of the U.S. Department of Health and Human Services. The NICHD sponsors research on development, before and after birth; maternal, child, and family health; reproductive biology and population issues; and medical rehabilitation. NICHD publications, as well as information about the Institute, are available from the NICHD Web site, http://www/nichd.nih.gov, or from the NICHD NICHDInformationResourceCenter@mail.nih.gov.

Glossary

Accommodation--Modification of an activity or ability in the face of environmental demands. In Piaget's description of development, assimilation and accommodation are the means by which individuals interact with an adapt to their world.

Acquisition--In conditioning theories, acquisition is sometimes used interchangeably with the tem learning. It mighty be used to signify the formation of associations among stimuli or between responses and their consequences.

Adaptation--Changes in an organism in response to the environment. Such changes are assumed to facilita6te interaction with that environment. Adaptation plays a central role in Piaget's theory.

Amino acids--Fast-action neuro-transmitters that include GABA (gamma aminobutyric acid) and gluta mate.

Assimilation--The act of incorporating objects or aspects of objects into previously learned activities. To assimilate is, in a sense, to ingest or to use for something that is previously learned.

Behavior management--The deliberate and systematic application of psychological principles in attempts to change behavior. Behavior management programs are most often based largely on behavioristic principles.

Behavior modification--The deliberate application of operant conditioning principles in an effort to change behavior.

Behavior therapy--The systematic application of Pavlovian procedures and ideas in an effort to change behavior.

Behaviorism--The school of psychology counted by S. O. Watson. The behaviorist believe that the proper subject matter is behavior, not mental events.

Chaining--A Skinnerian explanation for the linking of sequences of responses through the action of discriminative stimuli that act as secondary reinforcers.

Chunking--A memory process whereby related items are grouped together into more easily remembered "chunks" (for example, a prefix and four digits for a phone number, rather than seven unrelated numbers).

Classical conditioning--Involves the repeated pairing of two stimuli so that a previously neutral (conditioned) stimulus eventually elicits a response (conditioned response) similar to that originally elicited by a non-neutral (unconditioned) stimulus. Originally described by Pavlov. Clinical method and open-ended form of questions in which the researcher's questions are guided by the child's answers to previous questions.

Closure--A Gestalt principle referring to our tendency to perceive incomplete patterns as complete.

Cognitive strategies--The processes involved in learning and remembering. Cognitive strategies include procedures for identifying problems, selecting approaches to their solution, monitoring progress in solving problems, selecting approaches to their solution, monitoring progress in solving problems, and using feedback.

Cognitivism--A general term for approaches to theories of learning concerned with such intellectual events as problem solving, information processing, thinking, and imagining.

Combined schedule--A combination of various types of schedules of reinforcement.

Concept--An abstraction or representation of the common properties of events, objects, or experiences; an idea or notion.

Concrete operations--The third of Piaget's four major stages, lasting from age 7 or 8 to approximately age 11 or 12 and characterized largely by the child's ability to deal with concrete problems and objects, or objects and problems easily imagined.

Conditioned response--A response elicited by a conditioned stimulus. In some obvious ways a conditioned response resembles, but is not identical to, its corresponding unconditioned response.

Conditioned stimulus --A stimulus that initially does not elicit any response (or that elicits a global, orienting response) but that, as a function of being paired with an unconditioned stimulus and its response, acquires the capability of eliciting that some response.

Conditioning--A type of learning describable in terms of changing relationships between stimuli, between responses, or between both stimuli and responses.

Connectionism--E. L. Thorndike's term for his theory of learning, based on the notion that learning is the formation of neural connections between stimuli and responses.

Conservation--A Piagetian term for the realization that certain quantitative attributes of objects remain unchanged unless something is added to or taken away from them. Such characteristics of objects as mass, number, area, and volume are capable of being conserved.

Continuous reinforcement--A reinforcement schedule in which every correct response is followed by a reinforcer.

Control group--In an experiment, a group comprising individuals as similar to the experimental group as possible except that they are not exposed to an experimental treatment.

Counterconditioning--A behavior modification technique in which stimuli associated with an undesirable response are presented below threshold or at times when the undesirable response is unlikely to occur. The object is to condition a desirable response to replace the undesirable one.

Decay theory--An explanation for loss of information in short-term memory based on the notion that the physiological effects of stimulation fade. Similar to fading in connection with forgetting in long-term memory.

Dependent variable--The variable that reflects the assumed effects of manipulations of the independent variable (s) in an experiment.

Discriminative stimulus--Skinner's term for the features of a situation that an organism can discriminate to distinguish between occasions that might be reinforced or not reinforced.

Elaboration--A memory strategy involving forming new associations. To elaborate is to link with other ideas or images.

Elicited response--A response brought about by a stimulus. The expression is synonymous with the tem respondent.

Episodic memory--A type of declarative, autobiographical (conscious, ling-term) memory consisting of knowledge about personal experiences, tied to specific times and places.

Equilibration--A Piagetian term for the process by which people maintain a balance between assimilation (changing behavior; learning new things). Equilibration is essential for adaptation and cognitive growth.

Experimental group--In an experiment, the group of participants who are exposed to a treatment. (See Control group.)

Explicit memory--Type of memory associated with the hippocampus that involves memories of words, facts, and places.

Extinction--In classical conditioning, the cessation of a response following repeated presentations of the CS without the US. In operant conditioning, the cessation of a response following the withdrawal of reinforcement.

Fading--A conditioning technique in which certain characteristics of stimuli are gradually faded out, eventually resulting in discriminations that did not originally exist.

Fading theory--The belief that inability to recall in long-term memory increases with the passage of time as memory "traces" fade.

Fixed schedule--A type of intermittent schedule of reinforcement in which the reinforcement occurs at fixed intervals of time (an interval schedule) or after a specified number of trials (a ratio schedule). (See Continuous reinforcement, Interval schedule, Ration schedule.)

Forgetting loss from memory--My involve inability to retrieve; or might involve actual loss of whatever traces or changes define storage.

Formal operations--The last of Piaget's four major stages. It begins around age 11 or 12 and lasts until age 14 or 15. It is characterized by the child's increasing ability to use logical though processes.

GABA   (Gamma Aminobutgric Acid)--Very prevalent inhibitory neurotransmitter.

Gestalt--A German word meaning whole or configuration.   Describes an approach to psychology concerned with the perception of wholes, with insight, and with awareness. Gestalt psychology is a forerunner of contemporary cognitive psychology.

Higher mental processes--A general phrase to indicate unobservable processes that occur in the "mind"

Hippocampus--Structure located in the fore grain that catalogs long-term factual memories.

Hypothesis--An educated guess, often based on theory, that can be tested.   A prediction based on partial evidence of some effect, process, or phenomenon, which must then be verified experimentally.

Implicit learning--Unconscious learning, not represented in symbols or analyzable with rules. Roughly equivalent to procedural or unconscious learning.

Implicit memory--Involuntary memory such as the procedural emotional, and automatic memories.

Independent variable--The variable that is manipulated in an experiment to see if it causes changes in the dependent variable. The "if" part of the it-then equation implicit in an experiment. (See Dependent variable.)

Information processing (IP)--Relates to how information is modified (or processed), resulting in knowledge, perception, or behavior. A dominant model of the cognitive approaches, it makes extensive use of computer metaphors.

Insight--The perception of relationships among elements of a problem situation. A problem-solving method that contracts strongly with trial and error. The cornerstone of Gestalt psychology.

Internalization--A Piagetian concept referring to the processes by which activities, objects, and events in the real world become represented mentally.

Law of Effect--A Thorndikean low of learning stating that the effect of a response leads to its being learned (stamped in) or not learned (stamped out).

Law of exercise--One of Thorndike's laws of learning, basic to his pre- 1930s system but essentially repudiated later. It maintained that the more frequently, recently, and vigorously a connection was exercised, the stronger it would be.

Law of multiple responses--Law based on Thorndike's observation that learning involves the emission of a variety of responses law that Thorndike's theory is often referred to as a theory of trial-and-error learning.

Law of prepotency of elements--A Thorndikean law of learning stating that people tend to respond to the most striking of the various elements that make up a stimulus situation.

Law of readiness--Thorndikean law of learning that into account the fact that certain types of learning are impossible or difficult unless the learner is ready. In this context, readiness refers to maturational level, previous learning, motivational factors, and other characteristics of the individual that related to learning.

Learning--All relatively permanent changes in behavior that result from experience, but that are not due to fatigue, maturation, drugs, injury, or disease.

Learning theory--A systematic attempt to explain and understand how behavior changes. The phrase behavior theory is used synonymously.

Long-term memory--Process by which the brain stores information for long period of time.

Memory--The physiological effects of experience, reflected in changes that define learning. Includes both storage and retrieval. Nothing can be retrieved from memory that has not been stored, but not all that is stored can be retrieved.

Motivation --The causes of behavior. The conscious or unconscious forces that lead to certain acts.

Negative reinforcement--An increase in the probability that a response will recur following the elimination or removal of a condition as a consequences(s) of the behavior. Negative reinforcement ordinarily takes the form of an unpleasant or noxious stimulus that is removed as a result of a specific response.

Negative reinforcer--An event that has the effect of increasing the probability of occurrence of the response that immediately precedes it. Negative reinforcement ordinarily takes the form of an unpleasant or noxious stimulus that is removed as a result of a specific response.

Nervous system--The part of the body that is made up of neurons. Its major components are the brain and the spinal cord (the central nervous system), receptor systems associated with major senses and effector systems associated with functioning of muscles and glands.

Neural network--A connectionist model of brain functioning premised on the functioning of the parallel distributed processing computer. Neural networks are complex arrangements of units that activate each other, modifying patterns of connections. In this model, meaning resides in patterns within the network, and responses are also determined by patterns.

Neuron--A single nerve cell, the basic building block of the human nervous system. Neurons consist of four main parts: cell body, nucleus, dendrite, and axon.

Neuro transmitter--Chemical produced in a neuron that carries information in the brain.

Norepine phrine--Neuro transmitter associated with alertness.

Operant conditioning--The process of changing behavior by manipulating its consequences. Most of Skinner's work investigates the principles of operant conditioning.

Operant--Skinner's term for a response not elicited by any known or obvious stimulus. Most significant human behaviors appear to be operants.

Parsimonious--Avoiding excessive and confusing detail and complexity.

Parsimonious theories--Explain all important relationships in the simplest, briefest manner possible.

Population--Collections of individuals (or objects or situations) with similar characteristics. For example, the population of all first-grade children in North America. (See Sample.)

Positive reinforcement--An increase in the probability that a response will recur as a result of a positive consequence(s) resulting from that behavior (that is, as a result of the addition of something). Usually takes the form of a pleasant stimulus (reward) that results from a specific response.

Positive reinforcer--An event added to a situation immediately after a response has occurred that increases the probability that the response will recur. Usually takes the form of a pleasant stimulus (reward) that results from a specific response.

Pragnanz--A German word meaning "good form." An overriding Gestalt principle that maintains that what we perceive (and think) tends to take the best possible form where best usually refers to a principle such as closure.

Preconceptual thinking--The first substage in the period of preoperational thought, beginning around age 2 and lasting until age 4. It is so called because the child has not yet developed the ability to classify.

Premack principle--The recognition that behaviors that are chosen frequently by an individual (and that are therefore favored) may be used to reinforce other, less frequently chosen behaviors.

Preoperational thinking--The second of Piaget's four major stages, lasting from around age 2 to age 7 or 89, characterized by certain weaknesses in the child's logic. It consists of two substages: intuitive thinking and preconceptual thinking.

Primary reinforcer--An event that is reinforcing in the absence of any learning. Stimuli such as food and drink are primary reinforcers because, presumably, an organism does not have to learn that they are pleasant.

Reflex--A simple, unlearned stimulus-response link, such as salivating in response to food in one's mouth or blinking in response to air blowing into one's eye.

Refractory period--A brief period after firing during which a neuron is "discharged" and is incapable of firing again.

Rehearsal--A memory strategy involving simple repetition. The principal means of maintaining items in short-term memory.

Reinforcement--The effect of a reinforcer; specifically, to increase the probability that a response will occur.

Respondent--Skinner's term for a response that (unlike an operant) is elicited by a known, specific stimulus. Unconditioned responses are examples of respondents. (See Unconditioned response.)

Sample--A subset of a population. A representative selection of individuals with similar characteristics drawn from a larger group. For example, a sample comprising 1 percent of all first-grade children in North America. (See population.)

Schedule of reinforcement--The timing and frequency of presentation of reinforcement to organisms. (See Continuous reinforcement, Intermittent reinforcement.)

Schema--The label used by Piaget to describe a unit in cognitive structure. A schema is, in one sense, an activity together with whatever biology or neurology might underlie that activity. In another sense, a schema may be thought of as an idea or a concept.

Science--An approach and an attitude toward knowledge that emphasize objectivity, precision, and replicability. Also, one of several related bodies of knowledge.

Second-order conditioning--In classical conditioning, the forming of associations between the CS and other stimuli that take the place of the US (typically other stimuli that have been paired with the US).

Secondary reinforcer--An event that becomes reinforcing as a result of being paired with other reinforcers.

Sensorimotor intelligence--The first stage of development in Piaget's classification. It lasts from birth to approximately age 2 and is so called because children understand their world during that period primarily in terms of their activities in it and sensations of it.

Sensory memory--The simple sensory recognition of such stimuli as a sound, a taste, or a sight. Also called short-term sensory storage.

Shaping--A technique for training animals and people to perform behaviors not previously in their repertoires. It involves reinforcing responses that are progressively closer approximations to the desired behavior.

Short-term memory--Also called primary or working memory; a type of memory in which material is available for recall for a matter of seconds. Short-term memory primarily involves rehearsal rather than more in-depth processing. It defines our immediate consciousness.

Significant--In research, refers to findings that would not be expected to occur by chance alone more than a small percentage (for example, 5% or 1%) of the time.

Skinner box--One of various experimental environments used by Skinner in his investigations of operant conditioning. The typical Skinner box is a cage-like structure equipped with a lever and a food tray attached to a food-delivering mechanism.

Social learning--The acquisition of patterns of behavior that conform to social expectations; learning what is acceptable and what is not acceptable in a given culture.

Structure--A term used by Piaget in reference to cognitive structure in effect, the individual's mental representations, which include knowledge of things as well as knowledge of how to do things.

Theory--A body of information pertaining to a specific topic that makes sense out of a large number of observations and indicate to the researcher other factors to explore.

Token--Something indicative of something else. In behavior management programs, token reinforcement systems consist of objects like disks or point tallies that are themselves worthless but later can be exchanged for more meaningful reinforcement.

Trial and error--Thorndikean explanation for learning based on the idea that when placed in a problem situation, an individual will emit a number of responses but will eventually learn that correct one as a result of reinforcement.

Unconditioned response--A response that is elicited by an unconditioned stimulus.

Unconditioned stimulus--A stimulus that elicits a response prior to learning. All stimuli that are capable of eliciting reflexive behaviors are examples of unconditioned stimuli. For example, food is an unconditioned stimulus for the response to salivation.

Variable--A property, measurement, or characteristic that can vary from one situation to another. In psychological investigations, qualities such as intelligence, sex, personality, age, and so on can be important variables.

Bibliography

Achenback, T., & Zigler, E. Cue-learning and problem learning strategies in normal and retarded children. *Child Development*, 39, (1968), 837-848.

Ackerman, P. L. A theory of adult intellectual development: Process, personality, interests, and knowledge. *Intelligence*, 22 (1966), 227-257.

Alfassi, M. Reading for meaning: The efficacy of reciprocal teaching in fostering reading comprehension in high school students in remedial reading classes. *American Educational Research Journal*, 35 (2) (1998), 309-332.

Alliance for Childhood. Fool's gold: A critical look at computers and childhood. Available online: http://www.allianceforchildhood.net/projects/computers/Computersreports _foods_gold_contents.htm. (2000).

Amsel, A. *Behaviorism, neobehaviorism, and cognitivism in learning theory: Historical and contemporary perspectives.* Hillsdale, NJ: Erlbaum, 1989.

Anderson, R. C. Role of reader's scheme in comprehension, learning, and memory. In R. B. Ruddle, M. R. Ruddle, and H. Singer (Eds.). *Theoretical models and process of reading* (4th ed.). Newark, DE: International Reading Association, 1994.

Anderson, J. R., L. M. Reder, & H. A. Simon. *Application and misapplications of cognitive psychology to mathematics education.* Unpublished paper, Carnegie Mellon University, 1995.

Anderson, J. R. *The architecture of cognition.* Cambridge, MA: Harvard University Press, 1983.

Anderson, J. R. Acquisition of cognitive skills. *Psychology Review, 89,* (1982), 369-406.

Anderson, L. W., & R. B. Burns. Values evidence and mastery learning. *Review of Education Research, 57* (2), (1987), 215-223.

Andrews, J. E., & D. L. Jordon. Multimedia stories for deaf children. *Teaching Exceptional Children, 30* (6), (1998), 28-33.

Archambeault, B. Holistic mathematics instruction: Interactive problem solving and real life situations help learners understand math concepts. *Adult Learning, 5,* (1993), 21-23.

Arlin, M. Time, equality, and mastery learning. *Review of Educational Research, 54,* (1984), 65-68.

Armstrong, T. *Multiple intelligences in the classroom.* Alexandria, VA: Association for Supervision and Curriculum development, 1994.

Ashton, P. T., & Webb, R. B. *Making a difference: Teacher's sense of efficacy and student achievement.* White Plains, NY: Longman, 1986.

Atkinson, J. W. Motivation determinants of risk-taking behavior. *Psychology Review*, *64*, (1957), 359-372.

Atkinson, J. W. *An Introduction to motivation*. Princeton, NJ: Van Nostrand, 1964.

Atkinson, J. W. Michigan studies of the failure. In F. Halish & Huhl (Eds.). *Motivation, intention, and volition*. Berlin Springer, 1987.

Atkinson, J. W., & J. O. Raynor. *Motivation and achievement*. New York: Wiley, 1974.

Au, K. H., & J. A. Scheu. Journey toward holistic instruction: Supporting teachers' growth. *The Reading Teacher, 49* (6), (1996), 468-477.

Ayers, J. *Sensory integration theory*. Los Angeles, CA: Psychological Services, 1972.

Ayers, W. Childhood at risk. *Educational Leadership, 46*, (1989), 70-72.

Bader, B. Measuring progress of disabled students. *American Teacher, 15*, (1998).

Baddeley, A. D., & G. J. Hitch. Working memory. In G. Bower (Ed.), *The psychology of learning and motivation*. New York, NY: Academic Press, 1974..

Bakken, J. A. Evaluating the World Wide Web. *Teaching Exceptional Children*, 36 (6), (1998), 48-52.

Bandura, A. Psychotherapy based upon modeling principles. In A. E. Bergin & S. L. Garfield (Eds*.). Handbook of psychotherapy and behavior change*. Englewood Cliffs, NJ: Prentice Hall, 1971.

Bandura, A. Human agency in social cognitive theory: *American Psychologist, 44* (1989), 1175-1184.

Bandura, A. *Self-efficacy in changing societies*. Cambridge, MA: University Press, 1995.

Bandura, A. *Social Learning Theory*. Englewood Cliffs, NJ: Prentice Hall, 1977.

Bandura, A. *A Social Learning Theory*. Englewood Cliffs, NJ: Prentice Hall, 1970.

Bandura, A. *Aggression: A social learning analysis*. Englewood Cliffs, NJ: Prentice Hall, 1973.

Bandura, A. Human agency in social cognitive theory. *American Psychologist, 44* (1989), 1175-1184.

Bandura, A. *Principles of behavior modification*. New York: Rinehart and Winston, 1969.

Bandura, A. Psychotherapy based upon modeling principles. In. A. E. Bergin and S. L. Garfield (Eds.). *Handbook of psychotherapy and behavior Change*. Englewood Cliffs, NJ: Prentice Hall, 1971.

Bandura, A. Self-efficacy in changing societies. Cambridge, MA: University Press, 1995.

Bandura, A., D. Ross, & S. A. Ross. Transmission of aggression through imitation of aggressive models. *Journal of Abnormal and Social Psychology, 63* (1961), 575-582.

Bandura, A. Self-efficacy toward a unifying theory of behavior change. *Psychological Review, 84* (977), 91-215.

Bandura, A. *Self-efficacy: The Exercise Toward Control.* New York: W. H. Freeman and Company, 1997.

Bandura, A. *Social foundations of thought and action: A social cognitive theory.* Englewood Cliffs, NJ: Prentice Hall, 1986.

Bandura, A. Social learning analysis of aggression. In E. Ribes-Inesta, & A. Bandura (Eds.). *Analysis of delinquency and aggression.* Englewood Cliffs, NJ: Prentice Hall, 1976.

Bandura, A. Social learning analysis of aggression. In E. Ribes-Inesta, & A. Bandura. (Eds.). *Analysis of Delinquency and Aggression.* Hillsdale, NJ: Halsted Press, 1976.

Bandura, A. *Social learning and personality.* New York, NY: Holt, Rinehart, and Winston, 1965.

Bandura, A., & R. H. Walters. *Social learning and personality development.* New York: Holt, Rinehart, and Winston, 1963.

Bandura, A., Gusec, & Menlow. Observational learning as a function of symbolization and incentive set. *Child Development, 37,* (1966), 499-506.

Bandura, A., D. Ross, & S. A. Ross. Transmission of aggression through imitation of aggressive models. *Journal of Abnormal and Social Psychology, 63,* (1961), 575-582.

Bandura, A., D. Ross, & S. A. Ross. A. *Social learning and personality development.* New York, NY: Rinehart and Winston, 1963.

Bank, J. A. Multicultural education. For freedom's sake. *Educational Leadership, 49,* (1991), 22-25.

Bank, L., J. H. Marlowe, J. B., Patterson, G. R., & M. R. Weinrott. A comparative evaluation of parent-training intervention for families of chronic delinquents. *Journal of Abnormal Child Psychology, 19,* (1991), 15-33.

Barrell, J. Designing the invitational environment. In A. Costa (Ed.), *Developing Minds: A resource book for teaching thinking* (3rd ed.). Alexandria, VA: Association for Supervision and Curriculum Development, 2001.

Bauer, R. H. Short-term memory in learning disabled and nondisabled children. *Bulletin of the Psychonomic Society, 20,* (1987b), 128-130.

Bauer, R. H. Memory processes in children with learning disabilities. *Journal of Experimental Child Psychology, 34,* (1987a), 415-430.

Benderson, A. *Critical thinking focus.* Princeton, NJ: Educational Testing Service, 1984.

Bennett, C. Assessing teacher's abilities for educating multicultural students: The need for conceptual models in teacher education. In C. Heid (Ed.).

Multicultural education: Knowledge and perceptions. Indianapolis, IN: University Center for Urban Education, 1988.

Bennett, C. *Comprehensive multicultural education: Theory and practice.* Boston, MA: Allyn and Bacon, 1986.

Benson, G. D., & W. J. Hunter. Chaos theory: No strange attraction in teacher education. *Action in Teacher Education, 14* (4), (1992), 61-67.

Berk, L. E. *Child development.* Boston, MA: Allyn and Bacon, 1991.

Berk, L. E. *Child development* (4th ed.). Boston, MA: Allyn and Bacon, 1997.

Berliner, B. Reaching unmotivated students. *Education Digest, 69*(5), (2004, January), 46-47.

Berliner, D. C. The place of process-products research in developing the agenda for research on teaching thinking. *Educational Psychologist, 24,* (1989), 325-355.

Bert, C. R., & M. Bert. *The Native American: An exceptionality in education and counseling.* ERIC. 351168, 1992.

Best, D. L. Inducing children to generate mnemonic organization strategies: An examination of long-term retention and materials. *Developmental Psychology, 29,* (1993), 325.

Beyer, B. K. *Developing a thinking skills program.* Boston, MA: Allyn and Bacon, 1998.

Beyer, B. K. *Improving student thinking: A comprehensive approach.* Boston, MA: Allyn and Bacon 1997.

Beyer, B. K. *Practical strategies for the teaching of thinking.* Boston, MA: Allyn and Bacon, 1991.

Bigge, J. L. *Teaching individuals with physical and multiple disabilities.* New York, NY: Macmillan, 1991.

Biken, D. Making differences ordinary. In W. Stainback and M. Forest (Eds.). *Educating all Children in the Mainstream of Regular Education.* Baltimore: Paul H. Brookes, 1989.

Binker, A. J., D. Martin, C. Vetrano, & H. Kreklau. *Critical thinking handbook.* Rohnert Park, CA: Center for Critical Thinking and Moral Critique, 1990.

Bloom, B. S. The sigma problem: The research for methods of instruction as effective as one-to-one tutoring. *Educational Research, 13,* (1984), 4-16.

Bogdan, R. C., & S. K. Biklen. *Qualitative research for education: An introduction to theory and methods.* Boston, MA: Allyn & Bacon, 1992.

Bolger, R. Learning with technology. *Teamwork, 1,* (1996).

Booth, A., & L. Dunner. *Family school links: How do they affect educational outcomes?* Hillsdale, NJ: Erlbaum, 1990.

Borkowski, J. G., M. Carr, E. A. Rellinger, & M. Pressley. *Dimensions of thinking: Review of research.* Hillsdale, NJ: Erlbaum, 1990.

Bourne, L. E., Jr. Learning and utilization of conceptual rules. In B. Kleinmuntz (Ed.). *Concepts and the structures of memory.* New York, NY: Wiley and Sons, 1967.

Bourne, L. E., Jr., D. R. Ekstrand, & R. L. Dominowski. *The Psychology of thinking.* Englewood Cliffs, NJ: Prentice Hall, 1971.

Bower, G. H. Application of a model to paired-associate learning. *psychometrika, 26,* (1961), 255-280.

Bransford, J. D., & B. A. Stein. *The ideal problem solver* (2nd ed.). New York, NY: W. H. Freeman, 1993.

Brembs, B., F. D. Lorenzetti, F. D. Reys, D. A. Baxter, & J. H. Bryrne. Operant reward learning in a plysdia: Neuronal correlates and methanisms. *Science, 296,* (5573), (2002), 1706-1710.

Brody, G., & Z. Stoneman. Social competencies in the developmental disabled: Some suggestions for research and training. *Mental Retardation, 15,* (1977), 41-43.

Brooks, J. G., & M. G. Brooks. The courage to be constructivist. *Educational Leadership, 18-24,* (1999, November).

Brown A. L., A. S. Palincsar, & L. Purcell. Poor readers: Teach, don't label. *The school achievement of minority children: New perspectives.* Hillsdale, NJ: Lawrence Erlbaum Associates, Publishers, 1986.

Brown, A. L., & J. C. Campione. Students as researchers and teachers. In J. W. Keefe & H. J. Walberg (Eds.). *Teaching for thinking.* Reston, VA: National Association of Secondary School Principals, 1992.

Brown, A. L., & S. A. Palincsar. Reciprocal teaching comprehension strategies: A national history of one program for enhancing learning. In J. Borkowskit, & J. D. Day (Eds.). *Cognition in special education Comparative approaches to retardation, learning disabilities, and giftedness.* Norwood, NJ: Ablex, 1987.

Brown, J. L., & C. A. Moffett. *The Hero's journey.* Alexandria, VA: Association for Supervision and Curriculum Development, 1999.

Bruer, J. T. Education and the brain: A bridge too far. *Educational Researcher, 26*(8), (1997), 4-16.

Bruner, J. S., J. Goodnow, & G. Austin. *A Study of thinking.* New York, NY: Wiley and Sons, 1956.

Brunner, J. S. The act of discovery. *Harvard Educational Review, 31,* (1961a), 21-32.

Brunner, J. S. *The process of education.* Cambridge, MA: Harvard University Press, 1961b.

Brunner, J. S. *Toward a Theory of Instruction.* New York, NY: W.W. Norton, 1966.

Butler, O. B. Early help for kids at risk: Our nations best investment. *NEA Today, 7,* (1989), 51-53.

Caine, R. N., & G. Caine. *Education on the edge of possibility.* Alexandria, VA: Association for Supervision and Curriculum Development, 1977.

Caine, R. N., & G. Caine. *Making connections: Teaching and the human brain* (Revised). Menlo Park, CA: Addison Wesley Publishing Company, 1994a.

Caine, R. N., & Caine, G. *Making connections: Teaching and the human brain.* Alexandria, VA: Association for Supervision and Curriculum Development, 1991.

Campbell, J. *Winston Churchill's afternoon nap.* New York: Simon and Schuster, 1986.

Campbell, L. How teachers interpret MI theory. *Educational Leadership, 56*(1), (1997), 14-19.

Campione, J. C., A. M., Shapiro, & A. L. Brown. Forms of transfer in a community of learners: Flexible learning and understanding. In A. McKeough, J. Lupant, & A. Marini (Eds.). *Teaching for transfer: fostering generalization in learning.* Mahwah, NJ: Erlbaum, 1995.

Cannon, D., & M. Weinstein. Reasoning skills: An overview. *Journal of Philosophy for Children,* 6 (1985), 29-33.

Carmine, D. Curricular interventions for teaching higher order thinking to all students: Introduction to the special series. *Journal of Learning Disabilities, 24,* (1991), 261-269.

Carnine, D. Teaching complex content to learning disabled students: The role of technology. *Exceptional Children, 55*(6), (1989), 524-533.

Caroll, J. Self-efficacy related to transfer of learning and theory-based instructional design. *Journal of Adult Education, 22,* (1993), 37-43.

Carson, B. A journey from the bottom of the class to brain surgeon. *Education Update, 46*(4), 1. Alexandria, VA: Association for Supervision and Curriculum Development, 2004.

Carter, C. Why reciprocal teaching? *Educational Leadership, 54*(6), (1997), 64-68.

Cattell, R. B. *Intelligence: Its structure, growth, and action* (Rev. ed.). Amsterdam: North Holland Press, 1987. (Original work published 1971).

Chall, J. S. Two vocabularies for reading: Recognition and meaning. In M. G. Keown & M. E. Curtis (Eds.). *The nature of vocabulary acquisition.* Hillsdale, NJ: Erbaum, 1987.

Chance, P. Master of mastery. *Psychology Today, 21*(4), (1987), 42-46.

Charles, C. M. *Building classroom discipline.* New York, NY: Longman, 1985.

Chipman, S. F., & J. W. *Higher cognitive goals for education: An introduction.* Hillsdale, NJ: Lawrence Erlbaum Associates, 1995.

Choate, J. S. *Successful inclusion teaching.* Boston, MA: Allyn & Bacon, 1977.

Chomsky, N. *Language and mind.* New York, NY: Harcourt Brace, 1972.

Chomsky, N. *Syntactic structures.* The Hauge: Moutan, 1957.

Chugani, H. T. *Functional Maturation of the Brain.* Paper presented at the Third Annual Brain Symposium. Berkeley, California: 1996.

Church, R. M. Human models of animal behavior. *Psychological Science, 4,* (1993), 170-173.

Clinton, G. Setting up a school-based mentoring program. *The Prevention Researcher, 9*(1), (2002), 4-7.

Cobb, P., E. Yackel, & T. Wood. A constructivist alternative to the representational view of mind in mathematical education. *Journal of Research in Mathematical Education, 23*, (1992), 2-33.

Cognition and Technology Group at Vanderbilt. *The Jasper project: Lessons in curriculum, instruction, assessment, and professional development.* Mahwah, NJ: Lawrence Erlbaum Associates, 1992.

Coleman, J. S., E. Q. Campbell, C. J. Hobson, J. McPartland, A. M. Mood, F. D. Weinfield, & R. L. York. *Equality of Educational Opportunity.* Washington, DC: U. S. Government Printing Office, 1966.

Coleman, M. *Behavior disorders: Theory and practice.* Englewood Cliffs, NJ: Prentice Hall, 1986.

Collins, A., J. S. Brown, & S. E. Newman. *Cognitive apprenticeship: Teaching the craft of reading, writing, and mathematics.* (Tech. Rep. No. 403), Champaign: University of Urbana-Champaign, Center for the Study of Reading, 1987.

Collins, M., & D. Carmine. Evaluating the field test revision process by comparing two versions of a reasoning skills CAI program. *Journal of Learning Disabilities, 21,* (1998), 375-379.

Collins, T. W., & J. A. Hatch. Supporting the social-emotional growth of young children. *Dimensions of Early Childhood, 27,* (1992), 17-21.

Commission on Chapter I. *Making schools work for children in poverty.* Washington, DC: American Association for Higher Education, 1992.

Corcoran, K. Efficacy, skills, reinforcement, and choice behavior. *American Psychology,* (February 1991).

Cornish, E. The cyber future: 92 ways our lives will change by the year 2025. *The Futurist, 6,* (1996).

Council for Exceptional Children. *Brain Research Shed New Light on Student Learning, Teaching Strategies, and Disabilities, 10*(3), (2004), 1, 5, 7-10. Author.

Covington, M. V. *Achievement motivation, self-attributions, and exceptionality.* Norwood, NJ: Ablex, 1987.

Covington, M. V. *Making the grade: A self-worth perspective on motivation and school reform.* Cambridge, UT: Cambridge University Press, 1992.

Covington, M. V. The motive for self-worth. In R. Ames & C. Ames (Eds.). *Research on motivation in education.* New York: Academic Press. 1984.

Covington, M. V. The role of self-processes in applied social psychology. *Journal of the Theory of Social Behavior, 15,* (1985), 355-389.

Cowley, G., & A. Underwood. Memory. *Newsweek, 131* (24), (1998), 48-49, 51-54.

Crain, W. C. *Theories of development: Concepts and applications.* Englewood Cliffs, NJ: Prentice Hall, 1985.

Creswell, J. W. *Research design: Qualitative and quantitative approaches.* Thousand Oaks, CA: Sage publications, 1994.

352

Cskszentimihaly, M. *Flow: The psychology of optimal experiences.* New York: Harper and Row, 1990.

Cummings, C., & A. Rodda. Advocacy, prejudice and role modeling in the deaf community. *Journal of Social Psychology, 129,* (1989), 5-12.

Damasio, A. R. *Descarte's error: Emotion, reason, and the human brain.* New York, NY: Putnam Publishing, 1994, 3-19.

Damasio, A. R. How the brain creates the mind. *Scientific America, 6,* (281), (1999), 112-117.

Damon, W. *The social world of the child.* San Francisco, CA: Jossey Bass, 1997.

Danielson, C. & T. L. McGreal. *Teacher evaluation to enhance professional practice.* Alexandria, VA: Association for Supervision and Curriculum Development, 2000.

Darch, C., & E. Kameenui. Teaching LD students' critical reasoning skills: A systematic replication. *Learning Disabilities Quarterly, 10,* (1987), 82-91.

Delprato, D. J., & B. D. Midley. Some fundamentals of B. F. Skinner's behaviorism. *American Psychologist, 47,* (1992), 1507-1520.

deRibaupierre, A., & L. Rieben. Individuals and situational variability in cognitive development. *Educational Psychologist, 30* (1), (1995), 5-14.

Diamond, M., & J. Hopson. *Magic trees of the mind: How to nurture your child's intelligence, creativity, and healthy emotions from birth through adolescence.* New York, NY: Penguin Patnam, 1998.

Dochy, F., M. Segers, & M. M. Buehl. The relationship between assessment practices and outcomes of studies. The case of research on prior knowledge. *Review of Educational Research, 69*(2), (1999) 145-186.

Dodd, D. H., & R. M. White. *Cognition: Mental structures and processes.* Boston, MA: Allyn and Bacon, 1980.

Draganski, B., C. Gaser, V. Bush, G. Schuierer, U. Bogdahn, & A. Mary. Neuroplasticity: Changes in grey matter induced by training. *Nature,* 427 (6972), (2004), 311-312.

Druckman, D., & R. A. Bjork (Eds.). *Learning, remembering, believing: Enhancing human performance.* Washington, DC: National Academy Press, 1994.

Druckman, D., & R. A. Bjork (Eds.). *Constructivism and the technology of instruction: A conversation.* Washington, DC: National Academy Press, 1994.

Duffy, T. M., & D. J. Cunningham. Constructivism: Implications for the design and delivery of instruction. In D. H. Jonasse (Ed.). *Handbook of research for educational communications and* technology. New York, NY: Macmillan, 1996.

Duffy, T. M., & A. D. Johassen. *Constructivism and the technology of instruction: A conversation.* Hillsdale, NJ: Lawrence Erlbaum, 1992.

Dunn, R. *Strategies for educating diverse learners.* Bloomington, IN: Phi Delta, 1995.

353

Education Update. *How teachers are putting brain research to use?* 47, 6, (2005), 103. Association of Supervision and Curriculum Development. Author.

Eggen, P., & D. Kauchak. *Strategies for teachers: Teaching content and thinking skills.* Needham Heights, MA: Allyn and Bacon, 1996.

Emia, V. A multiple intelligence inventory. *Educational Leadership, 55,* (1997), 47-50.

Englert, C. S., & A. S. Palincsar. Reconsidering instructional research in literacy from a sociocultural perspective. *Learning Disabilities Research and Practice, 6,* (1991), 225-229.

Ennis, R. H. *Developed minds: A resource book for teaching thinking.* Virginia: Association for Supervision and Curriculum Development, 1985.

Ennis, R. H. A logical basis for measuring critical thinking skills. *Educational Leadership, 44,* (1986), 44-48.

Ennis, R. H., & J. Millman. *Cornell critical thinking tests: Levels X and Z.* Pacific Grove, CA: Midwest, 1985.

Epstein, J. L. School, family, community partnerships: Caring for childhood we share. *Phi Delta* Kappan, *77*(9), (1995), 701-712.

Epstein, R. Skinner, creativity, and the problem of spontaneous behavior. *Psychological Science, 2,* (1991), 362-370.

Eron, L. The development of aggressive behavior from the perspective of a developing behaviorism. *American Psychologist, 42,* (1987), 435-442.

Estes, W. K. New developments in statistical behavior theory. Differential tests of axioms for associative learning. *Psychometrika, 26,* 73-84.

Evans, R. *Albert Bandura: The man and his ideas: A dialogue.* New York, NY: Praeger, 1989.

Feigenbaum, E. A., & J. Feldman. *Computer and thought.* New York, NY: McGraw-Hill, 1963.

Ferguson, C., & J. Kamara. *Innovative approaches to education and community service: Model and strategies for change and empowerment.* Boston, MA: University of Massachusetts, 1993.

Fitts, P. M., & M. I. Posner. *Human performance.* Belmont, CA: Brooks Cole, 1967.

Flavell, J. H. Stage-related properties of cognitive development. *Cognitive Psychology, 2,* (1971), 421-453.

Flavell, J. H., P. H. Miller, & S. A. Miller. *Cognitive development* (3rd ed.). Upper Saddle River, NJ: Prentice Hall, 1993.

Fletcher, J. D. Individualized systems of instruction. In M.C. Alkin (Ed.). *Encyclopedia of educational research* (6th ed.). New York, NY: Macmillan, 1992.

Foder, J. A., T. G. Bever, & M. F. Garrett. *The psychology of language: An introduction to psycholinguistics and generative grammar.* New York, NY: McGraw-Hill, 1974.

Fodi, J. Kids communicate through adaptive technology. *Exceptional Parent, 36,* (1991).

354

Forest, M. *Maps and cities*. Presentation at Peak Parent Center Workshop. Colorado Springs, 1990.

Forster, K., Levels of process and the structure of the language processor. In W. E. Cooper and T. Walker (Eds.). *Sentence processing*. Hillsdale, NJ: Erlbaum, 1979.

Frayne, C., & F. Lantham. Application of social learning theory to employee self-management of attendance. *Journal of Applied Psychology, 72*, (1987), 383-392.

Frazier, M. K. Caution: Students on board the Internet. *Educational Leadership, 53*(2), (1995), 26-27.

Frederiksen, N. Implications of cognitive theory for instruction in problem solving. *Review of Educational Research, 54*, (1984a), 363-407.

French, J. N., & C. Rhoder. *Teaching thinking skills*. New York, NY: Garland, 1992.

Gagne, E. D. *The cognitive psychology of school learning*. Boston, MA: Little Brown, 1985.

Galloway, L. Bilingualism: Neuropsychological considerations. *Journal of Research and Development in Education, 15*, (1982), 12-28.

Garcia, E. Language, culture, and education. *Review of Research Education, 19*, (1993).

Gardner, H. *Frames of mind: The theory of multiple intelligences*. New York, NY: Basic Books, 1983, 1993a.

Gardner, H. *Multiple intelligences: The theory in practice*. New York, NY: Basic, 1993.

Gardner, H. *Intelligence reframed: multiple intelligence for the 21st Century*. New York: Basic Books, 1999.

Gazzaniga, M. S. *Nature's mind: The biological roots of thinking, emotion, sexuality, language, and intelligence*. New York: Bantam Books, 1992

George, T. Self-confidence and baseball performance: A causal examination of self-efficacy theory. *Journal of Sport and Exercise Psychology, 16*, (1994), 381-389.

Gilovich, T. *How we know what isn't so: The fallibility of human reason in everyday life*. New York, NY: Free Press, 1991.

Goldstein, C. Learning at cyber camp. *Teaching Exceptional Children, 30*, (5), (1998), 16-26.

Goleman, D. *Emotional intelligence*. New York, NY: Banton Books, 1995.

Graft, O. L., & B. Henderson. Twenty-five ways to increase parental participation. *High School Magazine, 4*, (1997), 36-41.

Green, F. R. Brain and learning research: Implications for meeting the needs of diverse learners. *Education, 119*(4), (1999), 682-687.

Green, W. T. Experience-dependent sunaptogenesis as a plausible memory mechanism. In I. Gormezano and E. A. Wasserman (Eds.), *Learning and memory: The behavioral biological substrates* (pp. 209-299). Hillsdale, NJ: Lawrence Erlbaum, 1992.

Griggs, S., & R. Dunn. Hispanic-American students and learning style. *Emerging Librarian, 23*(2), (1995), 11-14.

Grobecker, B. Reconstructing the paradigm of learning disabilities: A holistic/constructivist implementation. *Learning Disability Quarterly, 19,* (1996), 179-200.

Grossen, B. The fundamental skills of higher order thinking. *Journal of Learning Disabilities, 24,* (1991), 343-353.

Guild, P. *The cultural Learning style connection. Educational Leadership, 51,* (1994), 16-21.

Guild, P. B. Where do the learning theories overlap? *Educational Leadership, 55*(1), (1977), 30-31.

Guskey, T. R., & S. L. Gates. Synthesis of research on the effects of mastery learning in elementary and secondary classrooms. *Educational Leadership, 43*(8) (1986), 73-80.

Guskey, T. R. Rethinking mastery learning reconsidered. *Review of Educational Research, 57*(2), (1987), 225-229.

Guskey, T. R. The essential elements of mastery learning. *Journal of Classroom Interaction, 22*(2), (1987), 19-22.

Guskey, T. R. Cooperative mastery strategies. *Elementary School Journal, 91*(1) (1990), 33-42.

Guskey, T. R. Mastery learning. In J. H. Block, S. T. Everson & T. R. Guskey (Eds.). *School improvement programs.* New York, NY: Scholastic, 1995.

Guzzetti, B. J., T. E. Snyder, & G. V. Glass. Promoting conceptual chance in science: A comparative meta-analysis of instructional interventions from reading education and science education. *Reading Research Quarterly, 28*(2), (1993), 117-155.

Hall, M. H. An interview with "Mr. Behavior," B. F. Skinner. *Readings in Psychology Today.* Delmar, CA: Communications Research Machines, Inc., 1972.

Hall, R. H., M. A. Sidio-Hall, & C. B. Saling. *Spatially Directed Post Organization in Learning from Knowledge Maps.* Paper presented at the Annual Meeting of the American Educational Research Association, San Francisco, 1995.

Halpern, D. F. *Thinking skills instruction: Concepts and techniques.* Washington, DC: National Education Association, 1987.

Halpern, D. F. *Thought and knowledge: An introduction to critical thinking* (3rd ed.). Hillsdale, NJ: Erlbaum, 1995.

Hamilton, R., & E. Ghatala. *Learning and instruction.* Houston, TX: McGraw-Hill, Inc., 1994.

Hamlette, H. E. Effective parents: Professional communication. *Exceptional Parent, 27,* (1997), 51.

Hannafin, M., S. Land, & K. Oliver. Open learning environments: Foundations, methods, and models. In C. M. Reigeluth (ed.). *Instructional design*

356

theories and models: A new paradigm of instructional theory (Vol. II, pp. 115-140). Mahwah, NJ: Lawrence Erlbaum Associates, 1999.

Hart, L. A. *Human brain and human learning.* New York: Longman, 1983.

Hatch, T., & R. Johnson. Social skills for successful group work. *Educational Leadership, 47*, (1990), 29-33.

Healy, J. *Your child's growing mind: A practical guide to brain development and learning from birth to adolesc*ence. New York: Doubleday, 1994.

Hergenhahn, B. R., & M. H. Olson. *An introduction to theories of learning* (5ᵗʰ ed.). New Jersey: Prentice Hall, 1997.

Herman, J. L., P. R. Aschbacker, & L. Winters. *A practical guide to alternative assessment.* Alexandria, VA: Association for Supervision and Curriculum Development, 1992.

Hernstein, R. J. The evolution of behaviorism. *American Psychologists, 32,* (1997), 593-603.

Hicks, D. C. Narrative discourse and classroom learning: An essay response to Eagan's "Narrative of learning: A voyage of implications." *Linguistic and education, 5,* (1993), 127-148.

Hiebert, J., D. Wearne, & S. Taber. Fourth graders' gradual construction of decimal fractions during instruction using different physical representations. *Elementary School Journal, 9,* (1991), 321-341.

Hilliard, A. G. Teachers and cultural styles in a pluralistic society. *NEA Today, 7,* (1989), 65-69.

Hilliard, R. D., & J. W. Myers. Holistic language learning at the middle level: Our last, best chance. *Childhood Education, 73,* (1997), 286-289.

Holdstock, L. *Excerpts from "Education for a new nation."* Africa Transpersonal Association. (Reprinted with the permission of the author). (1987), http:/www.icon.co.za/-cogmotics/articles/new nation.htm.

Holland, J. G., & B. A. Skinner. *The analysis of behavior: A program for self-instruction.* New York, NY: McGraw Hill, 1961.

Hollis, K. L. Contemporary research on Pavlovian conditioning: A new functional analysis. *American Psychologists, 52,* (1997), 956-965.

Holloway, J. H. Caution: Constructivism ahead. *Educational Leadership,* http://www.icon.co.za/-cogmotics/drbruce.htm. Dr. Bruce Copley. (1999, November).

Holt, S. B., & F. S. O'Tuel. The effect of sustained silent reading and writing on achievement and attitudes of seventh and eighth grade students reading two years below grade level. *Reading Improvement, 26*(4), (1989) 290-297.

Honebein, P. C. Seven goals for the design of constructivist learning environments. In B. G. Wilson (Ed.). *Constructivist learning environments: Case studies in instructional design.* Englewood Cliffs, NJ: Educational Technology Publications, 1996.

Houston, J. P. *Fundamentals of learning and memory* (3ʳᵈ Ed.). Orlando, FL: Harcourt Brace Jovanovich, 1986.

Hudgins, B. B., M. R. Riesenmy, S. Mitchell, C. Klein, & V. Navarro. Teaching self-direction to enhance children's thinking in physical science. *Journal of Educational Research, 88*, (1994), 15-26.

Hudgins, B. B., & S. Edelman. Children's self-directed critical thinking. *Journal of Educational Research, 81*, (1988), 262-273.

Hughes, R. T. Computers in the classroom. *The Claearinghouse, 4*, (1996).

Hulse, S. H. C. The present status of animal cognition: An introduction. *Psychological Science*, 4, (1993), 154-155.

Hunt, L. C. Six steps to the individualized reading program (IRP). *Elementary English, 48*, (1970) 27-32.

Hunter, M. C. *Mastery teaching*. Thousand Oaks, CA: Corwin Press, 1982.

Hunter, M. C. Mastery teaching. In J. H. Block & T. R. Guskey (Eds). *School improvement programs*. New York, NY: Scholastic, 1985.

Hyum, J., & S. A. Fowler. Respect, cultural sensitivity, and communication. *Teaching Exceptional Children, 28*(1), 25-28.

Interdisciplinary voices in learning disabilities and remedial education. Austin, TX: Pro-Ed.

Iverson, I. H. Skinner's early research: From reflexology to operant conditioning. *America Psychologist, 47*, 1318-1328, 1992.

Jensen, E. *Teaching with the brain in mind*. Alexandria, VA: Association for Supervision and Curriculum Development, 1998.

Jensen, E. *Brain-based learning*. San Diego: Brain Store Incorporated, 2000.

Jensen, E. *Different brains, different learners: How to reach the hard to reach*. San Diego, CA: The Brain Store, Inc., 2000.

Jensen, R. E. *Standards and ethics in clinical psychology*. Lanham, MD: University Press of America, 1992.

Johnson, W., & R. Johnson. Social skills for successful group work. *Educational Leadership, 47*, (1990), 29-33.

Jones, B. F. Quality and equality through cognitive instruction. *Educational Leadership, 47*, (1990), 204-211.

Kagan, S. L. Early care and education: Beyond the school house doors. *Phi Delta Kappan*, (1989), 107-112.

Kahn, K., & J. Cangemi. Social learning theory: The role of imitations and Modeling in learning socially desirable behavior. *Education, 100* (1979), 41-46.

Kalecstein, A., & S. Norwicki. Social learning theory and prediction of achievement in telemarketers. *Journal of Social Psychology, 134*, (1993), 547-548.

Katayama, A. D., & D. H. Robinson. *Study Effectiveness of Outlines and Graphic Organizer: How Much Information Should be Provided for Students to be Successful on Transfer Test?* Paper presented at the Annual Meeting of the American Educational Research Association, San Diego, 1998.

358

Katz, L. G. *The Teacher's Role in Social Development of Young Children.* ED Clearinghouse on Elementary and Early Childhood Education. ERIC 331642, 1991.

Kauffman, J. *Characteristics of emotional and behavioral disorders of children and youth.* New York, NY: Merrill, 1993.

Kazdin, A. *Behavior modification in applied settings.* Homewood, IL: Dorsey, 1980.

Keefe, C. H. Developing responsive IEPs through holistic assessment. *Intervention in School and Clinic, 28*(1) (1992), 34-40.

Kimmel, A. J. *Ethical issues in behavioral research.* Cambridge, MD: Blackwell Publisher, 1996.

Kinnick, V. The effect of concept teaching in preparing nursing students for clinical practice. *Journal of Nursing Education, 29,* (1990), 362-366.

Klaus-Meier, H. J. Conceptualizing. In B. F. Jones and L. Idol (Eds.). *Dimensions of thinking and cognitive instruction.* Hillsdale, NJ: Erlbaum, 1990.

Klein, S. B. *Learning: principles and applications.* New York, NY: McGraw-Hill, Inc., 1987.

Klein, S. B. *Learning: principles and applications* (3rd ed). New York, NY: McGraw Hill, 1996.

Kohler, W. *Gestalt psychology.* New York, NY: Liveright, 1929.

Kohn, A. *Punished by rewards: The trouble with gold stars, incentive plans, A's, praise, and other bribes.* Boston, MA: Houghton Mifflin, 1993.

Kotulak, R. *Inside the brain: Revolutionary discoveries of how the mind works.* Kansas City, MO: Andrews and McMeely, 1996.

Kulik, C. L., J. A. Kulik, & R. L. Bangert-Drowns. Effectiveness of mastery learning programs: A meta-analysis. *Review of Educational Research, 60*(2), (1990), 265-299.

Kun, B. Stop studying and start learning. *IT Review, 2*(6), (1995), http://www.icon.co.za/-cogmotics/articles/stopstudying.htm

Kurtines, M. *The role of values in psychology and human development.* New York, NY: John Wiley and Sons, 1992.

LaBerge, D., & S. J. Samuels. Toward a theory of automatic information process in reading comprehension. *Cognitive Psychology, 6,* (1974), 293-323.

Lahey, B. B. *Psychology: An introduction.* New York, NY: McGraw Hill, Inc.

LeDoux, J. *The emotional brain: The mysterious underpinning of emotional life.* New York, NY: Simon and Schuster, 1996.

LeDoux, J. E. Emotion, memory, and brain. *Scientific American, 270*(6), (1994), 50-67.

LeDoux, J. *The emotional brain: The mysterious underlining of emotional life.* New York, NY: Simon and Schuster, 1996.

Leedy, P. D. *Practical research: Planning and design* (6th ed.). New York, NY: MacMillan, 1997.

Lefrancious, G. R. *Theories of human learning* (4ᵗʰ ed.). Pacific Grove, CA: Brooks Cole Publishing Company, 1999.

Lefrancios, G. R. *Theories of human learning*. Stamford, CA: CT Wadsworth/Thomson, 2000.

Leinhardt, G. History: A time to be mindful. In G. Leinhardt, I. L. Beck, and C. Stainton (Eds.). *Teaching and learning in history*. Hillsdale, NJ: Erlbaum, 1994.

Lerman, D. C., & B. A. Iwata. Prevalence of the extinction burst and its attenuation during treatment. *Journal of Applied Behavior Analysis, 28,* (1995), 93-94.

Leshowitz, B., K. Jenkens, S. Heaton, & T. L. Bough. Fostering critical thinking skills in students with learning disabilities: An instructional program. *Journal of Learning Disabilities, 26,* (1993), 483-490.

Lester, M. P. Connecting to the world. *Exceptional Parent, 26* (11) (1996), 36-37.

Levine, M. Hypothesis behavior by humans during discrimination learning. *Journal of Experimental Psychology, 71,* (1996), 331-2338.

Lingren, H. S. *Educational psychology in the classroom.* New York, NY: John Wiley and Sons, Inc., 1956.

Lipsitt, L. P., & H. Kaye. Conditioning sucking in the human newborn. *Psychonomic Science, 1,* (1964), 29-30.

Littky, D. C. *The big picture: Education is everyone's business.* Alexandria, VA: Association for Supervision and Curriculum Development, 2004.

Lord, L. H. *Using Literacy Centers to Differentiate Instruction.* IRA Convention, REO, May 2-6, 2004.

Lowery, L. How new science curriculums reflect brain research. *Educational Leadership, 55*(3), (1999), 26-30.

Lumsdaine, A. A. Educational technology, programmed learning, and instructional sciences. In E. R. Hilgard (Ed.). *Theories of learning and instruction.* Chicago, IL: University of Chicago Press, 1964.

Lysynchuk, L. M., M. Pressley, & N. J. Vye. Reciprocal teaching improves standardized reading-comprehension performance in poor comprehenders. *The Elementary School Journal, 90*(5), (1990), 469-484.

Macfarlane, A. What a baby knows. *Human Nature, 1,* (1978), 74-81.

Macinnis, C. Holistic and reductionist approaches in special education: Conflicts and common ground. *McGill Journal of Education, 30*(1), (1995), 7-20.

Mahoney, W. What was he thinking? *Prevention, 56*(3), (2005), 159-165.

Marshall, C., & G. B. Rossman. *Designing Qualitative Research.* Newbury Park, CA: Sage, 1989.

Martinez, M. E. What is problem solving? *Phi Delta Kappan, 70*(8), (1998), 605-609.

Maryland State Department of Education. *Teaching children with special needs.* Baltimore, MD: Division of Instructional Television, 1973.

Marzano, R. *A different kind of classroom.* Alexandria, VA: Association for Supervision and Curriculum Development, 1992.

Marzano, R. J. *The theoretical framework for an instructional model of higher order thinking skills.* Denver, CO: Mid-Continent Regional Educational Lab, 1994.

Marzano, R. J. Critical thinking. In J. H. Block, S. T. Everson, & T. R. Guskey (Eds.). *School improvement programs.* New York, NY: Scholastic, 1995.

Marzano, R. L. *What works in school: Translating research into action.* Alexandria, VA: Association for Supervision and Curriculum Development, 2003.

Maslow, A. H. *Motivation and personality.* New York: Harper, 1954.

Mason, S., & A. L. Egell. What does Amy like? Using a mini-reinforcer in Instructional activities. *Teaching Exceptional Children, 28,* (1995), 42-45.

Maszak, M. S. Mysteries of the mind. *U. S. News and World Report, 138*(7), (2005), 57-58.

Matsueda, R. L., & K. Heimer. Race, family structure, and delinquency: A test differential association and social control theories. *American Sociological Review, 52,* (1987, December), 826-840.

Mayer, R. E., & J. K. Gallini. When is an illustration worth ten thousand words? *Journal of Educational Psychology, 82,* (1990), 715-726.

Mayer, R. Learners as information processors: Legacies and Limitations of educational psychology's second metaphor. *Educational Psychology, 31,* (1996a), 151-161.

Mayer, R. E., & M. C. Wittrock. Problem-solving transfer. In D. C. Berlinear and R. C. Calfee (Eds.). *Handbook on educational psychology.* New York, NY: Macmillan, 1996.

McCormick, C. B., & M. Pressley. *Educational psychology: Learning, instructions, and assessments.* New York, NY: Longman, 1997.

McKenzie, H. S., M. Clark, M. M. Wolf, R. Kothera, & C. Benson. Behavior modification of children with learning disabilities using grades as tokens and allowances as back-up reinforcers. *Exceptional Children, 34,* (1968), 745-752.

McPeck, J. *Critical thinking and education.* Oxford: Martin Robertson, 1991.

Means, B., & M. Knapp. Cognitive approaches to teaching advanced skills to educationally disadvantaged students. *Phi Delta Kappan, 72,* (1991), 282-289.

Meichenbaum, D. *Cognitive behavior modification: An integrated approach.* New York, NY: Plenum, 1977.

Meichenbaum, D. Teaching thinking: A cognitive behavior approach. In Meier, D. (1985). New age learning: From linear to geodesic. *Training and Development Journal,* (1983). http://www.icon.co.za/-cogmotics/articles/new age learning.htm.

361

Meier, D. New age learning: From linear to geodesic. *Training and Development Journal.* http://www.icon.co.za/cogmotics/articles/new age learning.htm, (1985).

Meltzoff, A. Learning how children learn from us. *Education Update, 46*(4), 2. Alexandria, VA: Association for Supervision and Curriculum Development, 2004.

Meyers, I. B. *Gifts Differing* (2nd ed.). Palo Alto, CA: Consulting Psychologist Press, 1990.

Miller J. J. Making connections through holistic learning. *Educational Leadership, 56*(4), (1998, December and January), 46-48.

Miller, D. L., & M. L. Kelley. The use of goal setting and contingency contracting for improving children's homework performance. *Journal of Applied Behavior Analysis, 27*, (1994), 73-84.

Miller, J. P., & Y. Nakagawa (Eds.). *Nurturing our wholeness: Perspectives on spirituality in education.* Brandon, VT: Foundation for Educational Renewal, Inc., 2002.

Miller, N. E. Studies of fear as an acquirable drive: Fear as motivation and fear reduction as reinforcement in learning of new response. *Journal of Experimental Psychology, 38*, (1948), 89-101.

Miller, N. E., & J. Dollard. *Social learning and Imitation.* New Haven, CN: Yale University Press, 1941.

Miller, R. *Holistic Education, Paths of Learning Resource Center.* Retrieved January 30, 2007 from http://www.infed.org/biblio/holisticeducation.htm. 2005

Minsky, M., & S. Papert. *Perceptions.* Cambridge, MA: MIT Press, 1969.

Moll, I. *The Material and the Social in Vygotsky's Theory of Cognitive Development.* Clearinghouse on Teacher Education. (ERIC Document Reproduction Service No. ED. 346988). Washington, DC: 1991.

Moll, I. *The Material and the Social in Vzygotsky's Theory of Cognitive Development.* Clearinghouse on Teacher Education. ED 352186, 1991.

Monteceinois, C. Multucultural teacher education for a culturally diverse teaching force. R. Marth (Ed.). In *practicing what we preach: Confronting diversity in teacher education.* Albany, NY: Suny Press, 1995.

Moore, S. *Piaget and Bandura: The Need for a Unified Theory of Learning.* Paper Presented at the bi-annual Meeting of the Society for Research in Child Development. Baltimore, MD: April 23-26, 1987.

Moulton, A. K., S. Brown, & R. Lent. Relation of self-efficacy believes in Academic outcomes: A meta-analytic investigation. *Journal of Counseling Psychology, 38*, (1991), 30-38.

Murray, D. J. *Gestalt psychology and the cognitive revolution.* New York, NY: Harvester Wheatsheaf, 1995.

362

Mussen, P. H. *Handbook on child psychology* (4th ed.). New York, NY: Wiley, 1983.

Nagy, W. E., & P. A. Herman. *Limitations of Vocabulary Instruction*. (Tech. Rep. No 326). Urbana, IL: University of Illinois, Center for the Study of Reading. ERIC Documented Reproduction Service No. ED248 498, 1984.

Necessary, J. R., & T. S. Parrish, T. S. The relationship. *Education*, (1996), 116-117.

Neef, N. A., F. Mace, D. & Shade. Impulsivity in students with serious emotional disturbance: The interactive effects of reinforcer rate, delay, and quality. *Journal of Applied Behavior Analysis, 26*, (1993), 37-52.

Neef, N. A., D. Shade, & M. S. Miller. Assessing influential dimensions of reinforcers on choice in students with serious emotional disturbance. *Journal of Applied Behavior Analysis, 27*, (1994), 575-583.

Newberger, J. New brain development research: A wonderful window of opportunity to build public support for early childhood education. *Young Children, 52*, (1997), 4-9.

Newell, A. *Unified theories of cognition*. Cambridge, MA: Harvard University Press, 1990.

Newell, A., & H. A. Simon. *Human problem solving*. Englewood Cliffs, NJ: Prentice Hall, 1972.

Newman, F. M. Beyond commonsense in educational restructuring. The issue of content and linkage. *Educational Research, 22*(2), (1993), 4-22.

Nickerson, R. S. *Review of research in education*. Washington, DC: American Educational Research Association, 1991.

Nickerson, R. S. *Reflections on reasoning*. Hillsdale, NJ: Erlbaum, 1996.

Nickerson, R. S., D. N. Perkins, & E. E. Smith. *The Teaching of Thinking*. Hillsdale, NJ: Erlbaum, 1995.

Norris, S. P. Synthesis of research on critical thinking. *Educational Leadership, 42*, (1985) 40-45.

Nuthall, G. The way students learn: Acquiring knowledge from an integrated science and social studies unit. *The Elementary School Journal, 99*(4), (1999), 303-341.

O'Brien, L. Learning styles: Make the student aware. *NASSP Bulletin.* (October 1989), 85-89.

O'Keefe, J., & L. Nadel. *The hippocampus as a cognitive map*. Oxford: Clarendon Press, 1978.

Obiakor, F. E. Self-concept of African American students: An operational model for special education. *Exceptional Children, 59*, (1990), 160-167.

Opportunity to build public support for early childhood education. *Young Children, 52*, 4-9.

Ormrod, J. E. *Human learning* (3rd ed.). Columbus, OH: Merrill Publishing Company, 1999.

Ormrod, J. E. *Human Learning* (3rd ed.). Saddle River, NJ: Merrill Publishing Company, 1999.

Ormrod, J. E. *Human learning* (3rd ed.). New Jersey: Prentice Hall, Inc., 1999.

Osborne, J. G. Free time as reinforcer in the management of classroom behavior. *Journal of Applied Behavior Analysis, 2,* (1969), 113-118.

Oswald, D. P., & N. Sinah-Nirbay. *Current Research on Social Behavior Modification, 16,* (1992), 443-447.

Palardy, M. J. Mastery learning: A mixed view. *Education, 107*(4), (1987), 424-427.

Palincsar, A. S., & A. L. Brown. Peer interaction in reading comprehension instruction. *Educational Psychologists, 22,* (1984), 231-253.

Palincsar, A. S., & A. L. Brown. Interactive teaching to promote independent learning from text. *The Reading Teacher, 39*(8), (1986), 771-777.

Palincsar, A. S., & A. L. Brown. Classroom dialogues to promote self-regulated comprehension. In J. Brophy (Ed.). *Advances in research on teaching* (Vol. 1). Greenwich, CT: JAI Press, 1989.

Palincsar, A. S., & L. Klenk. Dialogues promoting reading comprehension. In B. Means, C. Chelemer, & M. S. Knapp (Eds.). *Teaching advanced skills to at-risk students.* San Francisco, CA: Jossey-Bass, 1991.

Palincsar, A. S., & L. Klenk. Fostering literacy learning in supportive contexts. *Journal of Learning Disabilities, 25*(4), (1992), 211-225, 229.

Palincsar, A. S., K. Ransom, & S. Derber. Collaborative research and development of reciprocal teaching. *Educational Leadership,* 46(4), (1989), 37-40.

Papert, S. Jean Piaget: Child psychologist. *Time, 100,* (1999), 105-107.

Pavlov, I. P. *Conditioned reflexes.* (G. V. Anrep, Tran.). London: Oxford University Press, 1927.

Pearson, P. D. Changing the face of reading comprehension instruction. *The Reading Teacher, 38,* (1985), 724-728.

Pena, J. M. How K-12 teachers are using computer networks. *Educational Leadership, 53,* (1995), 15-18.

Perkins, D. *Outstanding IQ: The emerging science of learnable intelligence.* New York: The Free Press, 1995.

Perkins, D. N., R. Allen, & J. Hafner. *Thinking: The Expanding Frontier.* Pennsylvania. Franklin Press, 1993.

Pflaum, W. D. *The technology fix: The promise and reality of computers in our schools.* Alexandria, VA: Association for Supervision and Curriculum Development, 2004.

Phye, G. D. Strategic transfer: A tool for academic problem solving. *Educational Psychology Review, 4, 3,* (1992), 93-421.

Piaget, J. Discussion. In J. M. Tanner and B. Inhelder (Eds). *Discussions on child development.* New York: International Universities Press, 1960.

Piaget, J. *The language and thought of the child* (3rd ed.). (M. Gabain, Trans). New York, NY: Humanities Press, 1959.

Piaget, J. *The origins of intelligence in children.* New York, NY: Basic Books.

Piaget, J. *Genetic epistemology* (E. Duckworth, Trans), New York: Norton, 1987.

Pilgreen, J., & S. Krashen. Sustained silent reading with English as a second language: High school students' impact on reading frequency, and reading enjoyment. *School Library Media Quarterly, 21-23,* (1993).

Polley, D. B., & M. A. Heiser. Brain can be trained to produce sound in alternate ways, study shows. *Medical News Today,* (2004, December 16). [htt://www.medicalnewstoday.com/medicalnews.php?newsid=17695.

Polloway, E. A., & J. R. Patton. *Strategies for Teaching Learners with Special Needs.* New York, NY: Merrill, 1993.

Powley, R. L. The ventro media hypothalamic syndrome, satiety, and a cephalic phase hypothesis. *Psychological Review, 84,* (1977), 89-126.

Presseisen, B. Z. Avoiding battle at curriculum gulch: Teaching thinking and content. *Educational Leadership, 45,* (1988), 7-8.

Pressley, M. *Reading instruction that works. The case for balanced teaching.* New York: NY: Guilford, 1998.

Pressley, M., & L. Yokoi. Motion for a new trial on transfer. *Educational Researcher, 23*(5), (1994), 36-38.

Price, E. A., & M. P. Drisscoll. An inquiry into the spontaneous transfer of problem-solving skill. *Contemporary Educational Psychology, 22*(4), 1997, 472-494.

Rachlin, H. *Introduction to modern behaviorism* (3rd ed.). New York, NY: W. H. Freeman, 1991.

Ramey, C. T., & S. L. Ramey. Early interventions: Optimizing development for children with disabilities and risk conditions. In M. Wolraid (ed.). *Disorders of development and learning: A practical guide to assessment and management (2nd ed.).* Philadelphia, PA: Mosby, 1996, pp. 141-158.

Reese, H. W., & L. D. Lipsitt. *Experimental child psychology.* New York, NY: Academic Press, 1970.

Reilly, J. M. *Mentorship: The essential guide for school and business.* Dayton, OH: Psychology Press, 1992.

Reisberg, D. *Cognition: Exploring the science of the mind.* New York: W. W. Norton, 1977.

Research Triangle Institute. *Developing Emotional* Intelligence. Research Triangle Park, NC: Early Childhood Resource Center, 2002.

Restak, R. M. *The modular brain.* New York: Touchstone, 1994.

Reynolds, R. E., G. M. Sinatra, & T. L. Jetton. Views of Knowledge Acquisition and Representation: A Continuum from Experience Centered. *Educational Psychologist, 31,* (1996), 93-104.

Ridley, L. Enacting change in elementary school programs: Implementing a whole language perspective. *The Reading Teacher, 43,* (1990), 640-646.

Rieber, L. Seriously considering play: Designing interactive learning environments based on the blending of micro-worlds, simulations, and games. *Educational Technology Research and Development, 44,* (1996).

Riesenmy, M. R., S. Mitchell, B. B. Hudgins, & D. Ebel. Retention and transfer of children's self-directed critical thinking skills. *Journal of Educational Research, 85,* (1991), 14-25.

Robin, D. H., & K. A. Kiewra. Visual argument: Graphic organizers are superior to outlines in improving learning from text. *Journal of Educational Psychology, 87,* (1995), 455-467.

Robinson, D. N. *Social discourse and moral judgment.* San Diego, CA: Academic Press, 1992.

Rosch, E. Principles of categorization. In E. Rosch and B. Lloyd (Eds.). *Cognition and categorization.* Hillsdale, NJ: Erlbaum, 1978.

Rose, C. P., & M. Nicholl. *Accelerated learning for the 21 century.* New York, NY: Delacourt Press, 1997.

Rosenshine, B., & C. Meister. Reciprocal teaching: A review of the research. *Review of Educational Research, 64*(4), (1994), 479-530.

Rosenstock, I., V. Strecher, & M. Becker. Contribution of HBM to self-efficacy theory. *Health Education Quarterly, 15,* (1988), 175-183.

Rotter, J. Generalized expectancies for internal versus external control of reinforcement. *Psychological Monographs: General and Applied, 30,* (1966), 80.

Rotter, J. *Social learning and clinical psychology.* New York, NY: Prentice Hall, 1966.

Rotter, J. Generalized expectancies for internal versus external control of reinforcement. *Psychological Monographs: General and Applied, 80,* (1954), 80.

Rotter, J. Internal versus external control of reinforcement: A case history variable. *American Psychologist, 45,* (1990), 489-493.

Rovee-Collier, C. Time window in cognitive development. *Developmental Psychology, 31*(2), (1995) 147-169.

Rumelhart, D.E., & D. A. Norman. Accretion, tuning, and restructuring: Three modes of learning. In J. W. Colton & R. Klazky (Eds.). *Semanticfactors in cognition.* Hillsdale, NJ: Lawrence Erlbaum, 1981.

Ryba, K., L. Selby, & P. Nolan. Computers empower students with special needs. *Educational Technology, 53* (1995), 82.

Salend, S. J., & C. R. Whittaker. Group evaluation: A Collaborative peer-mediated behavior management system. *Exceptional Children, 59,* (1992), 203-209

Santrock, J. W. *Life-span development* (7th ed.). McGraw-Hill Companies, Inc., 1999.

Semb, G. B., J. A. Ellis, & J. Araujo, J. Long-term memory for knowledge learned in school. *Journal of Educational Psychology, 55,* (1989), 137-155.

Scardamalia, M. *Creative Work with Ideas: A Luxury?* Paper presented at the Annual Meeting of the American Psychological Association. New Orleans, LA: April 2002.

366

Scarmalia, M., & C. Bereiter. Computer support for knowledge-building environments. *The Journal of the Learning Sciences*, (3), (1994), 265-283.

Schank, R. C. *Tell me a story: A new look at real and artificial memory*. New York: Charles Scribner and Sons, 1990.

Schramm, W. *The Research on Programmed Instruction. An Annotated Bibliography*. Washington, D.C.: U. S. Office of Education, 1964.

Schunk, D. Peer models and children's behavior change. *Review of Educational Research, 57*, (1987), 149-174.

Schunk, D. H. Self-efficacy and academic motivation. *Educational Psychologists, 26*(2), (1991), 206-222.

Schurr, S., J. Thompson, & M. Thompson. *Teaching at the middle level: A professional's handbook*. Lexington, MA: D.C. Health, 1995.

Seligman, M. E. P. *Helplessness: On depression, development, and death*. San Francisco, CA: Freeman, 1975.

Seligman, M. E. P., S. F. Maier, & J. Greer. The alleviation of learned helplessness in the dog. *Journal of Abnormal Psychology, 73* (1968), 256-262.

Seligman, M. E. P., S. F. Maier, & R. L. Solomon. Unpredictable and uncontrollable aversive events. In F. R. Brus (Ed.). *Aversive conditioning and learning*. New York: Academic Press, 1971.

Semb, G. B., J. A. Ellis, & J. Araujo. Long-term memory for knowledge learned in school. *Journal of Educational Psychology, 55* (1993), 305-316.

Shade, B. J. The influence of perceptual development on cognitive styles: Cross ethnic comparison. *Early Childhood Development and Care, 51*, (1989), 137-155.

Shore, R. *Rethinking the brain: New insights into early development*. New York: Families and Work Institute, 1997.

Shreeve, J. Beyond the brain. *National Geographic Society, 207*(3), (2005, March), 2-31.

Sigel & Hooper. *Logical Thinking in Children Research Based on Piaget's Theory*. Holt, Rinehart & Wilson, 1969.

Silver, H. R. Strong, & M. Perini. Integrating learning styles and multiple intelligence. *Educational Leadership, 55* (1), (1997), 22-27.

Skinner, B. F. *Beyond Freedom and Dignity*. New York, NY: Knopf, 1971.

Skinner, B. F. *Science and Human Behavior*. New York, NY: Macmillan, 1953.

Skinner, B. F. Teaching machines. *Science, 128* (1958), 969-977.

Skinner, B. F. The origins of cognitive thought. *American Psychologist, 44*, (1989), 13-18.

Skinner, B. F. The science of learning and the art of teaching. *Harvard Educational Review, 124* (1954), 86-87.

Skinner, B. F. *The technology of teaching*. New York, NY: Appleton-Century Crofts, 1968.

Skinner, B. F. The free and happy student. *Phi Delta Kappan, 55,* (1973), 13-16.

Skinner, B. F. The origins of cognitive thought. *American Psychologist,* (1989), 13-18.

Skinner, B. F. *Walden two.* New York, NY: Macmillan, 1948.

Skinner, B. F. What is the experimental analysis of behavior? *Journal of Experimental Analysis of Behavior, 9,* (1966), 213-218.

Skinner, B. F. *The behavior of organism: An experimental analysis.* Englewood Cliffs, NJ: Prentice Hall, 1938.

Skinner, B. F., & Epstein, R. *Skinner for the Classroom,* Champaign, IL: Research Press, 1982.

Slavin, R. E. *Educational psychology: Theory and practice* (6th ed.). Boston, MA: Allyn and Bacon, 1999.

Slavin, R. E. *Educational psychology: Theory and practice* (6th ed.). Boston, MA: Allyn and Bacon, 2000.

Slavin, R. E. Ability grouping and student achievement in elementary schools: A best evidence synthesis. *Review of Educational Research, 57,* (1986c), 243-386.

Sluyter, D., & P. Salovey (Eds.). *Emotional development and emotional intelligence: Implications for education.* New York: Basic Books, 1997.

Silver, H., R. Strong, & M. Perini. *So each may learn: Integrating learning styles and multiple intelligence.* Alexandria, VA: Association for Supervision and Curriculum Development, 2000.

Smith, G. P. Pavlov and appetite. *Integrative Physiological and Behavioral Science, 30,* (1995), 169-174.

Soloff, S. B., & J. C. Houtz. Development of critical thinking among students in kindergarten through grade 4. *Perceptual and motor skills, 73,* (1991), 476-478.

Soto, L. D. Enhancing the written medium for culturally diverse learners via reciprocal interaction. *Urban Review, 21*(3), (1989), 145.

Sousa, D. *How the brain Learns.* Reston, VA: National Association of Secondary School Principals, 1995.

Spiver, N. N. *The constructivist metaphor: Reading, writing, and the making of meaning.* San Diego, CA: Academic Press, 1997.

Sprenger, M. *Learning and memory: The brain in action.* Alexandria, VA: Association for Supervision and Curriculum Development, 1999.

Staats, C. K., & A. W. Staats. Meaning established by classical conditioning. *Journal of Experimental Psychology, 54,* (1957), 74-82.

Steinberg, L., B. Brown, & S. M. Dornbush. *Beyond the classroom: Why school reforms have failed and what parents need to do.* New York: Simon and Schuster, 1996.

Sternberg, R. J. "What is successful intelligence?" *Education Week, 16*(11), (1996, November) 37.

Sternberg, R. L. Investing in creativity: Many happy returns. *Educational Leadership, 53*(4), (1995), 80-84.

Strickland, F. Internal-external control expectancies from contingency to creativity. *American Psychologist, 44*, (1989), 1-12.

Stuart, R. B. Social learning theory: A vanishing or expanding presence? *Psychology: A Journal of Human Behavior, 26*, (1989), 35-50.

Suppes, P. Stimulus: Response theory of finite automata. *Journal of Mathematical Psychology, 6*, (1969), 327-355.

Sussman, D. M. PSI: Variations on a theme. In S. W. Bijou & R. Ruiz (Eds,). *Behavior modification: Contribution to education.* Hillsdale, NJ: Erlbaum, 1981.

Sylwester, R. What the biology of the brain tell us about learning. *Educational Leadership, 51*(4), (1993, December; 1994, January), 22-26.

Sylwester, R. How emotions affect learning. *Educational Leadership, 52* (2) (1994), 2226.

Sylwester, R. *A biological brain in a cultural classroom: Enhancing cognitive and social development through collaborative classroom management.* Thousand Oaks, CA: Corwin Press Incorporated, 2003.

Tait, R. W., & M. E. Saladin, M. E. Concurrent development of excitory and inhibitory associations during back conditioning. *Animal Learning and Behavior, 14*, (1986), 132-137

Tarver, S. Cognitive behavior modification, direct instruction and holistic approaches to the education of students with learning disabilities. *Journal of Learning Disabilities, 19*(6), (1986), 368-375.

Taylor, G. Impact of social learning theory on educating deprived minority children. *Clearinghouse on Teacher Education.* ERIC. 349260, 1992.

Taylor, G. *Curriculum strategies for teaching social skills to the disabled.* Springfield, IL: Charles C. Thomas, 1998.

Taylor, G. R. *Curriculum strategies: Social skills intervention for young African-American males.* Westport, CN: Greenwood Publishing Group, Inc., 1997.

Taylor, G. R. *Curriculum strategies for teaching social skills to the disabled: Dealing with inappropriate behaviors.* Springfield, IL: Charles C. Thomas, 1998.

Taylor, G. R. *Curriculum models and strategies for educating individuals with disabilities in inclusive classrooms.* Springfield, IL: Charles C. Thomas, 1999.

Taylor, G. R. *Impact of social learning theory on educating deprived/minority children.* Clearinghouse for Teacher Education. ERIC. 349260, 1992.

Taylor, G. R. *Curriculum strategies for educating disabled individuals.* Springfield, IL: Charles C Thomas, 1998.

Taylor, G. R. *Educational interventions and services for children with exceptionalities.* Springfield, IL: Charles C Thomas, 2001.

Taylor, G. R. *Using human learning strategies in the classroom.* Lanham, MD: Scarecrow Press, Inc., 2002.

369

Taylor, G. R. *Practical applications of social learning theories in education African-American males.* Lanham, MD: University Press of America, 2003.

Taylor, G. R. *Parenting skills and collaborative service for students with disabilities.* Lanham, MD: Scarecrow Press, 2004.

Taylor, G. R., T. Phillips, & D. Joseph. *Assessment strategies for students with disabilities.* Lewiston, NY: The Edwin Mellen Press, 2002.

Taylor, G. R. *Reforms in educating African American males in Baltimore City Public Schools.* In The State of Black Baltimore (Editors, Howard Henderson, and Stanley Battle). Baltimore, MD: Coppin State University, 2004.

Tennyson, R. D., & O. Park. The teaching of concepts: A review of instructional design literature. *Review of Educational Research, 50,* (1980), 55-70.

Thomas, L. M. *Comparing theories of child development (3rd ed.).* Belmont, CA: Wadsworth, 1992.

Thomas, L. M. *Comparing theories of child development (4th ed.).* Belmont, CA: Wadsworth, 1992.

Thompson, P. M., J. N. Giedd, R. Woods, D. MacDonald, A. Evans, & A. Toga. Growth patterns in the developing brain detected by using continuum mechanical tensor maps. *Nature, 404,* (2000), 190-193.

Thompson, R., & J. McConnell. Classical conditioning in the planarian, dugesia doroto cephala. *Journal of Comparative and Physiological Psychology, 48,* (1955), 65-68.

Toepher, Jr., C. Curriculum design and neuropsychological development. *Journal of Research and Development in Education, 15,* (1982), 1-10.

Tolman, E. C., & C. H. Hovzik. Introduction and removal of reward and maze performance in rats. *University of California Publications in Psychology, 4, 2* (1930), 57-275.

Tolman, E. C., B. F. Ritchie, & D. Kalish. Studies in spatial learning: Orientation and the short-cut. *Journal of Experimental Psychology, 36,* (1946), 13-24.

Tolman, E. C., B. F. Ritchie, & D. Kalish. Studies in spatial learning: Orientation and the short-cut. *Journal of Experimental Psychology, 36,* (1946), 13-24.

Tudge, R., & P. Winterhoff. Vzgotsky, Piaget, and Bandura: Perspectives on the relations between the social world and cognitive development. *Human Development, 36,* (1991), 61-81.

Turgi, P. Children's rights in America: The needs and the actions. *Journal of Humanistic Education and Development, 31,* (1992), 52-63.

Urban Education Project. *The urban learner framework: An overview.* Philadelphia, PA: Research for Better Schools, 1994.

Vasques, J. A. *Cognitive Style and Academic Achievement in Cultural Diversity and the Schools: Consensus and Controversy.* Edited by J. Lynch, C. Modgil, and S. Modgil. London: Falconer Press, 1991.

Vaughn, S. R., C. A. Ridley, & D. D. Bullock. Interpersonal problem solving skills training with aggressive young children. *Journal of Applied Developmental Psychology*, 5, (1984), 213-223.

Vygotsky, L. S. *Mind in Society: The Development of Higher Psychological Processes.* Cambridge, MA: Harvard University Press, 1978.

Waal, F. B. The end of the nature versus nature. *Scientific American*, 6(281), (1999), 49-99.

Wagner, R. K., & R. J. Stember. Alternative conceptions of intelligence and their implications for education. *Review of Educational Research*, 54(2), (1984), 179-223.

Walker, H., M. Irvin, K. Larry, J. Noell, & H. S. George. A construct score approach to the assessment of social competence. *Behavior Modification*, 16, (1992), 449-452.

Walters, S. P. Accessible web design. *Teaching Exceptional Children*, 30(6), (1998), 42-47.

Wanner, E., & M. Maratsas. An ATN approach to comprehension. In M. Halle, J. Bresnan, and G. A. Miller (Eds.). *Linguistic theory and psychological reality.* Cambridge, MA: MIT Press, 1978.

Wasserman, E. A. Comparative cognition: Toward a general understanding of cognition in behavior. *Psychological Science*, 4, (1993), 156-161.

Wasserman, E. A., C. L. DeVolder, & D. J. Coppage. Non-similarity based conceptualization in pigeons via secondary or mediated generalization. *Psychological Science*, 3, (1992), 374-379.

Watson, D., & P. Crowley. How can we implement a whole language approach? In C. Weaver (Ed.). *Reading process and practice.* Portsmouth, NH: Heinemann Educational Books, 1988.

Watson, G. & E. M. Glaser. *Watson-Glaser Critical Thinking Appraisal, Forms A and B.* Cleveland, OH: Psychological Corporation, 1980.

Watson, R. I. *The great psychologists* (3rd ed.). Philadelphia, PA: Lippincott. 1971.

Windholz, G. Hypnosis and inhibition as viewed by Hdidenhain and Pavlov. *Integrative Physiological and Behavioral Science*, 31, 1996a, 155-162.

Weaver, C. (Ed.). *Reading process and practice.* Portsmouth, NH: Heinemann Books, 1988.

Weaver, C., D. Stevens, & J. Vance. Alternative conceptions of intelligence and their implications for education. *Review of Educational Research*, 54(2), (1984), 179-223.

Weignan, O., O. Kuttschreuter, & B. Baarda. A longitudinal study of the effects of television viewing on aggressive and prosocial behaviors. *British Journal of Social Psychology*, 31, (1992), 147-164.

Weiner, B. *Theories of motivation: From mechanisms to cognition.* Chicago: Markham, 1972.

Weiner, B. *Achievement motivation and attribution theory.* Morristown, NJ: General Learning Press, 1974.

Weiner, B., L. Friezel, A. Kuklala, L. Reed, S. Rest, & R. Rosenbauj. Perceiving the causes of success and failure. In E. E. Jones, D. E. Kanouse, H. H. Kelly, R. E. Nisbett, S. Valins, & B. Weiner (Eds.). *Attribution perceiving the behavior*. Morristown, NJ: General Learning Press, 1971.

Weiner, L. *Preparing teachers for urban schools*. New York, NY: Teachers College, 1993.

Wenger, E. *Communities of practice: Learning, meaning, and identity*. New York, NY: University Press, 1998.

Wertheimer, M. Experimentelle Studien, Uber das sehen von Bewegung. *Zeitschrift fur Psychologie, 61*, (1912), 161-265.

What make teens tick? *Time Magazine Supplement*, 53-59 (2004, May). Author.

Wheatley, M. C. *Leadership and the new science: Learning about organization from an orderly universe*. San Francisco, CA: Berrett-Koehler, 1992.

Wickelgren, W. A. Learned specification of concept neurons. *Bulletin of Mathematical Biophysics, 31*, (1969), 123-142.

Williams, W. A. *Closing the achievement gap: A vision for changing beliefs and practices*. Alexandria, VA: Association for Supervision and Curriculum Development, 1996.

Willis, J. *Research-based strategies to ignite student learning*. Alexandria, VA: Association for Supervision and Curriculum Development, 2006.

Windholz, G. Hypothesis and inhibition as viewed by Hdidenhan and Pavlov. *Integrative Physiological and Behavioral Science, 31*, (1996a), 155-162.

Windholz, G. Pavlov's conceptualization of paranoia within the theory of higher nervous activity. *History of Psychiatry, 7*, (1996b), 159-166.

Windholz, G. Ivan P. Pavlov: An overview of his life and psychological work. *American Psychologist, 52*, (1997), 941-946.

Winn, W. Learning from maps and diagrams. *Educational Psychology Review, 3*, (1991), 211-247.

Wittenburg, D., & R. McBride. *Disposition for Self-regulation of Learning for Four Pre-service Physical Education Teachers*. Manuscript submitted for publication, 2004.

Wolf, D. P., P. G. LeMahieu, & J. Fresh. Good measure: Assessment as a tool for educational reform. *Educational Leadership, 49*(8), (1992), 8-13.

Wolfe, P., & R. Brandt. What do we know from brain research? *Educational Leadership, 56*(3), (1998), 8-13.

Wolfgang, C. H. *Solving discipline problems. Methods and models for today's teachers*. Boston, MA: Allyn & Bacon, 1995.

Wolraid, M. (Ed.). *Disorders of development and learning: A practical guide to assessment and management (2nd Ed.)*. Philadelphia, PA: Mosby, 1996, pp. 141-158.

Wong, B. L. Self-questioning instructional research: A review. *Review of Educational Research, 65*, (1995), 227-268.

Woodward. *Industrial organizations: Theory and practice.* London: Oxford University Press, 1961.

Wurtman, J. J. *Managing your mind and mood through food.* New York, NY: Perennial Library, 1986.

Yancey, W., & S., Saporito. *Urban schools and neighborhoods: A handbook for building an ecological database.* Philadelphia, PA: Temple University, 1994.

Yell, M. L. Cognitive behavior therapy. In T. J. Zirpoli and K. J. Melloy. *Behavior management application for teachers and parents.* Columbus, OH: MacMillan, 1993.

Yinger, R. J. New directions for teaching and learning: Fostering critical thinking. San Francisco, CA: Jossey-Bass, 1990.

Zaragoza, N., Vaughn, S., & McIntosh, R. Social skill intervention and children with behavior problems: A review. *Behavioral Disorders, 1*(6), (1991), 260-275.

Zazdeh, L. A., K. S. Fu, K. M. Tanak, & M. Shimura. *Fuzzy sets and their applications to cognitive and decision processes.* New York, NY: Academic Press, 1975.

Zeichner, K., & S. Melnick. *The Role of Community Field Experiences in Preparing Teachers for Cultural Diversity.* Paper presented at the Annual Meeting of the American Association of Colleges of Teacher Education. Chicago, IL: 1995.

Zull, J. E. The art of changing the brain. *Educational Leadership, 62*(1), (2004), 68-69.

INDEX

374

Brown, A. L., 211, 212
Brown, B., 261
Brown, J. L., 265, 266
Brown, J. S., 221
Brown, S., 101
Bruer, T. J., 252, 253,
Bruner, J. S., 168
Brunner, J. S., 46, 145
Brus, F. R., 32
Buehl, M. M., 5
Buka, S. L., 263
Bullock, D. D., 120
Burns, R. B., 66
Bush, V., 257
Butler, O. B., 83, 127

C
Caine, G., 246, 255, 266
Caine, R. N., 246, 255, 266
Calfee, R. C., 168
Campbell, J., 230, 255
Campione, J. C., 212
Cangemi, J., 84, 87, 93, 94, 97, 101, 106
Carmine, D., 80, 186
Carr, M., 188
Carroll, J., 99, 118
Carson, B. A., 259
Cattell, R. B., 5
Chaining, 55
Chall, J. S., 6
Chance, P., 62
Characteristic of scientific theory, 12
Charles, C. M., 108, 109
Chelemer, C., 211
Chipman, S. F., 174
Choate, J. S., 56, 73, 74
Chomsky, 130, 145
Chugani, H. T., 262
Church, R. M., 59
Clark, M., 69
Classical conditional model, 42
Classical conditioning in human learning, 46
Classical conditioning, 41, 42
Classification of learning theories, 10
Classroom applications, 66, 156, 160, 181
Clinton, G., 5
Cobb, P., 197
Coding data, 18
Cognition and Technology Group at Vanderbilt, 75
Cognitive and behavioral comparison, 142
Cognitive dimension, 272

Cognitive maps, 147, 148
Cognitive psychology, 129
Cognitive strategies and procedures, 163
Cognitive theories, 299
Cognitive theorists, 145
Coleman, M., 6, 92, 117
Collaboration with parents and teachers, 296
Collins, A., 221
Collins, M., 186
Collins, T. W., 115
Collins, T., 140
Colton, J. W., 256
Commission on Chapter I, 297
Commonality among theories, 85
Communication reasoning, 1
Compositions, 164
Computer advantages, 72
Computer technology and technological services, 71
Concept defined, 163
Concept learning, 165
Conceptual learning, 163
Conditioning theories, 298
Consent, 19
Constructing theory, 18
Contingency contracting, 71
Contributions of early theorists, 37
Cooper, W. E., 141
Coppage, D. J., 164
Copying behavior, 89
Cornish, E., 73, 77
Covington, M. V., 30, 32, 49
Cowley, G., 264
Crain, W. C., 152Berk, L. E., 153
Cresswell, J., 17
Critical thinking, 173, 180; principles and problem solving skills, 175
Crowley, P., 203
Crystallized intelligence, 7
Cskszentimihaly, M. 242
Cues, 87
Cultural and social values, 292
Culture to learning style relationship, 282
Cummings, C., 117
Cunningham, D. J., 75
Curriculum development, 229
Curtis, M. E., 6

D
Damasio, A., 29
Damon, W., 98, 118
Danielson, C., 62

Darch, C., 187
Darnasio, A. R., 245
Deception, 22
Delayed Conditioning, 43
Delprato, D. J., 50
Derber, S., 218, 221
DeRibaupierre, A., 152
Descriptive analysis, 17
Developing and evaluating long-term goals, 113
Development of testable hypotheses and Research questions, 16
Development of testable hypotheses, 16
Developmental approach, 132
DeVolder, C. L., 164
Diamond, M., 262, 264
Discrimination, 45
Dochy, F., 5
Dollard, J., 87, 97, 100
Dominowski, R. L., 169
Dornbush, S. M., 261
Dragnaski, B., 257
Drisscoll, M. P., 168
Drive theory, 31
Drive, 87
Druckman, D. 255
Duffy, T. M., 75, 248
Dunn, R., 271
Dunner, L., 76

E

Early contributors to learning theories, 9
Ebel, D., 184
Edelman, S., 173, 183
Edwards, 96
Effects of modeling influences, 97
Egell, A. L., 268, 272, 274
Eggen, P., 145
Ekstrand, D. R., 169
Ellis, J. A., 66, 76
Emotional intelligence defined, 25
Emotions role in learning, 28
Empirical reasoning, 1
Encouraging connections, 29
Englert, C. S., 211
Ennis, R. H., 179, 185
Epstein, J. L., 76
Epstein, R., 24
Ernia, V. A., 229
Eron, L., 98
Establishing reliability of instruments, 16
Estes, W. K., 143

Ethical issues in conducting research, 19
Evaluating learning styles, 273
Evans, A., 251
Evans, R., 92, 99, 101, 102, 103, 189
Everson, S. T., 61
Experimental conditions, 17
External rewards, 60
Extinction, 44, 53

F

Federal intervention, 297
Feigenbaum, E. A., 137
Feldman, J., 137
Ferguson, C., 287
Findings/Results, 18
Fitts, M., 257
Flavell, J. H., 163, 255
Fletcher, J. D., 55
Foder, J. A., 141
Fodi, J., 71, 74
Forest, M., 115
Forester, K., 141
Fowler, S. A., 289
Frayne, C., 102
Frazier, M. K., 71,
Frederiksen, N., 176
French, J. N., 173, 175, 180
Fresh, J., 229
Fu, K. S., 166

G

Gagne, E. D., 164
Gallini, J. K., 169
Galloway, L., 26
Garcia, E., 294
Gardner, H., 8, 223, 225, 226, 227, 228, 233, 241, 242
Garrett, F., 141
Gaser, C., 257
Gates, S. L., 61
Gazzainga, M. S., 28
George, H. S., 116
Gestalt psychology, 158
Ghatala, E., 122
Giedd, J. N., 251
Gilovich, T., 24
Glass, G. V., 254
Goals and philosophy of education, 1
Goldstein, C., 56, 74, 78
Goleman, D., 4, 263
Goleman, T., 25
Goodnow, J., 46, 168

376